SO-AKF-821

Many Mountains Moving

a
literary
journal
of
diverse
contemporary
voices

twelfth issue

Volume IV, Number 3

The Day When Mountains Move
Akiko Yosano

The day when mountains move has
   come.
Though I say this, nobody believes
   me.
Mountains sleep only for a little while
That once have been active in flames.
But even if you forgot it,
Just believe, people,
That all the women who slept
Now awake and move.

This poem was originally published in 1911 in Seitō ("Blue Stocking"), a Japanese literary magazine. It was reprinted from *The Burning Heart: Women Poets of Japan* (translated and edited by Kenneth Rexroth and Ikuko Atsumi, Seabury Press, 1977).

Publisher/Editor
NAOMI HORII

Art Editor
KELLEY JORDAN

Contributing Editors
MARILYN KRYSL
LUIS ALBERTO URREA

Fiction Editor
BETH NUGENT

Managing Director/Nonfiction Editor
HEATHER GRIMSHAW

Poetry Editor
ALISSA REARDON NORTON

Advisory Board
MASAKI HORII
MICHELE SPRING-MOORE
CASSANDRA VOLPE

Production Assistance
SEAN CAILLOUETTE

Cover Photography
WILLIAM RUTLEDGE

Cover Design
RICHARD JIVIDEN

Logo Design
CRAIG HANSEN

Production
SARAH B. PACE
ALISSA REARDON NORTON
JIM UBA

Technical Manager
JIM UBA

MANY MOUNTAINS MOVING (ISSN# 1080-6474; ISBN #1-886976-11-2)
is published three times annually by MANY MOUNTAINS MOVING, Inc.,
a 501(c)(3) nonprofit organization. First North American Serial Rights.
© MANY MOUNTAINS MOVING 2001. Many Mountains Moving,
420 22nd Street, Boulder, CO 80302, U.S.A. Distributed by Small Press
Distribution. Indexed by The American Humanities Index (Troy, NY;
Whitston Publishing Co.) and The Index of American Periodical Verse
(Lanham, MD: Scarecrow Press).

CONTENTS

NONFICTION

Acknowledgments

We would like to thank the many friends and supporters whose contributions and subscriptions have made this issue possible. Special thanks are due to the following:

Patrons
Susan and Jim Bell
Chuck Hebert
Pam Swanson
Vernie and Arthur Ourieff
Celestial Seasonings

Donors
Nancy and Chet Volpe

Supporting Subscribers
Rachel Dacus
William Marshall, Jr.

Organizational Donors
We gratefully acknowledge support from the **Arts and Humanities Assembly of Boulder County (AHAB)** through the AHAB/Neodata Endowment. We are grateful for marketing support from the **Council of Literary Magazines and Presses** and from **Small Press Distribution** through the New Readers for New Writers Program. Funded in part by a grant from the **Boulder Arts Commission**, an agency of the Boulder City Council. Also, we would like to thank Margaret Maupin and the Tattered Cover; Boulder Bookstore; James Lough of *The Rocky Mountain News*; Common Grounds of Denver; and the Women's Art Center—for their support in hosting Many Mountains Moving readings.

Finally, many thanks to our readers, who are dedicated to opening an exchange among cultures through art and literature.

Center for Arts Resources and Leadership

BOULDER ARTS COMMISSION

Many Mountains Moving, Inc. is a 501(c)(3) nonprofit organization. If you work for an institution or organization that supports literature and the arts and wish to make a tax-deductible donation, or know of any individuals who wish to make a contribution, please ask them to contact us at Many Mountains Moving, 420 22nd St., Boulder, CO 80302. Phone (303)545-9942. E-mail mmm@mmminc.org. Web address: www.mmminc.org.

Egg Girls
Lisa Glatt

I'm in Los Angeles, at a dingy clinic on Sepulveda Boulevard, with all these very pregnant girls. Being thirty, I've got ten years on them, at least. We're lined up on a couch, a couple girls reading magazines or pretending to, another few looking at the television, and every so often one girl tries to talk to another girl, asking some innocuous question, and is grudgingly answered or rebuffed, so Ms. Friendly goes back to her magazine or book or whatever.

We're in waiting room #4, our final stop before the procedure, which means we've left our husband (doubtful) or parent or boyfriend or best friend in #1, waited in #2 to give blood and urine, waited in #3 to be ushered towards a cubicle—behind a thin wall, and within earshot of the others—where we answered a stranger's questions about our sexual history in hushed tones.

This is the place they send problem cases. That's what I am, a problem. "We're having a problem, Amanda," they said on Saturday morning at The Family Center in Redondo Beach, a half block from where I live with my mother. In all fairness to the center, they'd warned me, told me I'd have to wait at least six weeks from conception—but, having found myself pregnant by a traveling Irish boy, a three-night stand ten years my junior with glittering green eyes, a speech impediment, and a defective condom—I couldn't wait. "Yes," I said, "I'm sure it's been six weeks, maybe seven." I calculated, counted in my head, and OK, I was early, a liar on top of everything else, but just by four days. I didn't think it would make a big difference, but apparently it did, because it's my second abortion—or attempt—this week, because here I am on this couch with these ridiculously pregnant girls, and I'm the only one not showing. I mean, they are big—-not the kind of pregnant that's a secret, but visibly, stomach out, swollen breasts, the whole thing. They come back three days in a row for what they call insertions.

"I'm just here for an insertion," the biggest girl of all tells me. She's got a white bow on top of her head. She's huge, massive, tall and fat, with long legs like trees. One tree leg is crossed over the other, or trying to, and because she's sitting next to me, the bottom of her blue bootie is just inches from my bare knee. In addition to the bow, she's wearing little baby barrettes, pink, one on each side, holding back her hair. The barrettes are extra tiny, absurd on a girl like her. Her hairdo is way too busy—just who would be with her, I'm thinking, who'd make her pregnant, who'd pull those barrettes out, who'd set that silly bow aside and fuck her, that's what I want to know—which isn't nice of me, I understand, but I'm thinking it. I'm blaming my hormones. I blame the Irish boy who mispronounced my name. I blame my mother's breast cancer, which recently, after three and a half years of silence, reoccurred, popped up, chewing and chewing at her hip until even she had to admit, arthritis doesn't feel like this, not a pinched nerve, not something twisted or sprained, not something I ate or cheap shoes.

I wonder if the big girl didn't know she was pregnant, like my friend Mitchell's sister who gave birth in the toilet. She thought she was taking a shit like any other shit, Mitchell said, and then wham—a baby boy. I wonder if this big girl had the same problem, if she kept growing and growing, from Monday to Monday, thicker and thicker, like a balloon or cream puff. Did she make excuses, like Mitchell's sister, when her pants wouldn't zip, when the button popped off her best skirt?

There's a half dozen of us, sitting on this couch, which is beige or gray, a cardboard color, and we're wearing white paper robes, and most of us, everyone but me, like I said, is obvious and round. We're watching *General Hospital* on a tiny television, the sound turned down low, quiet until the commercials begin. A commercial for eggs comes on, an animated thing, where a dozen eggs with faces pop out of their crate and dance around. They've got eyelashes, these eggs, and lipstick. They're blushing pink, singing a song. "Scrambled or fried, poached or baked," they squeal. A voiceover is telling us how eggs aren't nearly as bad for you as the healthy heart people claim. His voice is deep, serious when compared to the squealing eggs, and he's saying that they're wrong about cholesterol, that four eggs a week is good for you. I'm thinking that we look like eggs, us swollen girls in white, sitting on a couch the color of cardboard. I'm thinking maybe I'll go home and write a poem about us egg girls when the biggest egg of all, the girl next to me, says, "You know what they are?"

"Dancing eggs," I say.

"Not them," she says, rolling her eyes.

I shrug.

"Insertions. I'm talking about insertions."

"Oh."

"You know what they are?" she says again.

"No, I don't want—"

"It's seaweed or something," she interrupts.

I nod, but don't look at her. I stare hard at the television. *General Hospital* is back on, and I'm pretending the story line is more important than real life, that Luke and Laura's impending divorce outweighs what we egg girls have going on here.

"It's supposed to make me—or it, easier to get to. I've been here a couple times already. Someone said my vagina might be open enough today, but I doubt it."

"It's your cervix," I tell her, still not looking her way.

"What?"

"They want your cervix to dilate."

"Vagina, cervix, what's the difference?"

"There's a difference, believe me."

"Well, anyway, like I was saying, that nurse who took my blood, she said I might be open enough."

"That's nice," I say.

"Well, don't get too excited," she says.

"I won't," I tell her.

"Because I'm not lucky that way, if everyone but the lucky ones come back here three days in a row, then I'll be here four, maybe even five, you watch."

"Maybe not."

"It's true. I'm unlucky—well, that's obvious, isn't it?" She lets out a small laugh. She pats her stomach and sighs.

"Guess so."

"This is how it works. They've got you on a table, legs spread wide. I mean, they could stuff a TV in your honey pot if they wanted to." My pal's working with her hands and arms now, elbows together, making a V. "They take this stuff, it's seaweed, I think it's seaweed, is it seaweed?" she asks the girl on her left. The girl shrugs. She wets her finger with her tongue, then uses it to turn the page of the magazine in her lap. She lifts the magazine in the air, blocking the biggest girl from her view. "It's seaweed," she concludes, "and they've got your legs spread—"

"Look," I say, "I'm not here for an insertion, OK?"

"Suit yourself," she says.

"I'm early," I say.

"So?"

"I'm barely pregnant."

"I'm just telling you what they do. Don't you like to know what goes on behind closed doors?"

"No, really—" I begin.

"They stick this stuff inside of you and—"

"Please," I say. "Stop."

"What?"

"Can't we just wait our turn?"

"We are waiting."

"I mean, quietly."

"Oh," she says, sneering now, "you're one of those."

"Yes," I say.

"And you even admit it."

"That's right."

"You're not embarrassed about being a snob?"

"No."

"Well." She takes her leg in her hand, the one that's attempting to cross over, and sets it down, next to the other leg, which is now bright red, and maybe asleep because she's rubbing it. "I never.... You should be ashamed of yourself," she tells me, still rubbing.

"For other things in my life, yes, for wanting you to shut up, no."

"My god," she says. "You're a real weirdo. And a snob, too. A weirdo and a snob."

"I'm fine with it, the snob part, the weirdo part is inaccurate, but say what you want."

"Weirdo, weirdo."

"Look," I say, turning towards her, noticing for the first time that the other eggs, even the one next to her, are staring at the two of us, excited, enjoying our fight. "I've got problems worse than you not liking me. You understand?"

"Well," she says again, breathless.

"I'm not here to make friends."

"Maybe the rest of us are."

"Come on," I say. "The rest of us have friends at home. I bet a friend or two of ours is outside in the waiting room right now. You see what I'm saying?"

"I see that you're a wacko," she says.

"That's right."

"I see that you're a real nut."

"You should be afraid of me then."

"I see that you're a little old for an abortion, don't you think? You may be early, angel that you are, but you're old."

"Thank you, that's lovely."

"What are you, twenty-seven, twenty-eight?"

"Fuck you."

"Fuck you too, old lady."

"That's fine."

"Fuck you, fuck you," she says, and then, thank god, a door

opens and a woman calls her name. "Pamela?" the nurse says, smiling.

"Pammy," the big egg corrects her, almost yelling.

The nurse's smile disappears. She gives Pammy, who hasn't budged an inch, a puzzled look. "Come on," the nurse says.

"Call me by my right name," Pammy demands.

"What?" The nurse lets the clipboard fall against her thigh. She sighs. She stares at Pammy.

"Say who I am or I'm not moving."

"Good god," the nurse says. "I should have stayed in bed."

Pammy shrugs. She fiddles with one barrette, then the other, unsnapping and snapping.

"Pammy, it's your turn," the nurse finally says. "You coming or you just going to sit there?"

Pammy moves her fat ass, and there's one less egg on the couch. She's clutching that paper gown, hiding the ass. She's huffing and puffing, taking heavy steps in her blue booties. Before stepping inside, Pammy turns to me. "You better not be here when I get back, old lady," she says.

Whatever it was at that stage was too tiny to reach. The fetus, I mean. Last Saturday I woke up from what I thought would be my first and only abortion, and the doctor, a gray-haired man with a long, white beard that actually fell on my pillow as he spoke to me, said, "The procedure was unsuccessful." He identified himself as Carolyn—some inside joke between the man and his staff. "It was empty—you're empty," he said.

"Tell me something I don't know," I said.

"Seriously, uh, uh—" he began, looking at my chart, searching for my name. "Amanda, right?"

"Yes," I said.

"You're thirty, it says here."

"That's right."

"I couldn't find anything. In your uterus, I mean."

"You're joking. This is some weird joke, like your name, isn't it?" I was drugged, slurring my words, trying hard not to.

"No, not at all, I'm terribly serious, Amanda," he was speaking loudly now, enunciating each word.

"I have cramps, though. Here and here and here." I pointed at myself under the sheet, touched the places that hurt most.

"How about some codeine, Amanda? Want some codeine?"

"I want an abortion," I said, my voice cracking.

"There, there." He patted my arm, that beard getting closer and closer to my face. He motioned to a nurse. "Get her something for the pain, Margie," he said.

"I want an abortion," I said again, starting to cry.

"I tried," Carolyn said. "I worked and worked at it—there was nothing inside. Like I said before, I couldn't find a thing."

Margie returned, holding a Dixie cup, two white pills in her open palm.

"Give me those," I said.

Carolyn thought the fetus was in a fallopian tube, stuck there in-between, which I figured was fitting—my fetus lost, inches from potential nourishment, indecisive, unable to commit. He mentioned the threat of rupture, bleeding, death, and was sending me to a clinic on Third Street, a fertility specialist. From my grimace and sigh, Carolyn could tell I didn't appreciate the irony. "It's the only place in town with an ultrasound machine available on a Saturday morning."

"Wonderful," I said.

"Dr. Spookie is waiting for you. I've already called her."

"Nice name."

"Get going, Alison. She's opening her office just for you."

"My name's Amanda," I told him.

I sat with my best friend Kate at the fertility clinic, doubled over in pain, on codeine, trying hard not to throw up again. Against my wishes, Kate had called my mother, and now my mom was bursting through the door, her face scrunched up with worry. She limped towards me, a hand on that sore hip. "Oh dear," she said.

"You've got enough going on," I said.

It wasn't just that I was thirty years old, unmarried, but where was my boyfriend? What about precaution?

"He wore a condom," I told her.

"Who? That's a good question, isn't it? Who? Who?" she said, like a fucking owl. She motioned for Kate and me to scoot apart, then sat down between us.

"Never mind, Mom. Please, I'm in pain."

"I'm sorry. Where does it hurt?" she asked, and for a moment we were mother and daughter, just that, and she was going to make it better.

"Everywhere," I said.

"You could have told me, Amanda—that's all."

"I didn't want to."

"That's fine." She patted my knee. "You're a grown-up. I understand."

"Yes."

"You've got to stop worrying about me, though, acting out."

"Acting out?"

"You know, they talk about it on TV, Oprah and Geraldo, the talk shows."

"Whatever, Mom."

"You can't worry about me all the time, that's what I'm saying."

"Fine."

"A little bit of cancer is nothing. A couple zaps of radiation and I'll be OK. You know me," she said, looking at Kate to back her up.

"Absolutely," Kate said, nodding, trying to look hopeful.

"Where's Dr. Spookie?" I said.

"You shouldn't call the doctor names, Amanda—it isn't nice."

"That's the woman's name, Mom."

"Oh," she said. "Interesting," she said.

Dr. Spookie, a short woman, stocky, with red hair and freckles, helped me onto a table—the same table, I imagined, that other women wanted nothing more than to hop onto pregnant. I thought of those women, their loving men crouched beside them, holding their hands, waiting for heartbeats, dying to count fingers and toes, looking for little penises or tiny vaginas. Dr. Spookie moved the sonogram thing, which was cold and metal, across my stomach, the way someone else might have ironed a shirt. "Let's see," she said. "Let's take a look."

"I live with my mom in her apartment and she's sick…." I began.

"Eureka," Dr. Spookie said. "Right here. In your uterus, where it's supposed to be."

"How'd Carolyn miss it?"

"Who?"

"The doctor from The Family Center. He said his name was Carolyn."

"Why?"

"I don't know."

"His name's not Carolyn."

"I don't care, really."

"I wonder why he said that. That's funny," she said, staring at the screen.

"I don't think it's funny right now."

"He or she is in the corner," she continued, "clinging to your uterine wall."

"Great."

"Do you want to see?"

"No," I said.

"I'm sorry," she said. "I'm sorry. I shouldn't have asked you that."

"I'm not like the rest of your patients, I guess. I'm different."

"What was that you said about your mother?"

"Nothing," I said.

Last week, driving down Atherton, a familiar one-way street I use all the time, several times a week, I found myself going the wrong way. My first clue was going through an intersection and realizing that the cars opposite me were stopped. My traffic light was turned around, backwards, which I thought strange, but still it didn't register. Within seconds I saw the cars coming towards me, screeching to a halt. Smoking, the cars, with their drivers hanging out windows, cussing.

What the fuck's your problem?" one man hollered. I was turning my car around, trying not to see or hear him. Later, just before sleep, I kept seeing the image, all those cars, an SUV, a Caddy, a Jeep, that cursing man, his shoulder, one arm hanging out the window, coming towards me. I listened to my mother breathing in the next room. I played and replayed my drive down Atherton, thinking, cancer is just like that.

I'm turning in stiff sheets, coming to, with a terribly sweet taste in my dry mouth, when I see her ass. They've got us lined up on cots, and her ass could be any ass at all, but it's hers, I know it. The ass is white, wide and flat, with dimples, and there's something very sad about an ass like that, and a girl, an obnoxious girl, but a girl none the less, alone, leaning over, vomiting into a plastic dish. The barrettes are still there, but they've moved considerably towards the back of her head. She's holding the white bow in her hand, using it to wipe her mouth. She moans, throws those big legs out of the sheet, and crawls from the cot. "I have to pee," she says. "Someone, help me," she says, and she's crying now. I look around the room for a nurse, someone, anyone, but it's only us, the egg girls from waiting room #4.

"Hey," I say. "Someone here needs help," I call, but my voice is small, tiny in the room.

Pammy falls to the floor then, weeping, on her fat knees. I sit up, step out of the sheets. I've lost one bootie and the tile is cold on my foot. I stick my hand under her arm, and try to lift her, but she's heavy, and won't or can't budge. "Someone help us," I say. "Please." But no one's here, no one's coming. "Come on, try to stand," I say. "I'll get you to the bathroom if you stand up." Pammy takes a deep breath. She sighs, then makes an effort. Halfway up, knees bent, Pammy's eyes are level with my own. She looks into my face, squinting. "I can't see without my glasses," she says.

"It's me, the old lady," I say.

"Oh, you," she says, straightening up. She is a tower, a building. I'm helping Pammy the building to the bathroom. Halfway there, we stop in the hall a moment to breathe, rest. "You lost a bootie," she says.

I shrug.

"Isn't your foot cold?"

"Yeah," I say.

"Bummer."

"Sure is."

"I'm ready now," she says. And we continue down the hall, one foot in front of the other, taking little steps, baby steps.

When I was born
Jill Greene

my father was having sex in a hotel room
or on a brown office couch, the scent
of dim restaurants clinging to his hair, his fingers
sharp with the smell of onions. My mother
had felt their sting months before. She lived
on anger, drawn from anyone who came close,
her rage left behind a wake of silence.
When she could find no more anger, she took back
what little she'd given me, so I was born with a space
where mine should be. She made a gift in exchange:
swallowed salt I swam in for months. At the moment of birth,
as the contractions lifted my mother and set her down,
lifted her and set her down again like a lover,
as she rose and fell my father rose and fell, the pain
rising to her throat, to a groan, a scream his orgasm
rising to his throat, a groan, a scream and as
my head crowned the edges of air, a sister took root
in the womb of another woman, a sister
with anger intact, conceived as I was released
to this world, riding a wave of salt water, smelling
of onions and wailing for us all.

Dysplasia *(carcinoma in situ)*
Carolyn Kieber Grady

Crawling inside me
you are the flower I didn't want
in my garden—
a misplaced wild black-eyed susan—
spreading and changing the shape
of my cells

My sisters with their chattering infants
taunt me with vitality and female energy
like obscene ocher squash blossoms
The moon blessed *them* with ripening this season
It is not their fault they are so beautiful

You are the weed I want to rip out
—toss into the compost heap
to steam back into soil—
but you keep appearing
as thickened atypia
metamorphosing
inextricably a part of me

My mother—with sagging breasts
and the survival of harsh sunny days
built into her smile and the lines on her neck—
nods like a blue aster cooling the garden palette
She eyes me with the practicality of living
through many natural cycles
and holds me in an embrace so strong I feel the earth
must give way to her steady footsteps

I do not feel when dysplasia begins
yet I begin to shiver
with the early winter
the awkward ripening portends

My daughter—for whom even the sliver
of new moon smiles in joyful abundance—

holds my hand as we examine the chrysanthemums
bursting with orange blossoms

Every day we come into the garden
looking for what the sun has brought to fruit
or what the night has brought to flower
There something always manages to tease out our love

Today it was the wolf spider sitting on a pumpkin
Every spring it spins new threads on the leaf pile
Every fall its web hangs old and raggedy
accepting of the coming cold

        someday
     I'll climb on the roof
     and shout over the neighbors' leaf blowers
     and motorcycles and the heavy bass
     of the kids' rock 'n roll   My womb   my womb

Daddy

Doris Ferleger

This morning, my father enters our small, canary-yellow kitchen in his white boxer shorts and his Fruit of the Loom undershirt, stands at mock attention, and salutes. He puffs his lower lip out into an exaggerated pout, closes his soft blue eyes, and turns his large, shiny head from left to right. Like a happy parakeet, he sings, "Good morning to you, good morning to you, good morning and a happy 'Howdy Doody.'" He marches intrepidly in his underwear to the fridge for his prunes, or his self-made compote. "I need something to 'wettin' my whistle,'" he says. He likes using American expressions. If there are no prunes or compote, he settles for half a grapefruit. Digging in with an unserrated teaspoon, he squirts himself in the eye, but continues eating, undaunted. "Ach, Abram, eat like a 'mensch' not like a 'Chmielnicker,*'" scolds my mother. At the mention of Chmielnick, my father's eyes wander to another time and place. Or she might say, "If 'fressin' was a profession you would go in gold." But his urgent eating comforts her too. They are Holocaust survivors.

Forty years later, when my father is dying, my mother swabs my father's lips with chipped ice or a cold washcloth soaked in mint Listerine. She wishes he could dive into a grapefruit, head first, and suck up all its juices.

Daddy's round head looks extralarge this morning. The fifty or so strands of eight-inch hair he uses to cover his bald spot are all flyaway before breakfast. I like how straight and smooth those strands become under the hawk eye of my mother. I like the shiny, dark baldness peeking through. Daddy brings the tortoise-shell comb with him to the kitchen table, sits down like an obedient young schoolboy, and hands it to Mommy. He allows her the pleasure of doting, perfecting, loving him in this particular way. The ridges in the comb make straight, narrow roads in his black hair. He gets up before she is done. She follows him to the refrigerator like a fly on a sticky bun, hungry to get those last, stubborn, popping-up strands.

Daddy doesn't really need his hair to be perfected. He has already spent adequate time in the narrow, powder-blue master bathroom, oiling his hair down with Brillcream or Vaseline, whichever was in reach. "Oil is oil, grease is grease," he says.

At breakfast, Daddy's white ribbed undershirt covers most of his pendulous, hairy belly. It doesn't matter to him if the Fruit of the Loom label is on the outside or on the inside. Is it Chmielnick, the Holocaust, or neither that makes him not care?

I have my own view of my father's belly. Being a child given to perfection from a very young age, I wish his belly were flat, like an American colonel's, so it mould match the rest of his body. He has thin swarthy legs, narrow hips and thighs, and soft, lean arms. Though his hugs feel urgent, large, dense, scary. I wonder if I am one of his five murdered sisters. I wonder if he is hugging ghosts.

My father's hands are remarkably soft for a man who works embroidery machines, yanked pulleys in a candle factory, used chemical textile dyes, shoveled heavy snow and Jewish bodies under Nazi gunpoint. He holds my hand often, but never idly. His left thumb moves the thin olive skin on the back of my hand, up and down, or rubs my knuckles over and over again. My hand, his worry stone.

At the breakfast table, sometimes my father's private parts hang out of one side of his boxers. He doesn't notice. "Al, fix yourself!" my mother chides, and points downward, Dutifully he tucks them back in, though they don't stay long.

This morning after grapefruit, he decides on a piece of herring, slapped with sour cream and onions, straight out of the jar. My mother says, "You can take a man out of Chmielnick, but you can't take Chmielnick out of a man."

When my father is dying, at seventy-two, my mother wishes she could give him a sea of herrings to eat. She wishes he could savor them as he would a young lover. She wishes she could swallow her words.

When my father was in his last year of dying, he had a brief love affair with a herring, for which my mother not only forgave him, but was sorry to see end. They had moved from my childhood home into an apartment at Beaver Hill, so there would be no stairs to climb. The apartment's mauve carpets were stained from faulty IVs, flattened by Polish nurses traipsing in and out along the same runway in seven-hour shifts round the clock, and grooved from the wheels of my father's wheelchair. The actual affair started and ended in one day, though I believe my father's longing for herring continued until he died.

It was on a day my uncle Arthur was making his usual house call. Arthur was my father's first cousin who grew up with him in Chmielnick. Arthur remembered the same townspeople, the same sock they used as a ball, and the same "Vishedlenya" (Holocaust) that liquidated their town and their families, The two of them felt close in conversation or silence. This was good, because my father could no longer speak. His illness had taken so much of him.

On this particular visit, my father is seated in his wheelchair, which is rolled so his knees barely fit under the dining table, a napkin securely placed on his lap, even though he could only "eat" through a tube, the J tube in his stomach. The doctors provide "superalimentation," ample liquid nourishment through that tube. And though it is sufficient to keep his weight at 190, which my mother was very proud of, it neither "wettens his whistle" nor makes him "dakvik" (take deep pleasure, feel fully satisfied).

Arthur sits down at the dining room table, to my father's right. My mother is serving fresh rye with herring for Arthur and herself. All rye at my mother's is either fresh or thrown out. Fresh means same day, not refrigerated or frozen to be brought out for guests. Herring means a squat jar of gray fish with heads still intact, slumped in a pool of sour cream and cooked onions. The whole jar is on the table.

My father stares unabashedly at the jar. It is indeed love at first sight. He inches his shaky, weak hand toward the jar. No one notices. He tries to take hold of the jar but it is too heavy. Instead, he manages to squeeze a slippery whole herring into his fingers, draw it to his lips, and suck it into his mouth. It slides across his tongue and plunges right down his gullet.

Sour cream on his lips is the dead giveaway. My mother has not been paying attention for just a few moments and look what has happened. The herring was my father's sumptuous young lover, smelling like the sea, creamy and slippery, going down.

My mother catches him too late. It is like realizing your kid has swallowed a dime that you left on the kitchen table; no bad results in the moment, but terror about the next hour. Will the child be choking? Will it be your fault?

The herring doesn't hurt him. His eyes glide toward heaven.

A 'Chmielnicker' is a poor, unpolished Jewish man from Chmielnick, a small "shtetl" in Poland, liquidated of most of its Jews in 1943 by Nazi soldiers. My father was one of a hundred or so survivors.

What the Lines on My Hands Can't Tell You
Sandra Yannone

February is the month I fall
in love with women, the warm
smalls of backs, my mother

in her seventh month holding
out for spring. So I know
about desiring heat, how slowly

winter depreciates. I use the taste
it leaves on my tongue to teach
other mouths to taste. Always

the first stubborn child,
I have not yet become
my mother at twenty,

but when I finger the skin
surrounding my middle,
thinning in places where cells

lose their grip, I can feel her
deep pink scars stretching
four more years

to lose the third child
before it was born.
Mid-morning, we were alone,

snowed in. I flipped playing cards
to the living room floor
to ignore the fear of her

body crumpled in the pristine
wooden chair in the corner
of the pristine dining room,

the tight pull of phone cord
straining from the kitchen wall,
dividing her pain

from me. The same
familiar cold shoots through me
today as I watch the frost

fracture into uncertain webs
on the bedroom windows,
feel the temperature

catch my spine, my hands
instruments on the glass, laboring
to reach the hour all will melt.

Because I Tell Myself I Don't Want Children
Sandra Yannone

I sometimes star in my own TV
pregnancy. This time
I'm picnicking with only my women
friends. One assumes my husband
absent, on business in Michigan,
played a minor role in the uncut
version, clips of his small bit
scenes left for dead
on the editing floor.

There's a flea market in the hospitals
lobby, so I take my time
to examine all the domesticated
items women can't find the heart
to abandon, things they inherited
from their mothers. Things
they make a silent oath
to circulate among each other
in sanctioned summer rituals
on front lawns of churchyards.

I find a Fire King plate, a precursor
to Pyrex, with a map of Spain,
its rivers and roadways coursing
the clear glass. My friend
wants to buy it for me, wants
to give me another place
in the world. But I refuse as sometimes
for whatever lack of need
we refuse the most benevolent gesture.

But now labor has kicked in
the walls of my uterus. A nurse
issues a wheelchair. Before I descend
the maternal throne, my friend takes me
quickly, like a woman who turns her back
from a companion at the bar
and downs a shot, a small theft, wanting
at the expense of someone else,
and kisses "Have a nice daughter"
in my ear. Almost persuaded,
I know what she means.

Situation at the river

Eileen Hennessy

Yesterday I saw buds on branches.
This is March and the hatters are stricken.
Probably a toxin in the last
of the potatoes in the winter barrel.
Schizophrenia is endemic in these potato
lands. It's over-cold to search
for frenzied bottom-runners lounging
on the river bed. A lizard
may be no less a reptile
when made into shoes and a belt
to hold my summer dress close
to my body. It's too soon to know

what's bedded under the glass
blanket breaking up on the river.
The rising water's black, no matter
a white body was found in it once.
The lines of March-mad marathoners
toning on the road
flow past, their bodies gaunt. Mine's
a noisome watch, its ticking
just slightly off the wing-beat
of the watching robin. Tocksplash.
Mind the bed as it swims to me.

Situation with daughter and father

Eileen Hennessy

Not a day he doesn't think of her,
see her face, *his* face, in stones,
hear her steps, *his* steps,
on the flights of stars
that descend the sky.
In his dark lamp burns
the heart of a moth drawn
by the call of her bones,
his bones. He dates his birth
from the day she created light
around him, used night and day
as curtains to reveal and conceal
his book of private myth.
Will date his death from the day
her path diverges
in the ruined woods,
her footfalls in the leaves
no longer hint at where
she is. The question
of when she will go
is his river of darkness.

Fire Weather

Carol Quinn

for my sister

1.

With hips no more than a tiara of bone,
how will you have this child? You left home
because its windows leered from the night
inward, because blackberries and bamboo spilled
over the wall and mockingbirds stole *chanson*
from over the hills, because the San Gabriels
were on fire again, and the woman first told
to evacuate had set her thousand finches
free into the red smoke, darkening the land
while we stayed. You left because you needed
something else, methamphetamines, and there
was nothing left to steal from this house.
You left to become a mother, even though
this child will shatter your bones like glass.

2.

While you were missing, a girl your age
with your Joan of Arc hair was found
in the hills, her mouth cold with the ash
of San Dimas. Though she never told him
her name, a man claimed her by describing
her wounds, by revealing details kept from
the press, where she bruised easily while
the hills named for the patron saint of thieves
were burning. With a rock, he said,
he finished her like a window. An *eye
of the wind*, now broken and blind.

3.

From the air I see miles of ancient shores
in this Mojave you crossed. On the fire trails
at dusk, I climb canyons as they deepen

before the Santa Anas, ghosts of the waves
of an inland sea. This is how I know you:
in absence and effect, a shiver of brush,
a disembodied flood. Then a spark catches
in the dust, an irresistible pearl
in the body of the missing. Tinder simmers
at the edge of the known world. Days later,
you call. Where you are the leaves,
turning, carry the voice of the sea for miles.
You know the songs of waxwings and bluebirds
although you've never seen them before
this fall. Fissures creep across the panes
until your windows are brittle as ice,
but still you will not come home.

4.

I am picking up debris in the yard
after a windstorm. The rain
already finds its way in through
a dark scar in the roof. In the hearth
I burn shake-shingles and pine,
all that once sheltered us.

What He Tells Me

Christina Veladota

Since he tried suicide, my uncle has avoided
conversation beyond *yes* and *no*.
But today, of the woman who plays

piano in the boarding house: *She's quite good.*
She had a stroke, you know. She can only
play with one hand. By the baby grand

in the common room, he presses
an arm to his side, and with the other,
makes use of its raised hand,

mimicking the pianist claw, fingering air.
And I remember him as the man
who'd ride the *Jitney* from Brooklyn

summers we'd spend on the Harbor.
Grandma and Mother prepared,
wrapping liquor bottles in heavy towels,

locking them like small dead bodies
in the trunk of the Plymouth. Even then
his empty hands seemed like birds

hungry for the unspeakable. So much
fluttering, fluttering. And even now,
playing his silent music he proves

how a person can be like that,
caught in the paralysis of longing,
part helpless, part wanting to sing.

Watermelon

Joseph O. Legaspi

1.

This morning, thirsty from the drain of night's sleep, I ate a thick slice of sweet watermelon, cold, the kind of cold that could satisfy William Carlos Williams. Forget the coffee, the cream-cheesed bagel and bacon. I admit it: I'm fixated with this fruit, green outside, red on the inside, like Christmas, or my mother painted green, or like the Mexican flag without the eagle and the stripes, but with seeds, which, when sun-dried and salted, become the favorite snack food of Filipinos.

2.

I once told a tale to my younger sister of how I was conceived. Our mother went out for a walk one fine day in April, maybe June, and she walked down this path in the province, dried and brown and worn but teeming with butterflies, and the withered leaves and splinters on the ground crackled under her feet, sounding like wet wood placed on a bonfire. She walked until she stumbled upon a watermelon field where, overcome with thirst and hunger, she picked the largest, fattest one, cracked it open with her slim hand and found me in it. She carried me home and my true story ended. My sister rolled her ten-year-old eyes at me and said, "Mommy had sex with daddy."

3.

This summer night, I crave the satisfying sweetness of watermelon. I head down to the kitchen and open the refrigerator, searching, then remembering that my father had eaten it for dinner: there is no more watermelon. All that remains is a plum, burgundy, overripe, bitten, the teeth marks I know belong to my sister.

mindedness under a daytime moon
John Michael Cummings

while I sit on this bench, my mind clouds up, probably because my wife earlier this morning confessed that her marriage feels to her as though giving birth to a 30-year-old, and what a remark to hear even though understandably likely of me, me stuck with what liberal arts has generated, this head steaming, always fogging the windshield she laughs, always metabolizing like the body of a race horse she jokes, but in the heating sea breeze of this quaint street, my mind, I wish I could inform her now, squirts this way, then that, like an ice cube that, once starting to melt, slips and slides across a counter, this head of mine now acting psychic even though packed by her this morning like a paper shopping bag of duties: to the tense bank, to the grand post office where two aliens who never sweat instead puff smiles at me since I somehow know of the planetary invasion of their kind, Anne has guessed, has laughed, has rebuffed, having a mind whose flame conserves, being literal, sensible, patient as most women her age become even when her first marriage, she dares to enumerate as though foretelling a sequel, has felt as though birthing a grown man! oh, how horrible a comment for me to recall while sitting here like Socrates (Socrates? she would inquire, then refer to him as a prophet, to me as a fretful anemic, an old dog to refasten), yet I could divorce her if I were really cloyed, if, too, coaxed by another woman whose mind, unlike Anne's but like mine, consumes a raw steak of sensations every afternoon, say, like the New York poet friend of my friend Arte, a frail girl, he has described her, who cries whenever she ventures into the city, who, like me, races home disgusted by the dehumanization and, from her small bed I imagine, rocks herself asleep, the kind of woman whom artless Anne should envy at this moment since I yearn to walk across a mistress like rice paper, although no longer, not now, the urge away, my fealty strengthened by the outer sight of where Labradors, across the street, romp, three of them now stabbing paws into the belly of a family man, these pets slobbering, seen from my bench here as the Blackies, the Lassies, of a family, the social formation I wanted before, over the last few years, noticing the number of garbage bags outside every house (before wondering how the old man next door can last all week without filling more than one) before noticing, too, the interesting process of the mind, mine, that selects, subconsciously I guess, a different coffee cup from the china closest each morning, in which Anne, I love her, arranges them like

minutemen to start me every day, and, finally, before noticing how my
gold wedding ring never tarnishes after years now of being dunked in this
dish slime or that bathwater roux

how gold outwears the skin, while she names me too emotional or
while I impute her too grounded, blood and gold, bloody gold, a nice
image, despite her, lasts like memories, even those of hometown Whites
Ferry—wide brown rivers, lattice-iron bridges, sun-starred mountaintops,
flowerpot-red brick settlements, sand paths here and there, hot gravel and
printed souvenir cups, verdant lawns around molasses-brown park
buildings peppered with mud wasps—and of my family, my brother with
German buttocks, squatted until enormous, and my other one with a red
beard and soiled boots, and my father who wears a coal jacket during the
summer, all their faces so weirdly dazing during my most recent reunion
that I complained of fatigue from driving in order to lie in a back room
among guns and tins breathing the dank cool oxygen, so removed from
this lineage as to feel stuck in time, wedged sideways in sheets of schist,
like my brother with the boxy German behind whenever he squeezes into
any of my newer foreign cars and, stopping himself before landing on
whatever debris from my life in the city, suspends his backside in midair
as though the air itself has turned to syrup and glued him still, has ceased
his arrogance of me whenever I appear home-side, for he and the others
there have opted to resent me and even Anne, as well as our chaperon of
cheer and will, because this well-butted brother of mine, more than my
chilly father and bearded other brother, loathes anyone who has
experienced his hickish childhood yet has completed the interurban adult
curriculum required of those now employably educated, even though he,
in line with heritage, long ago deluded himself by regarding all others as
privileged without ever once assaying to overcome them, without ever
once submitting his set of chances upon the crucible—when childhood
and the twenties abut ungracefully—a coward, I today call him, and for
this punch into my past, Anne, while we drive home, rewards me by
rubbing my back, and for this pleasure, I say aloud she and I need now
our own family, as though to replant a field having perished in the storm
long ago, but rather than acceding, she worries while we ride home of the
time she still requires to complete a second degree, since I earn not quite
enough, so soon we both forget our hometowns and apologize mutually
for our having darker eyes recently because of lesser sex and more stress

because in the anxious struggle to find sleep, I have lately felt the
hardness of my wedding ring, unpinchable, solid, housing my flesh and

26

bone with curious defiance as this band slides when touched like a gentle implant by the younger alien in the post office, this gold band of mine around flesh, this tireless symbol of communion, proven true, too, by old men still married even if having resorted to hiding a girly magazine in the bathroom or ginger wine in the attic

but are we, Anne and I, searching for a family whenever we gaze into the yards across the road where tots wobble into play pools like battery-powered robots, or have we deprived ourselves of instinct and intuition to vector careers, have we sterilized ourselves into another Joe and Norma with baccalaureates in art and business, a starter IRA and already a litter of saving bonds, rather than knowledge of the whereabouts of the last drive-in theater in America, the last ventriloquist for hire, and the last brick bungalow in the county with a skylight in the kid's room for starwatching, our family redux, what we both pine, like scenic pines themselves, a glade in the sweet country, not these fire escapes and thin sidewalks and this lumpy futon   rising from which Anne decides this morning my brother is gay, being why he comports so secretively and antisocially whenever his father strains everyone together into one touchy room, and rising after her, I retort that unsuccessful men never answer their own phones, although she does not grasp my reference, one as indirect as I could render it, nor does she, when I comment that life has never been guaranteed, agree that everyone must willingly become a happy widget or that because a bird or dog will kill its young without conscience, whether by dropping it from a nest or by mouthing and crushing its small neck, the human choice to abort a fetus must also require reflex, instinct, not quibbling consciousness—my view of this issue—so that protesters, both those for and against, actually exhibit the problem with evolution once without basic nature? sleepy Anne inquires, still skeptical of herself as a widget and now of me as a bird falling from a nest, as well as of every living thing subject to termination whenever a certified letter arrives informing him or her of irreversible disease, as life, I have told her, has never been guaranteed, she the philosophaster, I the philologaster, both of us torching each other with our mouths like flame-throwers every night, although this late morning, this very second, I cannot understand, as my mind rises to the surface of being, why those three men across the street have gathered like telephone pole inspectors nor, as it then sinks again, why Anne believes my brother has clandestinely turned gay, a supposition announced upon me amid the night as though I possess the same atavistic tendency, perhaps because of my poor show of sexual intercourse early last evening, during which I kept thinking of telling Arte's poet friend a few parables to write, of men who collect garbage ought not treat themselves as same, of why Memorial Day vacates me of any kindred reckoning, being a day worse than Sunday, of the funny paradox of TV critics diametrically inaccurate, when badly rated movies seem oppositely great, and of a few others—foods triggering memories, for me pancakes without butter; a society gawking skyward for aliens (when two have already materialized in my town); the pointlessness of front-end alignments when roads up north connect sinkholes; and the crazy statute in this town permitting dogs to be transported in car trunks but not in truck beds—until all these thoughts did finally distract me of my erection and until Anne, seeming telepathic as she lay under me, grieved her detest of parents who allow their children to wear rat-tails, and of this last evening I think until these three men laugh so loudly as to interest me in whatever has humored them, until one of the two alien postal clerks emerges and passes me without sweating, heading, no doubt, to his spaceship, and, finally, until the bright surface of this town has fully contained me without any reverie, here where I spot an ant wiggling across the worn perforated toe of my Sears shoe and there where I notice a Labrador driving a fish truck...

what, yikes! yes indeed, over there, another anthropomorphized Lab, this one employed as a crosswalk monitor for the parochial school, and there, another black one walking upright, clad casually, looking leisurely about, now entering the library cupping books to return, a girl in style, and many more, two conversing at the sunny entrance of the corner pizza joint, where beyond, on a glistening green wrought-iron bench like mine reclines a blonde one, as I have surely gone mad, as I must have finally seen yellow, as the schizophrenics say, yet these scenes do tickle me into my first smile of the morning while waiting here for the bank to open, the world fully grown with Labradors, playing, prancing, a few older ones with whitened snouts gabbing by the card shop and a few adolescents ripping across the park toward the gazebo in the distance, but whether they notice me as the lone humanoid in their animal-land, I cannot tempt myself to speculate, because this mood feels too whimsical to touch and because I vaguely wonder whether these happy Labbies will prove to be the extraterrestrials the world has waited to welcome and the postal clerks to rejoin, those strange sweatless men who have never smelled of dog, I recall, yet why would aliens embody themselves as retrievers anyway? so indeed I must have smoked my brain during all this mental activity elapsing within seven minutes I count, glancing at my wristwatch faced, yes, with a grinning Labby whose little paw, while dotting a circle in the air around his robust head, functions as the second hand and his tail, curled behind him like a whip, as the minute hand, with no hours indicated on my watch now, as though any larger increment of time cannot serve me now, now when my reality on this street abounds with Labradors of interlocution and bipedalism, husky water dogs steering trucks, unpocketing change for meters, nodding politely to their neighbors, all having faces about to horselaugh, about to slobber, bodies about to wag, wiggle, sprint, and leap headlong into the trash, this citizenry of canines, one breed, the happiest, most affable breed, one licking a stamp over there, another buying a newspaper near me, the world as I imagine it, perfected by the nature of a Newfoundland aborigine

until I blink, and the humans resume, although not quite as de-humanizingly as before I sat, and, oh, here comes the prettiest one of all, Anne, out of the drugstore to check my progress with the bank, my ten minutes up

Slow dance
Mary McLaughlin Slechta

I'm dancing under a pavilion in paradise.

It's the last dance,
the slow dance,
and lover man, put off all evening,
has finally got me locked inside his arms
with his legs so close to mine
that I don't have to think about steps or rhythm
or losing a boyfriend because I couldn't merengue.

"This is forever," he may as well whisper in my ear:
where he turns,
        I turn,
                the pavilion turns,
                                the world turns.

No one comes forward to stop him when I cry out softly.

I remember a story they tell in St. James
of a man full of rum and madness
who raged a week on the abandoned roads.
I'm the foolish girl who read kindness
in his wicked smile and lingered.
In another story the earth swallowed a man
and threw him back before his widow could grieve.
My father, who knows the story, crosses his fingers for luck.
My mother, who doesn't, is the woman who covers her face in black.
She's shouting to my father that his stupid country
has cost her a daughter.

Will she come for me
when snow falls like ash in Montego Bay?

The scarlet heads of the tall hibiscus
hang ready to bawl their terrible tale.

Photo of Anita Cheng by William Rutledge
Copyright © William Rutledge 2001

Photo of Anita Cheng by William Rutledge
Copyright © William Rutledge 2001

Photo of Anita Cheng by William Rutledge
Copyright © William Rutledge 2001

Photo of Anita Cheng by William Rutledge
Copyright © William Rutledge 2001

Photo of Anita Cheng by William Rutledge
Copyright © William Rutledge 2001

Dawn, Stone Harbor, NJ

Melissa Kirsch

Good morning, flat-town, stiff-backed street town,
how'd you bleed the shame out of porcelain frogs
necking on limestone thrones in the garden,
tin angel on a wire hovering over the hydrangea?
I'm blushing for you, town rolled out,
splayed out on the ocean's left shoulder,
you've got your own language,
which is no language, which is mute-town,
frown-town, flat-chested, no gender,
mini-golf-town. Freezed-out, back-bled,
thin-skin, see-through, passed-out place.
I woke up here in the underbrush
of a dehydrated sea-shrub, chapped lips,
no new thing to be unveiled. The poem I write
is black and white with colors underneath, I say.
The painter said it's like the body,
the blood is down below the skin,
the color's in the veins of the slate-town.
The party's been evacuated in the sea's
sideyard, the lights are out indefinitely
and no one's home, no one's home.

Preliminary Notes for an Essay, Tentatively Titled "Why I Want to Go to Medical School"

Melissa Kirsch

Once and for all, not the heart. To finally be able
to stick the stigma of feeling on a more original organ.
Forget *heartache*, try *appendixache*. Perhaps Cupid could
send his arrow straight for the pancreas.
The corpse back flat and blueing, inside,
the poet's key. Michelangelo filched
a few in the name of art,
it's natural. To want my hand deep
in the viscera, to actually hold a lung.
To pull apart the tightest muscles between ribs.
The infinite Baudelairian possibilities of the spleen.

A high-school bio class cat will not suffice,
its gassed face frozen midshriek,
its brain too tiny
to weigh ponderously in my gloved palm.

The subtlety of a white labcoat,
the authority it implies. With this, secret knowledge:
the intimate acquaintance with marrow,
tracing the half-zipper of the spinal chord,
the sound of fascia ripping.

Labor Day, Burying Elliot

Melissa Kirsch

My mother is homesick for no one and no place
to which she can return. The mourners descend
like locusts, picking and chattering, flapping their wings,
leaving their shells behind. The bereaved come out in swarms
whenever there's food involved: cold cuts rolled up
like tiny newspapers, macaroni salad and casseroles,
paper plates and plastic forks. We measure our grief
by the number of grievers, the number of jello-fruit
suspensions received. The procession possesses
a theatrical quality, my mother's
the star, her friends play supporting roles:
The Marcias Bernstein, Berenson and Futerman,
like a law firm, or the better part of a bridge game,
gold bangles and tear-smeared eyeliner in threes.

> A neighbor steers my mother by the elbow, intoning
> meaningfully: *Elliot always loved living in South Windsor*
> *so he could look over the mall and be close to the racetrack.*
> *He loved the good things in life.*

> *The good things in death*
> *are a $65,000 casket, full copper,*
> *more for handles*, my mother returns.

> *It's not cheap to bury a loved one*, whispers a Marcia.

Another neighbor stops in
and shows us how to mourn properly: a bowl of water
on the stoop, we dip our hands on the way inside.
Soap the mirrors, light the candle, at sundown
we huddle in circles and pray.

When the throng departs, my mother and I
go behind the house, shake crumbs off
the tablecloth into the dark. And I know then,
because the clothesline stretched
between the two windows has more
romance and endurance in its D-cups and merry widows

than any evening spent holding back
what we really meant to say over prime rib and mashed potatoes,

I know from then on, I'll give in to anything:
an hour of sordid necking in the lobby, being flung
back against the bank of mailboxes, clutching fast
to whoever's heated utterance promises to save;
the false anything-can-happeness when you lose your stomach
forever on the last drop of the log flume.

In the silver urgency of twilight,
we are braced for the deluge to come.
My mother at one end, and I at the other,
we snap the tablecloth a final time
and fold it into a square.

Because

Khaled Mattawa

From the dust of volition a brick layer follows a pattern that leads to walls. Nothing in the world happens only once. Take a step. Now you're in the middle of a dance. Take the thief caught late one night, the soldiers slapping the back of his neck. Does he ask forgiveness? Does the officer seem unconcerned? For a year a man drives his mother to have her coffee grounds read. For another his father visited her grave and recited holy words. Once in a swimming pool a girl heard a word that made her head reel. Once a man heard a song and switched the radio off, and kept it off for months. Once you wrote a word and its sisters came tugging at your sleeves begging to be born. Deduction was a consultant then trying to sell a city a stadium it did not need. Percent. Percent. He said. Induction was a mad man on the verge of wisdom or a wise woman on the verge of something else. Now a squirrel jumps headlong into a garbage can. Another furiously climbs a tree in chase. The birds on the branches. The air you breathe. The asphalt's blackness and the snow's startling white. A canary in the mine. The hand that feeds lifts up to strike you. You switch off the light and go to bed.

The Metaphor of a Horse Can Be Folded and Kept in a Pocket

Jon Pineda

After he finishes the drawing, he leaves the napkin
on the table next to a pile of change, the shiny
heads of men scattered along
the thin body of an ink horse
seem to study the drawing, the sketch
of its weak jowls or the loose muscles
of its back, as if the body itself has never felt
the weight of a man. And those men looking on,
their faces, hardened, hold their pressed expressions,
even though they are bodiless and will always be,
even though they have known pain to some degree:
war, polio, infidelity, other fragments of loss.
The waitress scoops the coins into her hand,
drops them into the pocket of her apron,
then holds the horse as gently as she can.

Weight

Jon Pineda

On the steps of Santa Croce, a woman
held her child, his hand cupped above a plate
of coins. *Never mind them*, a guide said
to the group of tourists surrounding him.
Gypsies drug their kids to look like that.
The boy's eyes gazed into the roof of his skull.
His jaw fell and struggled to close, mouthing
a language he had found written on the walls
of blood. *The pieta is inside*, the guide said
as they filed, one by one, into the darkness,
over a roomful of bodies.

Willoughby Spit

Jon Pineda

In the middle of the tunnel, his car loses power and coasts,
but there is not enough momentum to push him through

the upswing. He stops, listens as horns begin to mimic
the beats of his hazards, drivers cursing behind the glass

are fish-like in the flashing light. *What,* he says, throwing his hands
in the air. There is no need to explain. Someone flips him off,

he does the same. When the wrecker arrives, traffic is backed up
past Willoughby Spit where, in this early morning, the thin boats tied

to the docks hint at some freedom for those stalled on the bridge.
And the silhouettes of the fleet across the bay start to move,

maybe en route to somewhere faraway, where life is
inconvenienced by more than this, then the cars in front,

their lights disappear inside themselves, inch forward as they prepare
to descend into the mouth of the tunnel, where there is some hope

of leaving it all behind.

[Auto]biography

Prudence Peiffer

I am in a car unraveling miles
distance a thing we pick up as it falls behind
You don't have to know how other
nights have lain in my arms
We aren't cubists driven only by the relative
when the colors accelerate to white

A startled doe locks me away in her eyes
and my mother yells at the hunter standing foolish
in our yard with a gun

The radio our moon tonight
flip flops, dress, and stranger taken off
Not just air, I want to leave an imprint
like the gravestone in the woods

someone lies down anonymous
to wild dogs and mopeds that pass by
someone lies down under our moon

I am smashing acorns apart with bricks
with hands propped against the door handle
and legs to the windshield
I am adding a little blue

In a ballet of thrown weight
I killed a frog once
stamped out its insides while
friends watched in sickened awe

Will you take me back, I ask.
Though some of it's been bulldozed, some let go
what never leaves? *the undiscovered*
seems to be the answer
though we are but an arms span away.

I am in a room unraveling
two elbows two knees one neck rhythm
listening for you in the driveway,
then turning low our crescent light

The murdered frog haunts my dreams for weeks

Goldilocks, Grown
Bertha Rogers

In the middle of my life, I came to myself in a dark wood.
    —Dante Alighieri, Canto I, *The Inferno, The Divine Comedy*

Can't seem to get the fire going.
Too much trouble stoking it, piling on wood.
Flu, in belly and bones, keeps me cold.

Three windows, each crowned
by three leaded, beveled panes,
bend cedar and fir, their everlasting reach.
My body hurts. A light rain falling.

When I was a child, on the farm,
Mother briskly handed me a dish—
blackberries in sugar syrup—to ease
a stomach ache. I ate the fruit, one glossy cap
at a time; lay back on my parents' pillows.
I watched the furrowed old walnut,
line trees between flat expanse. Slept.

Out here, as far west as I could risk,
I'm sick. The fire is fitful—everything else
provided—chair, bed, a bowl of soup,
sudden rainbows over stacked books.

The always trees talk, limbs crossing.
A dark wood. The wind in the canopy
                 calling, burning.

The Soul

Jay Rogoff

Flesh creates language, launching empty air
through her svelte throat's muscular double reed,
tongue and teeth drumming it to crescendo
up over her lips' sensuous sculpture.
Her word shrinks my world to a sheer idea.
And flesh makes paint: bones and muscles grind
earth, I daub with oil and sweat till I stand
in my round world with a flat pursuer
poking my personal space, offering me
a book, a blessing, a piece of fruit, salvation,
as if the flesh I paint could make me spirit.
Clothes make men. The dance drives ecstasy.
No fire to her beauty without ignition,
no life without the bed, the people in it.

Scenery
Jay Rogoff

Nature bores me so
    it's a relief to find out
        the Romantic landscape
            with its irradiated
                round trees or haystacks, its deep barred shadows,
    and its clouds galloping across the sunset
        is a painted
      backdrop,
          and the boisterous
          verdure of the lush

shrub lit
not
by sunset but
               by sun
a painted flat
            one
      dancer uses to prop
      herself up,
           and that the flowers
can bestow
         odors

only of tulle
    and sweat, and, faintly, dyes,
    paints, or appliqués,
        since those swatches
    of lilies
        and mums dancing against the painted sunlit bushes
        are, yes, ballet skirts, their hems and stiff stitches
the most unnatural
        thing in the world. I love to watch as
           art
        triumphs, as first one dancer in the wings snatches
            up her shoulder
            strap, then another
    and another, their preposterous

                       hair the red of matches,
their rapid steps burning the natural
                             air
until
          with a tempestuous
                         crescendo in the clear weather
                         it's over
                   and smoothing her floral skirt
         the prima ballerina curtsies
             and clutches
         the brilliant bouquet, flowers
                smacking of dreams, betokening lust, luscious
and unreal.

The Field

Jay Rogoff

But into what shall we beat our plowshares?
The grain strains skyward with the best of us,
but my love keeps its vigil in the furrows
where zygotes sprout in passion, where the source
suckles the jailbreaking seed, drunk with tears,
until, against the air, it joins the lace
lining the field's lips, only to shoot like rice
back earthward, raining on us in the mire's
embrace. So all aspiration recycles.
Love straitens us to drag us in the ditch,
one of the universe's dirty jokes
you wouldn't tell at the drunkenest party.
No, it's our joke, our love that's rude and dirty,
and when my lady suffers an itch, I scratch.

The Arc of Our Reach

Richard Ryal

pain behind the wound and the lake of light
below the ache, and the doctor looks in,
    her fingers reach in, slender precision
surprises a memory, sudden clasp of jasmine
grown at the back door while I was gone

the lake of light rises, stretches the hollow of me
to her, the healing a remembering,
    songbird face open over me, her wide
vision circle calm as few birds are, and light
rains into reflecting cells with the bend
    of water pouring from a good spout

my ladder of shadows has brilliant rungs,
guided by hand an arc appears from pain
    too lazy to shed me, our circles click,
agree on a common diameter, a current swells
and relents, tissue dreams of health

I climb lightly without leaving the table,
waiting, one foot on sand, one in sea,
    for an echo whose home
extends just beyond hearing, an expanse
habitable even to my fragility, its gate
    defended by a songbird

Out of Your Skin

Cameron K. Gearen

i.

I should have circled you with flowers, garlanded
your neck when you left. Instead I waved at the bus,
your face a speck smiling back, my feet in mud: rain.

ii.

You carried my letter for a month before you told me
        you shed the baby, dark mass in layers of your skin.
            At the clinic, girls ten years your junior cried
                into magazines, like a daytime soap.
                    You didn't cry, you write,
                        until you got home.

iii.

Remember that night on the path? Late wind roused
banana leaves, palm fronds, Orion slept on his side.

We knew the way by starlight, where the thin bridge
spanned water. Your foot dragged, suddenly heavy;

I found it in the torch beam, saw a snake
unwrap itself, flee to high grasses.

iv.

In Berkeley, you keep Indigos, cycle to the lab
Wednesdays for live rats. You stun them
with a knife's dull blade. Here—remember?—
snakes leave skin just outside gauzy mosquito nets.
In the morning, it flattens underfoot, rough as bark.
They pass days where bamboo and thatch meet,
wait out the heat until the world stirs at sundown.

v.

At night, while the canal ran toward the city,
you would consult the Tarot.
Son of Wands, Shaman of Cups,

the native man who loved you wordlessly.
Once, in your Outcome: the Devil;
he moved across the windless room
when you turned away.

vi.

I dream I am looking for you, friend.
Berkeley: no one has heard your name.

And on your parents' farm near Albany,
wood shed and barn, only my voice rings.

My letters to you, a sackful, spill and blow.
Prophecy of a world become vast.

vii.

Along the path, dust coated leaves brown.
        We waited for the first rain, everything streaming back
                into the earth, borrowed clothes. Now, the paddies are ponds.
Birds of paradise preen in the sun. I would pick one for you
        and send it. You search the cards for signs of your child:
                Priestess of Swords, Hanged One, Crone, Daughter of Discs.

The Woman Who Burned the World

Cameron K. Gearen

Nan, Thailand

First there was the matter of the rustling. All night
men parked motorcycles under bloody bougainvillaea
and circled her house. Thatch walls, cotton netting—
membranes holding her in. Dry grass scratched
their pants legs. She felt fear buzz the way
insects did her bulb. Strange world, always hot.
In the morning she found only the dry imprints of lizards.

Then there was the garbage. She learned the word,
tongue dizzy with five tones, and raised her eyebrows
when she said it, a question. The answer
escaped her. Bicycle to market every morning
for pineapple and pig's ear, on the look-out for the garbage
truck like home, men swinging on and off, trash in its belly.
But there was no truck. Searing day, the men,

night visitors, slashed and burned cassava fields.
She stood at the edge, watched earth blacken.
Days later, shoots crawled out of the ash, green as palms.
Parched air crackled. But the shoots were wet
as life on the bottom of a lake. When she set her yard on fire,
she started with the garbage. Lizards bit
each other's tails; she lit it. It burned

up. Then out. Flames bled in great circles, ever-widening,
the kind of fire that could leap a river, blaze an ocean,
leave us charred, an empty spinning earth. She stood
still. Her neighbor banged toward her from the east,
hungry chickens trailing, drained the cistern
into an aluminum basin. On the edge of flames she swung
her arms, hips, and great arcs of rainwater floated, crashed.

While Reading Plath

Catherine DeNunzio-Gabordi

I go quickly, safely to the familiar
where this was that, and even dancing things move
on a chalk black stage. There air turns inside out,
becomes a mattress for rest or a chest where
I might store my mind and breathe.
The beauty of the curls of essences
divvied into globes and swirls and smears
and then to beds of water, oceans, sheer
sheets of black, layered deep, The promise of feeling,
in my own cold ocean wrap. Yet even there
I know beyond resides a wormhole.
My salt at home. But friction, skin to water,
is something to believe in, safe and lost
in the last familiar; without the courage to divvy
up the rest of me, and wanting not to leave behind
my sons who know my smell, still need my curl of neck,
I went, go still toward friction. And there is the truth:
an extant fear, and then the salty sweetness of my sons'
sweaty nighttime scalps. I am only guessing,
but the wrapping of the other truth is soundless,
is in the beds of water.
Here, I'm an aria sung from a canceled opera.
There, inside, even gravity through water
is something I would feel were I not a speck
in space falling, free, blades cool and silky—
crossed like an axis through my core—
relieved and lost, undone, done.

Resurrection Fantasy

Gregory Brooker

1. Childhood

Olivines would not sparkle under that lake—
those were the times.
I saw them drag it after the limbo.
Who's having fun? Probably not the girl.
Fake gray angels misted up from the lake's winter sheet.
I saw birds and I got sick of them.
Across the neighborhoods and fields spread long months of snow.

To seal the snowy lakes, ghosts offered their backs and what the warm weather of
spring tried to expose they quickly covered upward with the cold white of their lives.

2. Easter

In rabbit-form I disappear.
Who is for hands becoming girls? I am.

3. Return

Finally spring melts the ghosts' white spines of ice
on the lake's winter top.

Their yellow serum melts into the water,
into the dandelions and elms at the lake's edge,
offering a bouquet for the deceased, a lustrous ring.

In a Palace of Snow

Alison Stone

In a palace of snow,
I lie in silk.
My powdered skin glows,
Closed lips gleam, and frost streaks my hair.
Frozen at my side, my dark
Dog snores while frogs croak
Beneath my window and the willows
Drop their secrets, Icy
Leaves mark streets that lead nowhere.
The clocks tock endlessly.

You are trapped in a desert, galloping knight
Burning in armor. Over
Your head the red sun pulses.
Topaz lizards crawl on rocks and bright
Flies dot the horse's
Side bleeding from your spur.
Bulging saddlebags contain
Swords and bones.
No room to carry coins
Or silk or milled grain.

Find me where the peacock spreads his feathers
And the thin moon rises from the south.
Touch me as night gathers
Shadows. Suck the ice from my mouth.

A Man Without Hobbies
Andrew Hoffmann

I'm a teacher at the college and each class I teach is an endurance test. It is a fucking twenty-mile race. I stutter and can't make connections. My students are bored and question the project. Today, I'm ambivalent. But it's not a bad day. Today I've a student who's curious and stays after. Would you look at my poem? she says, I wrote another poem.

She dresses like a parochial school girl, knee socks, knee skirts, broad-rimmed collars. And her eyes are large for her face. I can picture her my age, and I think, in twenty years her skin will have loosened and aged, her face will have filled out and she'll be beautiful. She writes first-person poems and uses images of passing, a lone goose at dusk, an elderly woman teetering on concrete steps in front of the nursing home, a white-bearded man in a hat crossing a river on a footbridge at night, all lights the sky, the music, the river, and somewhere out there, the city on the lost blue horizon. She shows me her poems, and I think she is writing these for me. Perhaps she sees me a solitary man, strong and making his way in poignant silence to some brittle edge of some brittle world. To be sure, I don't mind talking about death and disease, and she in turn seems concerned for my health. I hand her back her poems and she thanks me and I say good afternoon.

There are very few things I strongly believe in, but I do believe in cycles. I believe in reincarnation, in soulmates. I believe that there are people in the world I've known in another life, people I've been married to, parented by, people who've judged me and locked me in cells, who've fucked me and murdered me, people I've screwed in ever which way, and those I've intentionally harmed, murdered and loved, touched with the most tender hands and kindhearted listening, healed and been healed by, sacrificed for, acknowledged, cheated, mourned. I believe that in every life I'm born into I meet these souls again. This, this place, this circle, a swirling fever where with each birth is a new shell, or if not new, different, a changed shell, a turned image, a thing moving and alive and heading for I have no earthly idea where. Perhaps in one life I'm born as a man, perhaps in another a woman, me, born with ill luck and crazy fate to this mother under this sun, this time male, this time a teacher, this time a traveler with a fear of sluggish places. Yes, and the soul. The same soul? Yes, perhaps. But the question remains: what of each of us remembers the soul's old stories?

I have health problems. Buzzing in the ears, headaches, constipation, asthma, chest pains, a chronic cough. F. Scott Fitzgerald, for crissake. I go to the doctor, he laughs, says, your wheels are falling off. The doctor inspects my eyes, my ears, checks my pulse, my temperature, blood pressure, he pokes a finger in my asshole, no prostate problem. Thank god, that's what I say. About the sleep, the eczema, the headaches, he says, more exercise, less alcohol. 1 can't find anything wrong with you, he says. This costs me sixty dollars.

I walk through the old neighborhoods. This time of year, spring, ripe and blossoming, dew on the lawn, people at work in their yards. Children on bicycles. College students sitting on porches drinking beer in orange dusky sunset. Dogs chase dogs and I step around dog crap on the sidewalk. The sun is pleasant on the horizon. Peaceful neighborhoods. It is a flat three-mile walk from the college to my house. Exercise and fresh air, I feel better, I feel good, I feel spring from the inside out.

I'm a couple blocks from my house when a woman in a new twenty-seven thousand dollar four-wheel-drive truck pulls into a driveway of an apartment building across the street from where I walk. She puts the truck into neutral and leaves it running in the parking lot. As she hurries into one of the apartments, I cross the street, get in the truck, turn down the radio and back it out. The truck has a strong engine and as I turn the corner, obviously in a hurry, I see on the sidewalk, out the comer of my eye, I see my student, my young poet, there walking with an older woman, both women with arms crossed in front of their chests. You can imagine how this startles me, driving by my student in a stolen 4x4. I wonder who the older woman is. Something about her is familiar. I drive another mile or so and leave the truck in an alley beside a movie theater. I can't decide whether to keep or leave the keys. Finally, I choose a middle road and toss the keys in a dumpster.

When I come into the house, my wife asks if something is wrong.

You're sweating, she says.

The doctor says my wheels are falling off.

She laughs, offers to make a cup of tea.

I need a lifestyle change, I say. I'd like to move to the country. Maybe the desert. Walden Pond. Orondo by the river.

She doesn't like hearing this. No, she says, we can't move the kids to another school. We can't move again.

I need eyeglasses, I say. The vision in my left eye is blurred. I'm losing my sight.

She cleans the kitchen then reads to the kids and puts them to bed, then goes to bed herself. She's a mothering creature. She works at the aviary taking care of broken-winged hawks and falcons. She's a student of the habits of predators. Sweet angels, she calls her children, sweet saints. On her feet all day, I say, goodnight, Betsy, goodnight. An hour passes and I go into the bedroom and lean over her and smell her skin and kiss her lightly on the lips and think how lucky I am to know her. She is one of my very favorite people on earth.

I walk to the movie theater to see if the truck is still in the alley. Moonshine on the hood and over the pavement. I buy a ticket for the late show. The movie is a slow burner about a man, a dog, a train. At home I check on the kids, fall asleep on the couch to the sound of the TV.

The chiropractor adjusts my neck and gives me vitamins. He's into homeopathic remedies, tarot cards. He does muscle testing, kinesthesiology. Breathe, press out, release, he says. You've got some emotional stuff going on, he says, and shuffles the cards and holds them out and I draw one. The High Priestess. He nods. Womb, breast, vulva, heart, he says, the inner eye of wisdom. Your intuition is functioning more strongly than your intellect. Pay attention to lunar cycles. This costs me forty dollars.

I take the vitamins and piss bright orange. The moon is in the sky and the truck is gone. Sadly. I had visions of visiting it often, there in the alley behind the movie theater. I feel badly about throwing away the keys, but I'm not about to go searching through the dumpster. Really. What good are keys without a truck?

I saw you walking with a woman, I say.

Oh, my student says, my mother.

Today my student wears a sleeveless spring dress. And a ribbon in her hair above her ear .A young blossoming woman, dark gentian, I try to imagine what she'll look like in ten years, in twenty. What she'll speak of, what she'll know, what her curiosities will be. I can see her with many close friends and happily married. Last night I dreamed I helped a young couple repair the ceiling of their shack in the woods. Really, the shack was beyond repair and I suggested they tear it down and use the wood to build anew. Up on the hillside, I dreamed, in the rocks and the trees, safe from a valley of floods.

That's a nice thing, to walk with your mother.

She's my best friend. We talk about everything.

Like what?

Everything.

Give me an example. Be poetic.

You're teasing me.

I'm not teasing, I don't. I'm curious. What is it you talk about?

Well, we talk about lots of thing. Yesterday, it is kinda poetic. We talked about how there's a day we pass each year, the day we'll die on.

We don't know what day that is, but certainly we pass it every year. We were wondering what kind of things through a lifetime happen on that day, what kind of things are felt, what kind of things are seen, what kind of shadows, what kind of weather.

Who knows? Maybe this is the day. Forty years from now I'll die on this date. Maybe that's why we're talking about it today.

Our eyes meet and a wren's song passes through the open window. Beside her, I feel a stranger in this life, surprised at her sound, her dress, her pale arms. She looks like one who has never run, never exercised heartily, never really sweat. I like her in class, when I'm talking and looking around and I can't see her. I like the feeling of knowing she's listening, taking notes, thinking. That there is a merging between us. And when she speaks to me of the day she will die, I imagine little boys orphaned by a war sitting in windows in handsome patriotic coats.

Very poetic, I say.

Yes, she says. My mother.

You're full of poems.

She nods.

Of course, I say, it is your mother .

I'm up at dawn and watch sunrise and I eat breakfast with my family. The kids eat bacon and drink a lot of milk. Betsy eats grapefruit and a piece of buttered wheat bread. Betsy loves bread and bakes bread and looks a little breadish, hers the complexion of wheat. My daughter's name is Joey. My one-year-old son really doesn't have a name yet. Now we call him Boy. I've got the feeling Boy will stick. I don't feel good about it, Betsy doesn't feel good about it, but it seems nothing can be done. It seems like an infection in the neighborhood, the difficulty to name properly, if there is such a thing. They call the kid across the street Toolhead. Toolhead is worse than Boy. Honestly, every time I see the kid, I think phallic, I think prick, I think little utilitarian toolhead pecker. Ah christ. The kid across the street who, as time passes no doubt, my son will learn to look up to.

I walk across town with the sun on my face and stop at the armed services recruiting station. Inside I work my way to the desk looking at the picture posters of men in uniform with headphones and flashlights on the decks of ships. I also skim a pamphlet or two, so much information, so many possibilities for the future. At the desk the uniformed man stares right into me. He's my age and has lovely medals hanging from his shirt pocket.

I want to enlist in the Navy, I tell the man.

Just then two young fellows push through the door, hesitate in the doorway to inspect the place before coming forward. They too are interested in the posters and pamphlets.

The recruiter picks up a pencil and straightens a notepad in front of him. He asks my name.

Jones. Ben Jones.

Jones.

Yes. Jones.

Ben Jones.

Yes. Ben Jones.

How old are you, Jones?

I'm about forty.

You're about forty.

Yes.

He wrote something in pencil. Have you served your country before?

I've never served my country, no sir.

You've never been honorably or dishonorably discharged from any branch of the service?

No.

What do you need, Jones?

I want to enlist in the Navy.

He looks up. You're about forty and want to enlist in the Navy.

I nod. It seems like the concept is pretty clear to him. I ask if he's a captain.

No, not really. Do I know you from somewhere?

I teach at the college.

The boys come up behind me, they're ready to talk to the officer. He nods to the boys, then motions me back behind the desk. He leads me to the coffee machine and offers me a cigarette. He speaks in a low voice and I already like him. Let me tell you something, he says, even if the Navy would let you join, which it won't, what would a forty year old man want to enlist in the Navy for? Do you have any idea what a pain in the ass it would be? See those kids, you'd spend four years with kids like that. Not a pretty thing. And the barracks. No free time for yourself. No sleeping till ten. No movies, no booze, no babes. A drill sergeant always in the face. A Marine drill instructor. These guys are turds. And you being old and frail, he'd do everything he could to see you suck some light into your asshole. Why would you do such a thing? You teach at the college. I'd give my left nut to teach at the college.

I'd like to work on a boat, I say. I've never fought in a war. I want to fight in a war.

He looks anxiously to the kids. He wants to get to them, maybe he has a quota. It's not like kids are lined up and down the street to enlist.

The Navy's not about boats. The Navy's not about war. Christ, we'd all like to fight in a war. This office is the Navy. Does this look like a boat to you? I smoke two packs of cigarettes a day and drink chocolate milk because it makes the cigarettes taste better. This is no boat. Six weeks of boot camp is hell, shit, could I tell you about that.

I don't want to start smoking cigarettes, I say. I can't afford it.

Of course not. Nobody can afford it. Anyway, it's a moot point, you're too old.

We shake hands, he says good luck. He also says he can understand my wanting to fight in a war. It's a pipe dream, he says, let it go.

Betsy reminds me we're having a small dinner party for the bird people. I take a bath and rub on some cologne. Why, I don't know, I hate cologne, it gives me hives. I feel rushed, and by the time people arrive Betsy's drunk on wine. The talk naturally turns to birds, not enough funding for sick owls, this kind of thing. The children dip raw carrots and broccoli into mayonnaise. I go outside to smoke a cigarette I find in my shirt pocket. The air is cool and pure and I get sad thinking about the sea. Esther Chadwick follows me out and hands me a glass of wine.

Would you say you're a religious person?, she says.

I wouldn't say that.

My ex-husband, he was religious, but not spiritual.

I know the type.

Did Betsy tell you? I'm getting remarried. He's German. I'm flying to Germany tomorrow to be with him. We'll spend a month traveling. He speaks five languages. Of course he's got a Ph.D. Do you think you can help him get a job at the college?

A job? I say. Yeah, sure, no problem

After class I have a headache from the fluorescent lights and stagnant air so I ask my student if perhaps we could take a little walk, look at her poems at the coffee shop. She turns her eyes and steps away. Gives no answer, she doesn't speak. Her face turns red. She's embarrassed. She picks up her books and holds them close to her chest and abruptly leaves the room. Then, as if to underline a point, she misses three classes in a row and I miss her poems, miss our subtle communion. During these days, instead of teaching the white whale, I leap to the Pisan Cantos. Students are confused, of course, and all I can say is get with it, just write your goddamned papers. Am I cranky? easily irritated? At home I make a decision: the boy will be called something, something besides Boy. Betsy, I say, we've got to name this kid.

Betsy has no problem with this, and in fact is a bit relieved that I feel so strongly about it. She pours us each another glass of wine and we have no trouble finishing the bottle.

The neighborhood gardens are beautiful this year. I believe in progress. But am a religious man? No, not really.

The acupuncturist suggests I add more animal protein to my diet. Too much yin, she says. I can feel it in your pulse, she says, I can see in on your tongue. She plugs needles in the back of my neck and abandons me in a chilly dark room for an hour. This costs forty-five dollars. When I leave her office I make it a point not to say goodbye. Whether she knows it or not, some of us are afraid of the dark.

I start by ordering two eggs over easy, coffee and hash browns. The food is greasy and I order two more eggs. Then two more. Then I order six at one time, scrambled, forget the potatoes. The waitress keeps close tabs of the number. A clean dozen, she says. Can I get you anything else?

Standing, I feel a little dizzy, bloated and well greased. I try to speak. I want to say La Pasca because I want to say something of the future, the white temples of Mexico, the village into which I hope to be born next time, birthed through a hard-handed mother whom I will not resent.

The doctor finds nothing wrong with my eyes. If you have headaches, he says, perhaps you should see a neurologist. As far as I can tell, your eyes are fine.

Betsy fears I've been drinking too much and thinks I should see a counselor. For safety's sake, she says. She says she'll support me through it all, she'll even go to the sessions with me. I think it's a good idea and she calls for an appointment. Actually, I look forward to seeing a therapist, and on the day of the appointment I leave school early, taking my time walking through neighborhoods and enjoying the beautiful flower gardens. I meet Betsy in the waiting room of a dingy building. She's totally drunk and I spend most of the hour telling the therapist what a good mother Betsy is, a good person, my wife. This costs one hundred and fifty dollars. On the street outside the office Betsy and I kiss passionately.

My student comes to class with a new haircut. Her hair is very short. She dyed it white and combs it flat against her head with some kind of hair juice. She wears make-up, lipstick, powders her cheeks, she clowns around, new shoes and loose clothes. I'm surprised, moved. So after I deliver a sermon to end my discussion of the Cantos, I ask the class a serious question. Class, I say, are you religious? They're puzzled and, at first, silent. But then, one by one, nearly all nod yes, yes, religious. I can hardly believe the response, damn if the semester isn't ending on a high note. My student, the poet, is one of the few who doesn't nod, but smiles knowingly, as if she, and only she, has the correct answer .

I've decided I'd like to have coffee with you, she says.

The sun is bright and she has trouble walking in her tight little black shoes. She holds my elbow to steady herself as we move along. At the coffee shop she bends over the table to show me a new poem and part of a white breast. The poem, a love poem, is mediocre. The breast, however, is quite nice. The poem tries too hard to tell a story. The breast tells nothing at all but what it is.

I don't think this is an honest poem, I say. It lacks spontaneity.

I worked hard on this, she says. This is an honest poem.

I don't think so. It's a poem without poetry.

She pouts and I go into the bathroom. There are any number of things I can do in the bathroom but I decide to take a stall and sit on the toilet. For all I know, this could be a leaping point, the edge of the world. I hear somebody come through the door. Right away I'm struck with the feeling that something's up, so I pay attention. He moves quickly and takes the stall next to me. He bumps into the dividing wall. I look up and there he is, a young fellow standing on the toilet, leaned with his chin on the divider, staring down at me, his eyes are shaded by a ball cap.

Hey! What's this? Hey! Scram! I jump up and he hits the floor. I kick the stall door open and leap out and he's out of his stall too. I face him for a moment, then think, fuck this, and out of the bathroom I go and into the shop where my student frowns over her love poem. I sit at the table and keep my head down until the boy moves past. When he's out the door I look up, and there he is alright, on the other side of the window looking at me, his face shaded, just a young fellow. He turns and starts down the street.

Professor Jones, my student says, I think we need to talk.

So do I, so do I. Can you excuse me.

The sun hits my face. I look down the sidewalk and don't see the boy. And if I did? Perhaps I would follow him. I'm curious to know where he lives, what kind of house or apartment he lives in. I would like to meet his parents, sit at their table and share a cup of coffee or a drink. I would like to see the boy with his hat off, I would like to see his eyes. For now, there's my student, so much still to be confronted and adored. Clearly, she's disappointed and I sense her pain. Perhaps we're both feeling now some part of a day that is certain to come, the day on which we'll die. And wanting to keep that day as distant as possible, I sit back down at the table, reach and hold her hand. Hers is a young hand, cool and damp and pale. Mine is older and bears a few scars and a wedding ring. Together, they grip and twine and tremble.

Translation of Rainer Maria Rilke's
Sonnets to Orpheus (Sonnet No. 12, Part 2)
Translated by Cynthia Thatcher

Desire change. Be mad for the flame
in which a thing eludes you, splendoring changes.
That projecting spirit, which masters the earthly, most
loves in the figure's swing the inflecting point.

What locks itself into remaining already *is* rigidity;
does it think itself secure in the dull gray shelter?
Wait: from far away a hardest warns the hard;
watch—the absent hammer lifts—

him who pours himself forth as a source, recognition knows;
and she guides him rapt through bright creation
that often with starting out closes, and with end begins.

Every happy space they pass through, amazed,
is child or grandchild of parting. And altered Daphne,
since feeling the laurels,
wants you to turn into wind.

invitation to a disaster
Jeffrey Lee

Skin-hungry for your hands
she comes up to your bedroom as a fan
of your poetry, but you're Nobody, you say.
It doesn't matter, she says.
She's not the woman you love and can't have,
she's the baby you can have and want
in eccentric old clothes
and she keeps you up late cuddling her blues
which is fine except she takes off everything
(complaining *It's so hot!*)
except her worn-out panties
and it's late but she doesn't want to
so you sleep on the floor
on something rock-hard
in your clothes
and she wails her loneliness
and jealousy of your past
But we just met (!) you say.
It doesn't matter, she cries.
How can she be mad as a wife
on a first date? you think
but it's too late and sleep
overwhelms you and recedes
only near dawn when she stumbles by casually
half-waking and mostly naked
and you reach up hungry
for her skin and tug her in
your long dark sleeping bag
and roll with her in your lust
and she steams up like dunked toast
that is, till she crumbles into dripping sobs
and then you have to stop,
soothe and hold her together
tenderly as the non-drunk dad she never had.
It begins to dawn on you then
that she really wants something else.

the irrevocable awe

Jeffrey Lee

...once in a little Italian restaurant
when it was her (*my god...*)   birthday
       —yeah, that's what day it was,
you gave her a thoughtful gift which she adored
and—naturally enough—she kissed you,
but the old white waitress burned bright red:
       "You can't do that here!
       Not in our restaurant!
       You *whore!"*
And you see, she's crying again—
aghast at how much hate they have for you,
the sight of you together...
Violence won't help you
       —nothing'll do any good...
So you get up to leave, leaving extra cash
       —never even got served—
and the waitress yells louder:
       "You *whore!"*
The word tears through her mind like paper
       —no one ever called her that before!
So you yell back a first of your own:
       "Shut up, you evil bitch!"
She dials 9-1-1, threatening you both:
       "I'm calling the cops!"
You're hurrying outside now
and she's crying so blind she's stumbling.
Then the greasy-aproned cook leaps outside,
throwing a tin utensil that clatters and skitters
after you while he screams:
       "Come back! *I'll kill you!* You fuckin' chink!"
       "Just try it—you dumb fuck!"
But she's begging: "*Jeff—please!*"
so when he chases, you drive away jangling angry nerves
until sorrow like a whirlpool drains your heart-mind
       —and there's nowhere to go to—
and you hear her terrible sobbing: "*Why?*"
till she's almost hypnotized, asking the universe.

Slowly, what they thought dawns on you:
>   *Any pretty white girl with an asian had to be a prostitute.*
>   *They simply couldn't see her as just a person...*
Your mind breaks into irrevocable awe
at *how* they can hate you so deeply...

Stunned—you see her hands clutching the tear-stained gift
>   *happy birthday happy birthday happy birthday*
but not for you and her.

air and sampan and child / the first step
Jeffrey Lee

wade without sound into air   *—with nothing in the mind*

and soft currents   *but the one thing,*

move you—   *with nothing*

a white paper   *in the world*

sampan drifts   *but the one word,*

in shallows   *with nothing*

of a canal below   *in the words—*

and minnows taste   *but everything,*

your palm—   *every thing*

wade without   *I am,*

sound into air   *I write.*

and fingers   So I learn

let go   the first step

a pebble   is the point of

etched with   no return

crystal webbing—   as if starting guns

a white paper   aim at me

sampan drifts   spurring

and locusts cling   the cold-sweat race

to a sail   of a marathoner

that fills until   out of the old

shells sting—   hells and

wade without sound

into air

to fathom

the height

of sky that is

unknowingly

clear—

a white paper

sampan

drifts from you

who made it

as a child

but it releases you

at last—

wade without sound

into air—

a white paper

sampan

drifts

into the new

paradise of

misguided prayers

to be dancing

till my hands clasp

the bliss of

an ecstasy

unnameable

as you...

I am the shape

love takes,

surrendering...

I am the soul

love makes stronger,

singing

the only

immortal

part of me

—free.

a happy death / in this wild cold field
Jeffrey Lee

his side	*her side*
Tremors in	The winter grass
the lower spine	shimmers its seeds
spark vibes	as high as your
spontaneously in	shoulders in this
the belly's inner-	wild cold field and
most side—	those dead trees
like salmon	that rose above
thrashing over	the lesser ones,
falls diving	they stand out
up against	from those
gravity chasing	just living—
the scent of	they are like
a long-ago	great artists—
home passing	lightning struck
banks like	to make them
guiding thighs,	unique, and now
it is like that	little black birds
shivering	like clothespins
shimmering body	cling in their
in air out of	bare arms with no
its element,	clothes, no

71

an engine of

generation

with perfect

concentration,

one with more than

itself, one with

you—a poplar

a gale ripples

like water dancing

warm as a fire

yet liquid

as tangerines,

sweet as the

smell of the

rain-polished

peach—from the

weight of thighs

and the slippery

tides between and

the rocks that

would crush the

flow that must

always push—

I wash assured

in the wave

leaves like streams

running through

the breezes—

they are made

more beautiful

because of death,

like skeletons

over green youths

they reign as

the winter grass

hovers over

shoots of spring

and shelters

the fresher

stems that burst

into tufts of

bright light greens

like salamanders

against dark mud—

and all the

seeds slipping

down your legs

from long spears

seep deeper down

till rain makes the

and foam and am

free in this now

dying moment—

free from the

doubts always

in our eyes,

love is free

to die

a happy death...

soil a womb—

and you see—

your vision goes

beyond you

because the

worlds within you

seek without you—

like seeds

seeking the womb

the lambs
Jeffrey Lee

the love that is most unforeseen
unpreventable, incorrect
rains around you
like fog exploding into blossoms
like slow-motion bombs
erasing a city's streets
(in the time of love that was never a place)
yet she comes, the love
before you can discriminate
or discern who or what
to love
let alone how—

              At first,
you love the lamb you feed as a child
nursing its plump musk warmth,
a baby bottle in its hungry mouth
dribbling milk across the glaciers
of soiled newspapers
where you slide and run across
the whole basement floor
chasing his bright wool,
but then you never foresee
the night you ask, "Where is he?"
and your mother will show you
guts in a freezer bag
pressing your hand on to the frost,
stinging your skin with its blood-ice
making you cry
tears that splash
into lenses in that snow
showing through the plastic
the blood, body and screams of—

                        "Where is he?"
"We slaughtered him—This is him."
                  "But, you can't—you can't!"
"We did—it's done! He's dead! he's dead!"

There was a fall
before that winter's broken tongues
when we ran with our lambs
(they were brothers)
before mine was also killed
and your mother almost hit me for crying—
if only that fall came again
or comes again—
if only there were a Someday to come
when we could—
       if only...

       I heard the ghost coo out
over a woman's silent sleeping
I heard her husband's even breathing
and I was in another child's bed (yours?)
just a thin door away
where I worried into sleep
no shouting, screaming, laughing
not even tree leaves rattling
or beams creaking
no sound
but her cooing crying
piercing and sighing
making the darkness into endless fields
of the bones of air-raid evacuees,
       but dawn with its running waters
running machines and revving motors
over the hills flaring green and icy mirrors
to the frostlight-sun came
       and I saw the sheep rising to a standstill
still damp with dew
drugged on their feet
like ancient addicts staring
but I can only think of them
as if they were
still promised
the milk of infancy—

       In a train's café car
a drunk man takes my hand,
timid at first, but he ventures,

"Brother, you a minority—'m a minority,
we both God's. We *all* God's.
He made us—all o' us..."
He laughs but his wife doesn't,
I'm afraid he may cry right there
but the train rocks and he knocks
his beer over the table.
He dodges the dripping puddle;
I hand over a fistful of napkins.

        So many years have slid by
I can't tell you anymore
what happened or why;
I only remember
once there was a time of love
(though never a place)
when we weren't just islands
in the sea of newspapers
but children nursing animals
and animals cradling innocents.
There is no knowing in the end
but *what* we love,
and the fact *that* we love
escapes us...
        that is
until she comes again,
the loves that grieves
to such extremes
her sky is a rapture of pain
—like mary's over a forgotten god—
her rain erasing
every once-beautiful
thing of earth
but one.

the guard's reverie
Jeffrey Lee

1.

he thinks he must have done this hundreds of times
because one of the naked mothers hid her kid
in the rancid heaps of clothing,
so after the screams and the futility
of clawing, clutching and climbing over each other
(as if escape were ever possible atop another naked body)
leaving a pyramid of the tangled dead;
he hears a muffled shriek
and dredges up a boy who could be
three to four-years old who, just like himself,
has wide blue eyes.
The boy is dragged from the darkness
by the man crouching in the dirty daylight
who calls him: *little escapee,*
you missed your chance to go with your mother
and worse yet—you'll make me miss my lunch.
He lifts him up so easily
the boy forgets himself
and hangs on to the guard
who only remembers himself at the door
dropping him to be presentable
to the Sergeant who sighs *I should report this*
but the guard whines *I'd really rather eat now*
because I haven't eaten today.
Can't we just toss him in with tomorrow's—
Who gives a crap?
The sergeant asks *Why didn't you eat?*
and seeing the embarrassed downward look guesses,
The shits? All right—get out of here.
Then he walks the boy across to a different barracks
bangs the door in and tells some startled women
nothing—but seeing the boy, they understand...

2.
—he thinks he must have done this hundreds of times
but he is still standing by the trash heap
because there never was a boy,
and if there were, no Sergeant would let it live.
Instead, there is only a stink so filthy and strong
it ices over his eyes
as he sees them again in his mind
because he has done this hundreds of times:
he has to open that door and begin again
the work of tearing each body
from the others' still clutching arms.

Dr. S

Jeffrey Lee

I was surprised to see Dr. Syoenidz in dark glasses; they seemed incongruous with his middle-aged paunch that stretched out his light blue short-sleeve shirt. And his too short, too skinny tie was limp in the early morning humidity. But however he looked, he was bothered by how *I* looked.

He exclaimed: "Cayle! Why aren't you ready? Did you forget our trip?"

"Of course not," I shook my head. "You're thirty minutes late, so I started to fall back to sleep." Since it was early spring, it was almost pleasant on my street for once.

He seemed annoyed. That was a shock considering how patient and nice he'd always been before. In fact, he'd befriended me during the darkest months of my life. He had done me so many favors and spoken to me so regularly that I'd really started to think of him as a friend even though his daughter, who was a few years ahead of me and at the same college, was close to my age. He bought me sandwiches from the snack bar when I was starving (which was always). He often invited me up to his very nice, secluded office atop one of the houses on campus that contained faculty space. Though he was in the foreign languages, he'd shared with me his own art and poetry books. He'd read me poetry by Esenin and Mayakovsky in the original and lent me his copy of *Russian Poets on Poetry*, which I devoured. It was a really mind-expanding series of essays by the greatest futurist and modernist Russians. I'd never read them before, so that was the most important thing I read all year; that is, as far as developing a greater understanding of the passion of poetry and its too often tormented makers.

He'd also started saying that he truly admired my work as a poet. He insisted I had the spark of genius. He must have genuinely grasped some of what I was doing because he understood how much Mayakovsky and Esenin meant to me. He knew I could absorb them like a sponge, but at the same time, he had no pretensions about his own abilities as a writer. He told me: "I am merely one who can appreciate the beauty of poetry and art that others create. Really, Cayle, I feel honored to know someone like you."

That wasn't the only time when I wondered if he was patronizing me. One late afternoon in his office he'd said, "I admire your courage for being able to actually go through with it, you see, because—I never could bring myself to do it."

At first I didn't understand that he meant my suicide attempt several weeks before. Then I must've looked at him like he was crazy; I was thinking of his beautiful wife and three children and his wonderful house, and I asked, "But why would *you* feel that way?"

He got very agitated, but he explained how miserable his life had been in his youth and how he'd contemplated doing it but his nerve had failed. But I had a strange feeling he was withholding something.

Usually, though, he won my trust. There were just a few odd moments, like once he asked me to call him by his first name, Drivas, or "Driv" for short, instead of Dr. Syoenidz or Dr. S, as most students did. Even *I* thought "Driv" was ridiculous as a name. So I only said it after he practically demanded it.

Anyway, I was taken aback by his rushed demeanor and almost rude stare. But after scanning my twelve-by-fourteen room for a few moments, for a long time he focused in on my self-portrait where it sat on the old dresser. It was technically inept, and to make up for the lack of verisimilitude, I'd added a lot of moody, overexpressive shading. That made it look too brooding and androgynous in the wrong way. But it did convey some of my desperate feelings, so I liked it. Besides, one of the only entertainments I had in this new place (I'd left the old address in an ambulance) aside from reading was drawing. I only had a crappy old AM radio alarm clock to listen to.

Nonetheless, Syoenidz gazed reverentially at this sketch: "It's very beautiful!" Then he actually held it up and looked at me and smiled.

I was more surprised when he added: "It has a—a passion—a sensuality to it."

He was right, in a way, but I was embarrassed and said, "I don't think so."

I didn't have much to bring along: a few clothes, a toothbrush, and tablets that I carried in my ever-present army-surplus backpack. He was surprised at how little I was bringing for the overnight trip.

He drove too fast even though his BMW rode smooth no matter how many cars he raced around. He was delivering a talk or something at an academic conference. But he said he had lots of free time before and after his work so we could explore New York City together. He'd told me every young poet within a hundred miles of New York City should see as much of it as possible. Since I had almost no money to go myself, this seemed reasonable to me. I'd never been there overnight in my life.

Once he'd parked under his hotel, though, he acted strange at the registration desk. The clerk asked him, "How many rooms?"

"One," he said.

"Don't I get my own room?" I asked, surprised.

He shook his head. "It would cost too much."

The clerk noted down our room and started to hand over a key, but Syoenidz became agitated and asked nervously, "How many beds are in the room...."

"Two," the clerk said, momentarily startled out of his I've-seen-everything-too-many-times stupor. The clerk looked me over quickly before his pall fell over him again.

"Could we have a room with just one bed?" Syoenidz anxiously asked.

I was really taken aback, so I said, "Hey. Where'm *I* gonna sleep?"

I thought something was wrong, but I asked as though I thought he was just too cheap to do the usual thing. That way we might both be spared this embarrassment.

He got too flustered to talk, so I told the clerk, "I want my own bed."

Syoenidz got even more upset but at last snatched the key from the clerk's hand.

As we walked away, he complained, "Don't you trust me, Cayle? I'm really quite offended that you would—you would—embarrass me this way!"

I didn't say anything.

"What did you think? Something was going on? Cayle, don't you trust me?"

I kept silent.

"Cayle," he clutched my arm, "I just want to be close to you, that's all, my friend... It's a thing with us Slavs. We East Europeans are not so—so cold like the Americans who are forever afraid to touch each other or be close together. I'm your friend, you know that. I'm a happily married man. You've met my wife and actually eaten her homemade bread!"

It was all true, and there was more. His daughter wanted to be the first ordained Lutheran woman minister. He seemed impeccable—he was even loved by many students. On the other hand, almost every time I'd spent time with him before, he always parted with what now seemed a very perverse—and not just corny—joke: "Don't do anything I *would*."

Seeing my anxious expression, he kept defending himself: "Relax! First of all, we have two beds now, but even with one bed there would have been no problem. I have three children older than you, Cayle! I'm astonished at your suspicious mind!"

His speech was wearing me out as if his words were sandpaper and my mind was wood. When at last he whispered again, too harshly, "I just want to be close to you like a friend, that's all," I tried to think very clearly.

I asked, "Why didn't you want me to have my own bed?"

He was exasperated, and then he got angry. He shook his head, but he seemed determined to ignore what I thought. So he changed the subject.

He was very excited about showing me "the real life" of New York—so we went to 42nd Street and descended to a basement with a crudely painted "LIVE NUDE GIRLS" sign up over it. The cement stairs were heavy with the smell of cigarettes, vomit, shit, and rancid filth. The once white tiled floor was graying rapidly despite the efforts of a sullen, exhausted janitor with a large rolling bucket and mop. But I noticed the janitor was mopping out little flat-black painted stalls, each of them smaller than a telephone booth. An overpowering odor of detergent came from the steel bucket.

"I don't know... I don't wanna go in here," I said.

A couple of very grungy, depleted men looked at me and smiled. They were not exactly sleazy smiles but more like the smiles of the defeated who are glad to see someone less decimated joining their ranks. They were the most effete men I'd ever seen. If I hadn't been afraid of them, I'd have pitied them. They were standing by the sex toys and handling monstrous-looking plastic erections and foam rubber pussies and other things on a table.

"Oh, I'm surprised at you, Cayle. How can you be afraid to face the true decadent underside of the city? How can you call yourself a poet? There's nothing to be afraid of here! Besides, you have to see everything in the world if you want to be a poet!"

There we were, him in his bad tie and conference clothes and me in my oversized T-shirt and faded army surplus pants. I relented, thinking that the experience would be, if nothing else, fodder for poems. What a mistake.

He wanted to see the show, and it was worse than I feared. We had to step into these stinking black stalls and feed quarters into tiny black boxes after which a curtain would rise on a smudged plastic window. Then for a minute one watched the "live nude girl."

She was my age, or less. But she was aged in all the wrong ways. She was horribly pale under the fluorescent light—almost bluish white. It exacerbated her body's blemishes and dark bruises. Despite her youth, she had wrinkle lines and saggy bulges even though she was not fat. She did not have any clothes on except for these very big, clunky tennis shoes. The floor that she was walking on was covered with gym mats like the kind high schools have. She was not doing anything except walking around very flatfooted and bored. Sometimes she went nearer to the little windows where dollar bills appeared. She seemed about three weeks behind on her sleep; the rings and bags under her eyes were really so dark make-up wouldn't have helped. She made a kind of empty smile now and then; I couldn't help thinking that she looked like she was losing her mind.

Instead of feeding in more quarters, I stumbled quickly out of the darkness, feeling depressed. I hadn't shut the door behind me, but I'd begun to feel as caged as she was. I didn't see Syoenidz anywhere, then I realized he'd shut himself in the stall beside mine. He popped out with a lurid grin that actually frightened me.

"Isn't this great?" he asked. Then, seeing my face, he turned very serious, "Aren't you amazed at this decadence?"

I shrugged, "I've seen it," and he looked crestfallen. So I added, "It's amazing. Can we go now?"

"But you have to immerse yourself in this to understand the sufferings of humanity, you know, Cayle... There's no other way to really understand humanity. You have to experience everything, even the scum of the earth have feelings. Besides, when else will you have an opportunity like this?" He dropped several dollars in quarters into my hand and urged me to go back in.

I hesitated for a moment, but then I thought he was right that I'd never come back to a place like this myself. So I went back in and put a few quarters in.

It was getting worse. The girl was on the far side facing me, but she was squatting for a window behind her. She was showing her pale gray genitals to some guy steaming up his own window. She straightened up her legs a little while holding on her big tennis shoes. It looked like she was doing stretches in gym class, badly. Some more money fell on the floor near her feet, and her empty smile appeared. In a little while that window's curtain closed. She looked around and did the same thing for another window where a few dollars fell into her cage. I suddenly realized that the dark purple bruises on her inner arms and on the backs of her knees were overused tracks from shooting up. I felt this gut-wrenching horror at her life, then nausea—the smell was getting to me. I stepped back out into the light. The janitor looked up from his work. His mop was dripping with what I realized was fresh semen.

Syoenidz was in his dark stall for a long time. I was relieved to be alone for a while. I gathered my thoughts and looked at the men around me. They looked so impoverished and wasted. I realized this was their regular hangout—the horror of a whole life like that really struck me. I started to feel bad for them, but then one of them leered at me too intimately. Syoenidz was right about at least that—I didn't understand the "sufferings of humanity," and I wanted to contemplate this place, but from a distance.

Syoenidz was excited when he did finally pop out of his stall. When it dawned on him that I'd been standing around by myself for quite a while, he was dismayed. But he was eager to show me more though I didn't want to look at anything else. But he insisted, gesturing without words, as he pulled me over to his stall and pointed at a perfectly round hole two inches in diameter in the thin plywood wall between the stalls where we'd been standing. I didn't comprehend.

"Don't you see?... Don't you know what this is for?" he asked, very pleased with himself for having this piece of knowledge.

Then I realized what it was, and nodded, feeling suddenly sick in my stomach. But he eagerly explained anyway, "This is where you stick your penis through so that someone else—even a total stranger—can suck it off. Or—even fuck!"

Looking at me, his eyes were so huge I could tell he was really stimulated. I started to leave, but he grabbed my arm. "Wait, listen."

I heard it then, a low moaning, a shaking of wood here and there, and soft panting.

I nodded so he knew I heard it, and I really wanted to leave and started to quickly walk out. He caught up with me by the stairs, and then we were bathed again by the bright daylight, the traffic's roar and crowds of people, drug dealers, young girl and boy prostitutes and overdressed pimps. I was so glad to be able to walk quickly past everything. I hadn't eaten anything all day, but I wasn't hungry, anymore.

He dropped me off at the huge public library for a couple hours while he did his conference thing. I couldn't think very clearly. The only thing I remember was that he was late again, and that while I was waiting on the steps for him to reappear, a middle-aged man in his thirties wearing a very nice suit came up to me without smiling and asked, "Hey, ya wanna make fifty bucks?"

"No," I said, too surprised to say anything else.

After he was gone, though, I realized that he must have wanted sex. Then I realized, incidentally, that I didn't have any money on me except six crumby dollars—not even enough to get home on the most horrendous bus. Shit, I was counting on Syoenidz for everything. I hoped he wasn't going to get weird. Or weirder! I thought about all those Tae Kwon Do classes I'd had, and I thought that if he did anything, I'd be able to defend myself—I mean, he was an old middle-aged guy!

When he did finally come, I was so hungry my stomach hurt. He apologized for being late and offered to take me to dinner. The restaurant was a very dark German place with huge sausage, potato, and sauerkraut dishes. That was all they had, so we ate this immense, very salty, heavy dinner with which we only had very dark, thick beer to wash down. I never drank, though, and beer—especially this beer—got me drunk after a few sips. He kept talking cheerily about poetry, especially Mayakovsky and his tragic suicide and Rilke as a letter writer to a young poet, for some reason.

It wasn't till I actually started to feel my mind was buzzing that I realized exactly how I was being set up.

I stopped drinking the beer and insisted on water. Before he caught on that I had him figured out, I ordered coffee. He actually tried to object to my drinking coffee, too. It was so clear that he wanted me drunk, vulnerable, and sleepy. He was making me eat greasy food to knock me out. Then there was that whole thing with the beds in the hotel room. And where could I go?

I stopped talking completely so that he had to ask, "Cayle, what's wrong? Are you feeling ill?"

Actually, I was, but not in the way he was hoping.

Then, oddly, he praised Mayakovsky's suicide again: "I think that it revealed his greatness, Cayle. He was not afraid to sin boldly!"

I didn't respond.

"And, isn't it tragic that Esenin had to repress his homosexuality, and that he loved and married a beautiful dancer?"

Until that moment, my sympathies would have been with Esenin. But then I asked pointedly, "But how could he do that to her if he loved or cared about her at all as a human being?"

He stammered, "Why... Why—what do you mean?" He paused as if struck, "What do you care about her for? She was not a poet..."

I just stared at him and repeated the question because he was really bothering me.

Only much later did I realize that I should have picked up how little respect he had for women, any women—including his wife. I realized he wasn't truly able to love them. He'd complained they were unequal to men in genius, so he felt he couldn't communicate his true soul to them. He'd even once told me, "Women can never understand the way a man really feels because they don't have the same kinds of genius, the same kinds of souls—just look through history, Cayle." It was confusing to sort out his public pronouncements supporting women's rights and his boasting about his daughter who wanted to be a minister from his private confessions. Maybe he couldn't sort them out either.

He changed the subject and kept patronizing me with a steady blathering stream. I started assembling the facts. Having so little money, I had no way home—without him. I saw then with perfect lucidity that he was looking at me like a piece of meat.

"I'm done," I said.

He looked so dumbfounded that I almost laughed at him.

"But you must eat! You're so skinny you look like you're starving. Please, allow me to feed you."

"I don't want any more. I'm not hungry anymore," and in fact, I wouldn't really feel hungry again for a very long time.

"I won't have you leaving food like this! You're being ridiculous! You just have to wait a while, then eat more."

I waited and didn't eat. He waited and kept urging me to eat. It really was like a terrible game we were playing, except he thought I had no idea what he was up to. Or maybe he thought I was so trapped that it didn't matter... The beer was still making my mind fuzzy as we got up to go. I thought that I would still have the edge because he had eaten and drunken so much that I figured he'd have to fall asleep pretty soon. But I was wrong.

He kept raving at me, "Cayle, you have to experience everything!"

So he took me to a movie, Andy Warhol's campy 3-D remake of *Frankenstein*.

I knew it was another distracting, delaying tactic on his part, but I couldn't get out of it. Besides, anything seemed better than being alone with him in the hotel. I don't think he knew anything about the film except that it was an "art film" that I'd heard about and wanted to see because I liked Warhol. He didn't know how boring it would be or how oddly poignant it would be almost in spite of the bad acting and the perversely flat script. The "monster" and his "bride" in Warhol's version were too self-consciously gorgeous, bland, and existentially aware of the emptiness of the universe. Verifying his poor creations' intuitions about the universe, the doctor raped the female while she was still unconscious. Aside from that degrading moment, the film almost put Syoenidz to sleep, which in itself made me feel better. I even started to really like the movie for its honest portrayal of perversity.

When we got to the hotel room, I had to walk a very fine line. He became startlingly awake. He called room service for wine and started reading Rilke's *Sonnets to Orpheus* to me, in honor of me, he said. For a while, I didn't mind this because he had given up on insisting that we put the beds together without much of an argument. I'd simply said firmly, "No, I don't want that," several times.

But he kept drinking wine and urging me to drink. He kept reciting these sonnets to me, forgetting that I didn't know German. His face was red, his voice began to boom, and it seemed like he'd never get tired. Maybe he took drugs to wake himself up, but he was relentless. I stayed awake, sitting on the edge of my bed, pretending to be alert. I didn't want him to see me weakening. It really disturbed me because he also recited love poems to me, and these he read with special passion and pleading in his eyes. I was feeling more and more exhausted and afraid. My eyes were beginning to close when he finally gave up and said we could go to sleep. It was way after midnight by then, and he took a long time in the shower. I refused to shower, myself—even though the bathroom had a lock, it just seemed like the wrong move. It didn't occur to me till the morning—that is, too late—that I could have hidden in the bathroom.

There was a reprieve while he was showering, and I took advantage of that time to rest a little though I was careful to stay awake. I figured that as long as I kept all my clothes on and kept under the covers, I'd have some protection—at least enough to wake up before anything happened.

The disadvantage of being under the covers was that I wouldn't be able to hit him easily. All his limbs would be free and clear—and above me. So I had to remain on my back at all costs....

He finally came out in his pajamas. He still seemed wide awake, which was crushing. He said quietly, "Cayle, are you awake?"

"Yes," I said loudly.

"Aren't you tired, though?"

I said nothing for a long time.

"You must be tired after such a long day. Are you sure you don't want us to put our beds together?"

"I'm sure I don't want that."

"But I just want to be close to you as a friend. You don't understand. I care about you, really."

The silence seemed to fill with his semidrunkenness.

"I said I'm sure I don't want that. Please. Leave me alone."

"I'd never do anything to hurt you, Cayle. Really, you must trust me."

"Aren't you tired at all?" I was irritated.

There was a long silence. I knew he was planning his next moves. I could almost feel each step clicking into place in his mind.

"Yes," he admitted, and then he yawned a real yawn.

He turned the light out but seemed wide awake anyway. After only a few minutes he asked again, "Cayle, are you awake?"

"Yes." I was mad and I was so exhausted!

"Why won't you take off your clothes? You must be uncomfortable..."

"I'm fine."

"You can trust me, Cayle. I'm your friend, really."

I was starting to really hate him.

There was another long reprieve when he seemed to give up. His breathing changed from its short loud rhythm to a longer calmer rhythm. I started to feel more sleepy, but then a strange thing happened, I mean, strange for me, anyway. I prayed. Since I generally didn't believe in God, I only prayed in extreme emergencies. But this seemed like one to me. I wanted this night to be over so badly, and I wanted to be alone, home, and safe. I felt true despair.

I was still anxious when much later he got out of bed silently and walked around my bed on the way to the bathroom. I heard him close the door, hit the light, lift the toilet seat, and piss. I tensed up. But I was so exhausted that it was hard to do more than just feel tense. I was listening to his every little move: his hand on the doorknob, his first step out, his hand on the light switch, his steps quickly around my bed again, and then the sudden squeaking of his feet as they swivelled on the carpet away from the direction of his bed and toward my own.

Suddenly he leaped on me and pinned down my arms and legs with his. He was much heavier than I imagined. I couldn't lift him an inch. It was horrible—even more horrible than I feared, for he was trying to kiss me with his big wet slobbering mouth, which was rasping desperately straight into my ear: "I love you! I love you! I love you Cayle! I must have you! I must have you!" He went on and on like that, slobbering on the side of my face.

Terror seized me. I knew as I jerked my face away from his toward my left and struggled with all my strength to get out from under him that I had to think of something fast. I was so panic-stricken that I started to hyperventilate. The adrenaline was pumping so hard I could hear my heart in my throat. I was struggling in vain—he was only getting more excited.

Then I got a sudden inspiration about the one thing I could do that would totally turn him off: *If he thought I was laughing at him, he would stop being excited because he would feel deeply humiliated.* So I started to laugh a high-pitched, screeching, out-of-control laugh, a laugh that was at once eerie in a falsetto range and yet real in that it seemed to be laughing at *him.* Of course, I wasn't really laughing—I was too terrified to find him even slightly humorous. But this laughter kept searing through the air, filling the room; it was painfully grating even to me. It was almost witch-like as it rang out of my lungs, which were heaving like a machine, and happily I realized he was becoming deeply insulted. So I laughed even higher and louder until this hysterical surge, like a fountain, slowly pushed his face away.

I finally had my arms free again and was at last able to push him away with my own strength, but by then I didn't have to. He was so mad at me! And even then I did begin to realize that this injury he felt meant that he did love me, really, albeit in his own demented way. And that made me sad even in the midst of this laughter, which had a life of its own. I really couldn't stop it even ten minutes later.

The laughter prevented him from saying anything gushy anymore; it protected me every time he seemed to want to approach me, even when it began to pour out sporadically. He made a few attempts to scold me, and protested in his humiliation, "What are you laughing at? How can you be laughing at me? What are you laughing at?"

Then I was sure I was safe because he believed I'd found him totally ridiculous. He was decimated—brooding. He hardly said anything after my last laughs. He flung a few angry curses at me from behind his bed, shouting "Fuck you! You ingrate! You're so ugly anyway! You're a talentless good-for-nothing, Cayle! You'll never amount to anything!"

I knew better than to say anything. He finally went to sleep with his back to me.

Ironically, I was too pumped up to feel tired. I had the luxury of being free to fall asleep when I wanted to, which wasn't till I'd heard him snoring very loudly for a long time. But then his tremendous snoring kept me awake almost all night. And then I was so exhausted that being kept up was a kind of endless torture. But I was glad because I knew I'd won at least this battle.

But the next day was hell. When he woke me, he was hostile. Yet he was adopting a new kind of pretense in the gray daylight: "Nothing happened here last night. And if you tell anybody about it, ever, I'll say you were lying. *And you'll pay for it. I promise you!*"

"What are you talking about? You can't deny what happened here to me. If nothing happened, you'd have nothing to deny.... *I was here.*"

"You ungrateful son of a bitch! You can find your own way home!"

Logic was futile, so I said nothing.

After a few minutes of awful silence, we were checked out and on the sidewalk.

Suddenly, he turned and sneered at me, "Who do you think you're kidding, Cayle? *Nobody would want to fuck you anyway!*"

It hurt when he said that just because it was so insulting. He was so vicious and childish all at once. It was horrible yet fascinating to observe, in a way. He was lashing out at me with the same kind of contempt that he had previously reserved only for women.

I knew he could never appreciate what he'd just put me through, so I only said: "I don't have any way to get home. You said you'd take me to and from the city."

He just glared at me, but eventually, after many more insults, he grunted he'd take me back. It wasn't for my benefit, though. He could have far more easily given me money to get home. What he did was use the two-hour drive as an opportunity to outline all the ways in which he would retaliate if I said anything. He even threatened me outright and said he could—or would—have me expelled. He tried very hard to make me feel unworthy of his friendship.

After a while I tuned him out—I was numbed with fatigue. I knew he had to get back to his wife and his beautiful home. But I also realized that in his own way, he had been in love and suffered total humiliation, and now he hated me. How much he hated me was actually a sign of how hurt he was, but that just made him more dangerous. I realized then that my troubles from him were only just beginning.

L

Hugh Steinberg

I
wish to
feed
you
black
grapes,
watch you
eat
them
judiciously,
watch
you
split
each
one
apart
in your
mouth,
cup
the
seeds
between
your
fingers.
You
don't
know
this
yet.
I am
half
empty
with
you,
and I
want
to be
full.

Green Prevailing

Eric Elshtain

Rationalizing a thousand small starvations
I grow flora in her addict's heart:
its fixed pitch the rhythm
of whom she's always wanted
but who's already dead
in the aftermath of a garden scene.

Without you I sleep with vague pharmacies
filled with messages—
You need me or *I need more light.*

But it's beautiful that nothing happens between us—
in theory, you'll never walk in here again

implanting gardens in the soil
of our understood mornings
imprinted with the negative of your features.

I say a cold word for the parity
of her forms & my allergies
to the plant banished

in her kingdom's low-water hierarchies—
a locked green knee
shaped like its thicknesses.

Requiem

Eric Elshtain

She crushes saltines
to dust
in their cellophane,
pulls open & pours.

She collects
air with her nose,
keeping still
the pile
on her tongue.

She re-rehearses
him home
from duty, words

starting
in short breaths.

Dog; cradle;
frigate.

Her throat
behind the crumbs
aches to swallow

& unclenches
as she fights
the fact
of a child's fist
filled with dirt

& irises
readied
for a toss.

Fluid Mechanics

Jack Martin

At the urinal, a big friendly man
threatens my limbs,
my life
in the narrowest bar
in northern Colorado,
pokes me in the chest with *the Super Bowl*
      was more than weird,
      Goddamn it, an ass-whuppin—
      don'tcha think?
      Not WEIRD,
he's big in my face now.
(Zzip.)
      an ASS-WHUPPING—
and nervous, sort of,
I don't even care,
I could wet his shoes
and bash his face square

until later, rocking to the guitar of the hundredth monkey
with the green-eyed waitress while she works—
washed in the arms and faces in this lucky reggae
I remember how to love

and order more beer, nervous,
sort of, knowing the bubbles,
the bottom of this glass, the shrink
and vanish,
the amber sky

Hearing Sandy Bull Play Manha de Carnival
Michael Calvello

I see age
all around me
my father
a darkness growing
darker my mother
around our eyes
an ancient sadness
in our closet universe

please look in my eyes
and touch me
deep in the place of my spinning bone

Misconception
Jeff P. Stein

"Somebody's going to live through this. Suppose it's you?"
—Mark Doty

I. Waiting to Be

I wonder sometimes if she knows,
is waiting. Waiting
for us, watching over us until we
can join enough to bring the lightning
moment of her liberation—at which point we'll be
transformed from parent to child and child to parent.
This play of seeds and eggs in which we come
together all elbows and thumbs,
a certain smoothness brushing against an awkward
tossing, trying to find the right position—
what is the right position for conceiving?

Does she dream about us? Does she wonder
about our fingers, our quirks, our laugh?
It's trying—waiting for a baby,

waiting to be born.

II. Ultrasound

He keeps looking, sliding the jellied knob over
and over; I see only gray shadows, maybe a crescent
where the sac—what I can't understand is where,
nine weeks, where is this child?

I must not understand.
Somehow we cannot grow fast enough.
We've gone from forest to desert—her breasts still filling, veins coming in.
But he wants to take some blood in two days.
Wait until it passes he says; then collect the sick fish.

This world is too much to be weak.

I can't believe we're losing
this—a little spoiled fish swimming upside down.
What happened to our shine?

III. The Cannon River

The water catches my eye—it says,
"We are rushing along together;
        what is it with you?"

The waters shimmer past, leaving nothing.
All flowing by and always flowing by,
unable to miscarry, separate, or exclude
any of itself   together   one body.
And I wonder if we were a river
where would an unborn daughter go?

IV. Overdue

This morning the hospital bill overcame the mailbox.
Suction, surgical drapes, anesthesia.
No diapers, no formula, no blankets. Nothing but
untouchable cool techniques of jargon.
Blue ink pressed into layers of thin paper with
more force than it took—more time than it took—
to scrape away two months.
Your whole life in that five minutes. All that you
know of this world hollowed us to empty stumps.
You died inside; a hurricane tore through
when you ripped a hole out of my back.

V. Stones

This morning jogging, found myself turning
into the cemetery. Phantom cramp in my left side, sucking
for something like air.
Dusty monuments surrounding a quiet path of stones:
Timmerman, Crottendon, Horowitz, Paltz.
Marbled forgotten memories.

I was a father for two brief months. You were a
fixative we hoped for. Little undersized   fading rattle
in a shrinking sac. Who thinks of you now?
Teaches you the jazz greats?

I remember when everything but dating was easy.
More concerned with basketball scores and girls than debt.
Getting into every college I applied to.
I don't remember how to do this, don't remember
instructions for loans, miscarriages, flushing the radiator.

Nothing in this cemetery remembers you.
Not even these old stones will look after you now.
        this is what loss is like

The Famous Artificial Heart Experiment

Glen A. Mazis

There were no boundaries for him
once they removed his heart.
The bedside lamp broiled his liver
with its scalding light, the chill
draft running across the hospital floor
went straight to his tongue—
it froze in midsentence waggle—
and the nurse's hips
crushed his squeaking lobes,
surrounding them with their fleshy elegance.

Tied by throbbing hoses
to the clanking Jarvik Seven,
he was propelled relentlessly into space,
pushed assertively further
since his blood no longer
danced with the moon,
but was driven by metallic fanaticism.
The beats hammered at his mind
until holes opened
and he leaked away.

The doctors had feared
his senses would become too mechanical
paced by a cast iron pump,
after the pulpy center was removed.
How his thoughts got dispersed
was a puzzle, since clever with gears
and tubes, they never felt how we think
from the body's rhythmic kinship
with all that beats around it,
in time with clouds scudding skyward,
the bobbing of flowers on their stalks,
and even the ebb and flow of traffic:
the way the beating of the world
beats out its time in our hearts,
and so in our heads.

There is an ancient ability
of cells to listen
while pumping, to receive
in the midst of pushing,
that allows the world
to herd our feelings,
like wayward cattle,
into the corral of who we are.

Deconstruction
Jennie Pak

My spine's caught in the bedspring, if I rise
To meet brightening day's willing breath as I
Should, metal will cut through the mattress and
I, bloody, with springs attached, will walk to
The shower and bathe each coil purring; my delightful

Body—what have I done to deserve these
Extras, clinging as I am clanging and
Bouncing off walls? Will my daughter notice
When I walk into her room and as
Usual, she pains herself not to see me;
My hair is thinning and what good is
Garlic shampoo, the lies told us, that we tell
Ourselves as we fight to keep ourselves same. No, yes,

I don't know. I'm careful not to step
Beyond the doorway. Where you going? What time
Will you be home? Her shoulders, smooth doorknobs,
Dismiss me but I'm carrying more weight
This morning and not easily discouraged,
Movement is possible now—change, although
This house laughs at springs sticking out of
My back—automaton, android; turn what's
Human into what's not or something in
Between and maybe there is courage

To try again. You need a haircut, I say,
Reaching for greasy strands hanging
Unhappy in front of her ear. She pulls
Away so my fingers freeze midair, midpoint
She and I: these hands growing brown spots,
A leopard in her eyes. Lotions don't help, seaweed wraps;
Everything I touch cries: Look what happens—

How will I sleep tonight. Curly spine twanging
Through dreams: country tune, a challenge, cure—
Don't sleep, grab a jackhammer and tear the
House down. Watch tiles separate, ceilings
Exhale; smash the PC, VCR, radiators
Hissing, zipped in hard, black skins. I will stand
Outside my daughter's room struggling
To find last words before the heaving walls
Throw down their bones and regretless, cave in.

Make-Believe
Jennie Pak

I want to turn the page and be Simple Hans
Who can't be trusted to do a single thing,
Or the giant cyclops with the one chandelier eye.
I want to be the woman whose goose
Lays a hundred golden eggs, the world coated,
Suddenly, with promise, with miracle's strange paint.
Yellow, orange, silver: trees sprouting jewelled leaves,
Sparkles like a countess or queen; I want to pluck
Diamonds like plums, climb a castle looming across the sea—
I feel like swimming, but there's no water,
No way to peel the page in half and crawl through, torch it with a
Burning third eye, think: mosaic, waiting for the sun
And moon to part; west of the stars and north o' nothing.
Bronze, blue, purple: bodies in glass cases, axes and lances
And a witch's crooked smile, her finger waving
In front of the oven: Come here my love, come closer.
Who will solve the riddle, inherit a kingdom,
Curse one glass slipper, wield that knife
Piercing the goose's heart; magic, magic everywhere
And coma and awake to a stranger's face.
Red, violet, green: shine, shine, more of everything:
Castle's highest room, the invisible cloak, a potion that lets you
Stretch your body for miles; the warm kiss, the wrinkled face
Rolling across the floor, all happy ever, rainbow's shimmery dress
I put on, blasting into show of fireworks, bang-bang
The arc and bloom: dazzle out of nowhere.

Vampire
Jennie Pak

I will leave the window open.
So, come undo zippers of sleep,
Wrap me in tunneled whorls
Spinning around this empty spool
Like a clatter of silk. Just hold me

Close, lift my clumsy angles
From the bed's rectangle.
I am square: four closet corners,
Equal sides; what I learn in school
Breaks my circumference,

Viruses all stories. Makes no sense
To sit in the chair, listen to
Bells ring wrong ways home
Where plates of glass will
Never break, the potted gardenia

Should not die. I want to
Feel just what you feel—
Exactly the same clappered heat
Rising till fangs, illumined
icicles, show their intentions

Off. I mean to write my name,
Rip open that frog's slender thighs—
Such jumpy brilliance, no more
Wide chapters I must fill; I'm not interested
In exponents: arm after swinging arm

A discus I will throw off—
You won't make a sound, will shoot
Through me two comets
So far, so deep into the wood
It will burn the whole house down.

Legs
Neil Carpathios

Not the invention of kindness,
or hope,
or self-pity.
Not the punishment of too much longing,
the black bile of memory rising,
Earth's spinning.
Not Schopenhauer, Gandhi, Spinoza, Plato.
Not the crossing of a room, the sitting on a chair.
Not Mozart.
Not thighs fluting into rippling globes
of chiseled shanks,
the comparison of skin
to a horse's velvet haunch.
Not the rhythmic flex and release
of each calf as she walks.
Not the instep kissed.
Not the ankle.
Not the tendons beneath her knees.
Not what words can graze or grip.
Not extending this education
of her body or desire.
Not even this not knowing
where or how
to begin.

Pretending to Read

Neil Carpathios

By the reclining body
of the woman he loves,
magazine pages turn themselves.
She sips a margarita
through a straw
letting August sun
turn her brown.
Last night she sat brooding
on the stoop watching cars,
upset about some way
he'd hurt her. It happens.
She thinks he's hoping
time softens anger
between a man and a woman,
that he's wondering
how to say he's sorry
without having to say it.
He pretends to read
behind a newspaper,
she thinks he'll put
it down and wonder
out loud about weather,
state of the economy,
last night's scores.
She picks up the magazine,
pretends to read about
diets and Southern cooking.
She turns pages. He turns pages.
Neither gives in.
He sniffs cocoa butter,
thinks of the heart, the size of a fist,
how it holds all that's good,
bad in the world, how
it's awkward and stupid,
how it thinks it knows best,
how we reward it by loving
any person or thing,

punish it by doing the same.
Her hand reaches down
to the cluster of grapes.
Her jade bracelet clinks.
It happens. A bead of sweat
rolls down her wrist.
He says he wonders if
the mail came.
She offers him a grape.
He puts down the newspaper.
She puts down the magazine.
It always happens.
His heart bangs its tin cup
wanting more.
She says she's tired of reading.
He says he likes how
the wind ropes her hair.

My Father Come Back as the Dawn

Neil Carpathios

At the end of a rickety pier staring down
into green murk, haze layering
surface tension thick as gauze
unspooling further out-before my eyes,
all I want is at the center of a moment, here:
low-flying honker, cool air, stillness
and him beside me again, wordless,
pointing to where the mallard skids
into mist, skating, disappearing,
leaving a trail in water fading,
as if wanting to make sure I don't miss
the seamless line between the seen
and almost seen suddenly revealed
in air like milk, as though
what is here is always almost there,
as if to point the way toward
where he went, gliding, effortless,
toward the beauty of a thing in its body
pulled onward, opalescent, hush
of lake and sky, of everything inbetween,
marsh weeds erect, dragonfly lifting,
light piercing fog, him now gone,
even his abrupt leaving a pointing
toward a greater hush I can't name.

Only Envy
Daisy Fried

Some kids scoop handfuls of exploding caps out of big denim pockets,
hurl them down by ones and threes, ratatat,
boys lean against a green wall eating pizza shiny with grease,
my shadow over the face of a sleeping flatnosed drunk,
my shadow over the snob boy drawing him badly,
sex going on all over the place,
the rankness of garbage and
the bimbo of the world. Not jealousy, not lust.
                                        Only envy,
which walks streets at their most crowded hours,
stales and sours like milk in the brain,
like virgins who stay virgin past health and all believing.

Romance Novel

Daisy Fried

Smoky cold air came in when he opened
the door. He's brighter than the world behind
him, certainly more solid. There's hello
and damn you all in his smile for the room

and he makes for me and I am his straight
away, in the first few glimpses. I dreamt
I had many gowns, that this hard hard hand
ripped them off, one after the other. Green

one, *rip*. Blue, *zap*. Yellow with red flowers,
gauze insets. *Kazut, ffffrrrrrrrrttt*. We reached the zig-
zag, came to the honeydew—

The industrial laundry's heady bleach
dizz seeped into the gray gold street I
walked on alone. As if a bird formed itself out of my breastbone and flew off. As

if I walked through stands of blasted cedars
shaking down sapped drops of leftover rain
from prehistoric crooks and limb lops—

Breast. Mouth. Thigh. Zipper. Cream.
Repeat.
Breast. Mouth. Thigh. Zipper. Cream.

Make babies. Here come the babies. The End.

Dream Puzzle

Ran Huntsberry

On a brown card table in a dining room corner
two pieces of an old puzzle
slide into place. We are embracing
in a long hall with jigsaw edges.

Men in white coats
deliver crates of computer paper
to dab the ink
running down your cheeks.

I wash my lips in the black flood, press them
against your dry breasts like a rubber stamp, wait
for the missing words to dry.

Punched for Nothing

Peter Reynolds

Radio, I prefer bed to this driving
the 6 o'clock East of red tongs
tipping a serpent's tongue.
I'm not the one meant for your broadcast. Whatever language,
I'd fail it. Play fox hunt trumpets,
Napoleon drums, anything
to quick-widen Olympic these biceps,
my chest my chest until the seat belt snaps.
I need them full right now—that sorrow,
so long toughening himself into grief,
has named this the day he knocks
aside the "versus" that's kept us apart, kept me
safe since I first learned how a simple
silence in the chest makes people cry.

Yesterday was the birthday of my dead son.
My wife, hive-headed with confusion,
scissored boxes sealed since the funeral,
found a sweatshirt for the team
that left our city years ago—"What a nice gift,
I need to buy that." She carried it all the way
to Clawson's Sporting Goods, the checkout,
and when the register displayed
"This Item Not On File," collapsed. Love,

in your cold hospital,
please understand—I'm not there,
couldn't be—last night was punched
for nothing. I hope
that the next rest stop's trash can
has a lid weighted with stones. A shield
and something to sling into
those gladiatorial eyes of grief filling the horizon
before he grows too tall and can see
I won't outrun, will never
shrink him enough so he feels
this car's tires
squeal up his abdomen.

At Grandfather's House

Deborah Byrne

I have little waffle marks
from pressing my nose into the screen
door. Outside, the wind hits the trees.
Loosening leaves slap my grandfather
like hundreds of little hands. He has
just pruned his roses for the last time
this season. Before he pruned the roses,
he kicked the dog. Behind a tree,
the dog shivers and waits.
Beside grandfather, a bucket of water.
In it are dead chipmunks
who had made a maze of tunnels
a few inches under his lawn. They
made him angry. he says. *Makes my yard cave in*,
he says. He lives in a neighborhood
where everyone is "nice."
They have that look.
In his house, an immaculate den—
dark leathers, plaid cushions,
animal heads on the walls. Above the desk,
a painting of a DeLorean with red interior.
A handprint smudge on the right rear fender.
At night, spirits of the dead moan
and try to clean house.
Scattered dust falls on the wings of moths
and is flown away before dawn.
In his garage—shovels and sledgehammers
with dark stains. He lives near
a vacant lot that looks like someone's been
digging in it. You could trip
trying to cross that lot. He has taken his knife
and scratched his name into every tree
on his property. Yesterday, he pried the mailbox
off the front door and put it in the basement. I turn
and watch him as he goes into the bathroom
at the end of the hall. For a long time
he looks at himself in the mirror.
As he crosses the kitchen, he looks at me
with his bathroom eyes.

My Uncle's House
Alex Stein

In my uncle's house there was no bullshit. Or, rather, it was all bullshit, but bullshit was understood to be an ineluctable element of the human condition.

"We arise from a seedbed of bullshit," my uncle pronounced fondly, puffing on the evening's first joint.

He worked as a university physics professor. "If," as he said, "you could call it working."

"It is more like acting out a part in a theater of the absurd," he said. "The only difference is that all the while you are performing Eugene Ionesco's *The Rhinoceros*, your audience is convinced that they are witnessing a production of William Shakespeare's *Macbeth*. The trick is in helping them to understand that at a fundamental level there is no actual difference. Everything arises out of a seedbed of chaos. Nobody can say where any of it has really come from or what any of it really means. Tragedy may be comedy; the joke of which simply eludes us."

It was my uncle who first made it clear to me that the nature of "truth" was to be unknowable. "All fixity is falsehood," he said.

In the back of my mind, I had always known this, I felt. The truth was something more fluid than they had taught us in school. It was not simply this or that settled response, but a floating point, dependent upon context.

In what year did Columbus discover America? Answer: by which calendar? The Chinese? The Mayan? And with what colossal pretension do we use the word "discover" of a land-mass already long occupied?

"Questions," my uncle told me, "are not just means to ends, but ends in themselves."

You can well imagine that I soon began smoking a fair amount of marijuana myself.

"How do I know who I am?" I asked one night, as he was licking the seam on a third large spleef. "Slow process of discovery," he replied. "Trial and error." "No sudden flash of illumination?" I asked. "Not for those to whom it is not given," he replied.

My uncle is not the Buddha and neither am I the Buddha. We are just two swimmers in a sea of delusion, trying hard not to drown by the weight of our own vanity.

Some afternoons I stare at the sun as if from the deep reaches of cold space, thinking under what a tiny prick of the full Light, canopied, we all live and die.

110

My Aunt

Alex Stein

My aunt read tea leaves.

"This one was Darjeeling," she'd say, going around the table after the guests had departed and looking into their mugs. "This one was Earl Grey. And this," she'd say, pulling up a tea bag by its dunking string, "was definitely a Lipton's."

She also read auras, runes, and salt spills.

The only thing that she did not read was books. Reading books, in her opinion, constituted a failure of the imagination.

It was all right to write them, she supposed; although she really had to wonder "for whom?"

"It is a fine thing for your spirit that you are a writer," she said to me. "I just hope that you do not expect anything more from it."

My first published novel had been a runaway best seller.

I was appearing on television talk shows, for god sakes!

I got letters offering proposals of marriage.

I had a bank account. I went to interesting dinner parties.

But, by these things, my aunt was unimpressed.

"Once you have entered this earth's plane," she said, "you are sure to find yourself somewhere."

On Losing One's Virginity Again
Karen Propp

On Tuesday, I underwent minor surgery that retrieved my eggs from my ovaries. Wednesday, Thursday were long days while my husband and I waited to learn if his sperm had successfully fertilized my eggs in a petri dish. Finally, on Friday, I returned to the hospital to have the embryos transferred into my willing womb, What a strange, two-part, out-of-the-body conception! I feel as if I've lost my virginity again. Like the first time, I have lost innocence, but gained knowledge and a new sense of self. The world has shifted on its axis.

How can I articulate this surreal experience of losing my virginity for a second time, to the high ceremonies of assisted reproductive technology, at the age of nearly forty?

The first time, I giggled about it with friends at slumber parties. I pawed through *The Heart is a Lonely Hunter* and *Lady Chatterly's Lover* seeking words for what I felt. But now I cannot draw from any wellsprings of literature or history, I have few associations or comparisons to describe this new rite of passage that an increasing number of women are experiencing.

Nor do I have access to a vast store of women's tales like those available for pregnancy and childbirth. *We think back through our mothers if we are women*, as Virginia Woolf reminds. Tell your mother, aunt, cousin, or hairdresser that you are pregnant and she will invariably recall an incident from her own childbearing. But there were no petri dishes in what Alice Walker calls our mothers' gardens—those fertile beds of artistic and biological creativity from which we contemporary women grew. During our efforts to create new life with the new technologies, not one of our mothers can tell us, "I learned to shift my weight so the injections didn't hurt," or "The medications didn't bother me as much as the uncertainty." Some of our sisters and some of our friends may say this, but none of our mothers. We will have to be those mothers.

I think back to feminists such as Adrienne Rich who demand that we struggle to speak in the mother tongue and dream in a language other than that of the patriarchy. Rich reminds me to speak in my own voice rather than in the jargon voice of medicalized terminology. For medical language, despite all the sanctified power it suggests and projects, objectifies our bodies and reduces our individual experiences to anonymous events.

If I think back through Virginia Woolf, who so passionately urged women to write the truth about their own bodies, I am inspired to narrate the simple truth about my body—which is also my mind, emotions, experience—during the high ceremonies of assisted reproductive technology. *This is the way it happened to me.*

Monday, the evening before the egg retrieval, I follow my clinic's instructions to give myself an enema. Before these infertility treatments began, I never knew there were so many ways to poke and penetrate the body. Here is yet another: I kneel on the bathroom floor, face to the tile, ass in the air. In this humbling position I twist my right arm to squeeze a bottle of clear fluid into my anus. Erotic ritual? Fertility prayer? Torture? And a short while later, sitting on the toilet, my bowels convulsing in spasms, I am purged of my accumulations. Cleansed now, I can sleep a fitful sleep.

In the morning, Samuel and I drive our thirty-minute route to the hospital without saying much of anything to one another. He concentrates on the highway traffic and I on taking deep breaths to remain calm. At the hospital, we report to an unfamiliar wing where a nurse shows us to a private room. I hang my clothes in the closet, and slip into a cotton johnny so threadbare that as soon as I put it on I start to shiver, whether from an actual chill or from fear I do not know. Nothing could have been farther in elegance from the black evening dress about which Samuel and I used to fantasize, back before any of these treatments began. We imagined that I would wear that slinky dress to become impregnated with his banked sperm! In this pitiful hospital gown and under the bright fluorescent lights that wash out my skin, I feel myself becoming weak and vulnerable—a patient. As a patient, I lie down on the white gurney and cover myself with blankets. As a patient, I offer my bare arm to the technician who bustles into the room, rather deftly inserts an IV tube into a vein in my hand, and leaves a bag of fluids to slowly drip into my blood.

Samuel and I have exchanged few words this morning. Even so, I am glad he is here, a familiar figure sitting on a tan vinyl chair to remind me that there is a life we share outside this hospital room. He takes a yellow notepad from his briefcase to prepare for a meeting he must attend later in the day; I turn on the Walkman I have brought and listen to one of my relaxation tapes. We could almost be at home, each of us engaged in our own activities, but feeling the other nearby.

At home, for the past two weeks, morning and evening, I have injected myself with Fertinex, the newest FDA-approved ovum-stimulating drug, and as a result I have grown five mature eggs. There is about a five percent chance of impregnation per embryo, so the more embryos that are transferred, the better the odds for overall success. I have heard about the fifteen or twenty eggs other women produce, and when I compared myself to them I felt a bit like I did in junior high school when I envied Dawn Weaver's svelte figure and flawless skin. But I remind myself that five eggs is a good number for me, since the previous cycle I produced only two. Indeed, I feel proud of my five egg follicles, which I have seen as tiny dots on the ultrasound screen.

An aide comes into the room where Samuel and I are waiting and dutifully wheels me into the elevator that will take me upstairs to the pre-op room. She is young, with teased and treated hair, and long fingernails painted platinum blue. The elevator buttons light up: 2, 3. Samuel is quiet; I am quiet. The young woman's gum-chewing and spunky demeanor make me feel that were she not working these dour corridors, she would be in a place that's lively with music and conversation—a disco where I could wear my black dress. "Ready for your procedure?" she says rather brightly to me, as if asking whether I like the band Procedure. I have developed an aversion to that word. The egg retrieval is yet another procedure. in my experience, "procedure" is an all-purpose euphemism to cover events that usually involve speculums, catheters, needles. They take place in antiseptic rooms with bright lights, involve few words and many steady breaths. I've looked it up. The dictionary defines procedure as "an act composed of steps," and "procedure" originates from the word "proceed" which means "to go forward."

A medical term, procedure does nothing to help us women invent vocabulary for our newly scripted lives or tell the truth about our bodies. Everything in my infertility career has led up to these oh so post-modem rites of female passage: egg retrieval and the later embryo transfer. If I am to carry new life, these will be the determining moments. The word "procedure" and the accompanying hospital instructions about where to report and when I can or cannot eat are not sufficiently heroic for the great journey on which I and Samuel have embarked. For me at least, the steps the doctor will perform in a certain order—and make no mistake, they must be performed precisely is our signal for an end-of-the-century metaphysical breakthrough.

The aide pushes me, or should I say the gurney, into another brightly lit room. Again, Samuel and I have to wait. This room is a holding area, a passageway to the operating room. Out of the comer of my doped-up eye, I see a man with black wiry hair hurrying in our direction. From a distance, he resembles someone I once met on a blind date, The only topic we could find to talk about was downhill skiing, which at that time I hadn't done in fifteen years, and at the end of the drink or dinner, I forget which, I was terribly relieved to go home to my cat, attic room, and book-lined walls.

Mr. Blind Date saunters up to the bed on which I lie and looks into my face. I see by a momentary dip in his winning smile that he doesn't find me his type either. "We can't be sure of retrieving all five egg follicles," he says, voicing his disappointment. "Yes, we usually get 70%.... We'll do our best."

Can't be sure of retrieving all five! Wherever that was written it must have been in a fine print I missed. Already, my five eggs seem less golden. *Egg harvesting*, it's sometimes called, as if a woman were a ripe field. I feel rocky and dry.

A tremendous set of doors opens and I wave good-bye to Samuel as I am wheeled into the operating room. Scattered around me are little tables, metal instruments, objects covered in aqua plastic bags. A blond woman appears at my side and puts her hand on my shoulder. "I'm Stephanie. I'm your embryologist today."

My eggs will soon be her responsibility. It will be Stephanie who looks through the microscope at the semen sample and chooses for each egg a single sperm, a sperm that came from my husband's body. Stephanie will cut off its tail, and by manipulating the robotic arms of the micropipettes, inject that sperm into my egg

"You'll be careful to use the right sperm?" I ask tentatively.

"We match everything very carefully. Everything has your and your husband's names on it." I'm wearing a plastic bracelet with my name and address and I realize now why the admitting nurse, the IV tube technician, the anesthesiologist, and the doctor all turned my wrist to check it this morning. Stephanie tips my wrist as well. Apparently, I am still who I am supposed to be.

The bearded anesthesiologist, who glides about silent as gas, appears at my side, "We're giving you something is to make you comfortable," he tells me.

As if I could ever be comfortable amid all this strangeness. With the gas man's drugs, I will fall to, a deeper sleep than Sleeping Beauty knew. My blind-date doctor will use his special needle to puncture my vaginal walls. Up, up, he will go, to get what he wants. With his sharp needle and ultrasound guidance, he will penetrate farther than any other lover. Who has ever seen my anatomy with such intimacy? Who has ever known me like this?

I take a deep breath and feel my legs pulled open and then I know I must surrender my eggs to this new conception.

I wake woozy and a little sore, A nurse slips next to the bed and checks my pulse.

"Any pain? We have something if you do."

I query my belly and legs. Nothing stabs or pierces. I shake my head.

"You may spot a little."

I check the sheet and the pad between my legs for blood, wanting some visible sign that I have, indeed, lost my virginity this second time, but there is none.

By the clock on the wall I see that I have lost forty minutes of consciousness. Where did I go? Sweet nothings were surely whispered while I dozed and slipped dreamlessly to some mythic place where babies begin.

The wiry-haired doctor appears again at my side. "We retrieved four eggs, four good ones." And then he is off, with the bemused but harried air of a man who is used to leaving one woman's bed for the next.

Another bed is wheeled and placed next to mine. I turn my head and see a woman I recognize from the clinic's waiting room all those early mornings when I sat until my name was called for my blood to be drawn. This woman sat in a comer, her head bent, wearing a blue pea coat. Now her long-lashed eyes open and she turns her head groggily from side to side. I want to call out, *They did you too?* Against the hospital sheets, her copper-colored arms look incongruously healthy. Earlier, in pre-op, I'd glimpsed another young woman being wheeled out, her cheeks flushed pink, her hair lustrous. In a hospital setting, we infertility patients are instantly recognizable as neither ill nor injured.

How are you feeling?, I want to ask the woman in the bed beside mine. *Isn't this strange?* Are we egg retrieval companions? Synchronous ovulators? Above us both, neon green lines on monitors rise and fall to chart vital signs. No words rise from my muffled, medicinal rest. A nurse pulls a striped curtain around my bed and checks the round rubber pieces taped to my chest. It is December and over her scrubs she wears a smock covered with pictures of a jolly Santa Claus. My eggs have been taken and soon I will be sent home.

At home, I sleep off the anesthesia and wake feeling that I've been punched in the gut. This, I've been told, is a normal reaction following the emptying of my ovaries. I call a few friends. I call my sister. I call my mother.

"There were four eggs," I tell my mother, "and now they must fertilize." The words sound stiff in my mouth. Am I reporting on an operation or announcing news concerning her future grandchild?

There is a silence on the other end of the line. I can feel her searching out what say. She settles on "How are you feeling?"

"Everything went well," I try. But that sounds vague and insufficient. I am fired, apprehensive, and relieved. I tell her this, but my words have no history and cannot resonate off of anyone else's experience. Who ever talks about eggs fertilizing in a glass dish? It sounds like an exhibit for a science fair, I could aim to be a scientist at that fair and say *The injection pipette pushed through the zona pellucida into the ooplasm.*

I could draw associations. *In vitro* is Latin for "in glass," I could say, Remember Duchamp's art piece, his large glass, *Bride Stripped Bare by Her Bachelors, Even*. I was a bride and you could call me stripped bare. Remember his mounted bicycle wheel and urinal as sculpture? Maybe it's a matter of stripping away preconceptions in order to say: *This is a new female experience.*

The truth is, during the following two days, I become sentimental. I think often and fondly about my eggs, Eggs in a laboratory twenty miles away; eggs joining to my husband's sperm as I shop for groceries or read a book. The entire chromosomal structure for a new human being could be coming into play while we eat dinner or pay the bills. These possibilities will never cease to amaze me.

Late Thursday afternoon, the call comes. Four eggs were successfully injected with sperm; four eggs fertilized; there are four possible embryos.

I walk around the pond near my house to breathe in the wintry air and admire the season's starkest trees, bare now of buds, arching against a silver gray sky. A runner in a yellow sweatshirt speeds around the bend. A shaggy dog lopes by, his red tongue lolling. A stout woman in a parka huffs along. Every one of these living creatures began, it suddenly occurs to me, as an embryo. The globed streetlights come on. Four embryos, I say to myself, and the words finally begin to sound familiar. Hallelujah. Four possible embryos.

It is mid-December in New England; the days shorten and then shorten more, until darkness falls by 4:15. Soon it will be the Solstice, the darkest day of the year. I think about how the winter dark makes one travel inward, and I feel that is a good thing, for I want now to keep my energy quiet and introverted, near where the embryo might grow. By traveling inward, I find a new self to replace the one I shed when I lay down on the operating table in a drugged oblivion and allowed my vaginal walls to be punctured. The old self was nulligravid, fearful of pain, and wedded to the idea of a man and a woman alone in a bed where passion reigned. The new self was born from the daily discipline of measuring medicine into the syringe, and from the sixty-five injections administered into the fleshiest parts of thigh, buttocks, arm. The new self was born from the urgent air of the operating room, and from her name on the hospital identification bracelet, The new self does what is necessary without complaint, The new self believes in the seasonal dark and is ready for the best odds science can give.

That dark winter evening, as we have done every evening between the oocyte retrieval and the embryo transfer, my husband and I stand before the Chanukah candles. Thursday night, the night before the embryo transfer, the last night of the holiday, we set eight candles in a row. Samuel lights a match and then hands it to me. "You say the blessing tonight."

I light the center candle and hold it up. "Baruch a ta adonoi, we recognize the many miracles you have done for our people in history, but please, God, grant us one miracle in this house."

Samuel shakes his head. "You have to be more specific for what you ask. We don't want an ectopic pregnancy." He takes the candle from me and begins to light another tall red one. "We want the eggs to attach to the uterine wall and then we want one to grow into—"

"A child. A baby. We ask for the miracle of a baby growing inside me."

He hands me the candle and I ignite the remaining wicks.

We stand there awhile with our backs to the dark window. I feel strangely calm. Whatever happens next the eight small flames flickering in their brass Menorah have drawn me into their light.

Morning. Hospital. Operating room. I am lying on a white bed with a white sheet draped over my raised knees. Surrounding me, dressed in blue scrubs, are Samuel, a cheery nurse, a stone-faced technician, and a tall, gangly doctor. The silence in the room is like that on a mountain peak. Miles and miles of thin air, clear sky, and a silence that fills you up and creates secret pockets, reservoirs of calm.

The doctor on duty today has the geeky look of someone who spent his adolescence at science fairs. Clipboard in hand, he leans into the bed, his bony elbow resting on my side. He shows Samuel and me a chart rating our embryos. One is five cells but with fragmentation, one is four cells with no fragmentation, one is three cells. Fragmentation, which the doctor explains is not a good thing, can occur when the cells divide. My fourth egg, although fertilized by the embryologist, never went on to divide. "That's the best one," the doctor says, pointing to the middle line where he's listed the four cell, no fragmentation embryo. "The other two, wel…" he shrugs his shoulder. "We'll transfer them anyway.

I am disappointed and disheartened. The embryos are described as "Fail" (rather than "Good" or "Poor") as in a school report card. "But people do get pregnant with three embryos, right?" I ask. My voice sounds more desperate than I'd intended.

The doctor purses his thin lips. I want him to say "Yes, absolutely, you never know." But he knows his business. He sees the aggregate picture, the statistical probabilities, the plethora of pregnancy tests that turn up negative.

"At your age," he begins, and at that phrase, which I have heard too often of late, I cringe. Do the bright lights show up every wrinkle around my eyes, every graying hair in my head? "At your age, you have a fifteen to twenty percent chance."

He must see my face fall. "Okay, maybe eighteen."

The technician slips a sonogram wand onto my belly and beside me, the monitor lights up. We are back on the mountaintop and I am taking in great draughts, of the giddy air and letting my knees flop open against the bed railings. The doctor takes his seat on a stool and proffers a long catheter which he will use to deposit the embryos into my uterus.

My uterus! It is up on the monitor screen for everyone to see, and it is a cavernous terrain with peaks and valleys. To think there was a time, back when I was still a virgin,when I never looked into my interior space, To think that I was ever alone with my body. To think....

But there is no thinking in this room, there is only breath and light. We are wrapped again in miles of billowy silence while Samuel, myself, the nurse, the technician, and the doctor train our gaze. Samuel takes my hand. We are staring, staring.... I am tempted to say we are staring at the future but in fact we are staring at the thin white line on the screen that is the catheter coming though with our three fair embryos.

Did my mother sense this white light in the room the morning my father reached for her and she forgot to put in her diaphragm and I began? Where she had passion, I have precision. Where she had desire, I have a terribly conscious intent. I will proceed. M y pelvis is tipped and my breath is steady. My eyes are open. The ceiling is white and so are the walls.

Coal

Kathy Ackerman

From inside the earth
his point of view is limited
by the grime of the grind
where canaries cannot hide.
He passes time with histories
digs them from his mind
slightly curved as through a ball
slightly stooped in the underground.

With gloved hand he brushes the deep
grooves of his mother's face,
Cherokee, storyteller
she taught him nothing of value
can be stripped from the earth
and nothing of value returned.
It is folly to chip at the layers with picks,
to scoop black rocks of time into cars,
into the air to breathe in
it is folly to go down
where the spirits haven't been

and he coughs up her wisdom in black
in the yellow gray of his days;
he's sold his lungs to the trickster
who promised to pay his way.

An Itinerary for Michael

Vivian Shipley

So alone, you write, "Lord. Sometimes, I'm pleased this is our *only* life..."
It's not as if you need to structure a sonnet every day but writing *love*
would be harder for you than chiseling a headstone. My solution? Head
for the armpit of Florida and workshop your senses.

At Cape San Blas, a fishhook of sand jutting into the Gulf of Mexico,
we'll drive north on Rt. 98 although the first ten miles will be empty
beach screened by cabbage palms and pines, edged with water layered in
green, turquoise, slate, and brown. Off the horizon, thin and dark, a line
of barrier islands can become a metaphor for your heart. Keep an eye out
for life, alligators crossing from the right, snakes or turtles on the left.
Smell palm rot, oyster shells, low tide, shrimp boats, For no good reason
you can think of, fill your mouth with: Carrabelle, Sopchoppy, Panacea,
Tallahassee.

At Big Bend, mangrove swamps will pull out beads of our sweat. Air,
thickening to Jell-O, will lure sandflies and us to white sand, fine as flour
that my father used to barrel, ship up to Kentucky for square dances in our
barn. If you still feel lonely, Michael, create a family, learn the names of
hurricanes: Camille, Opal, Kate. Like distant aunts without uncles, there
is more than one story for each of them, detailed by houses on one side of
the road, foundations on the other, washing machines in shallow water
that keep company with air-conditioning compressors, patio furniture,
kitchen cabinets.

For a change of pace, let's turn off the main road and float down the
Wakulla River where life is the way you want it to be with no surprises in
water so clear every rock in the riverbed can be seen. Steering the boat,
you'll feel secure enough to define *fecund* for a dictionary: deer, osprey
nests overhead, night herons, anhingas drying their wings in cypress trees,
Spanish moss, wood ducks, grebes.

Circling back home, take the Oyster Route but be prepared to give up
control to taste, to touch, to smell. Bolster your confidence, quote Eliot's
J. Alfred Prufrock: *And sawdust restaurants with oyster shells.* Repress,
restless nights in one-night cheap hotels. First stop, Posey's in St. Mark's.
Fishermen in white rubber boots, crackers, five kinds of sauce for pearly-

gray oysters just tonged up with a wooden rake from the bay. Actually, Posey's has cleaned up its act, serves smoked mullet on plastic plates instead of blue gas station paper towels. Prehistoric looking, the mullet bends plastic forks. Be a cave man, don't use one. No need to use your sleeve, wipe your mouth on the 200 napkins kept on every table. If you're not afraid of falling, dance the two-step, the reel, jitterbug, twist macarena in the hall overlooking but remember there's no more chicken wire to keep you from going through screens into the river.

After the second dozen oysters, we should move on to Boss Oyster in Apalachicola. Ignore the roll of paper towels, suck or lick your fingers in between each course of steamed blue crabs, heads-on-shrimp, hand cut onion rings and barbecue out of the pit. Judge how sober you are by naming shrimp boats: Rosa Marie, Marla J, Nixie, Bay Wolf Pitcher after pitcher of beer will have a cup of ice floating. The trip will be complete when you can't pronounce *aphrodisiac* for oyster, our workshop will be over if you can see mermaids lounging by our table on the shells piled into mounds the size of a mall, if you can hear *the mermaids singing, each to each.*

7 AM

Marilynn Talal

Leaf mold tattered under foot, branches of sunlit
    curls, birdsong chipping the morning, wind sigh
        through trees shaking spirit wings—

my lost loved ones form invisible weaving
    that braids daily miracles: butterflies
        come in ones, twos to savor

zinnias that poison deer. Or hummingbirds dart
    to windows, hang wingless then flee, etching
        s's suspended in air.

A green-headed body comes on the wind rattling
    like ducks above yellow almond blossoms
        that button along a branch.

One day I will join them in vines climbing treetrunks,
    kiss you, reader, with buds flaming branches
        varicose against white sky.

My Daughter's Hands
Marilynn Talal

Words wing by her ears
unnoticed. Each thumb touches
each finger repeatedly, tip to
tip in a rhythmic pattern,
a dance for the air.

Her nails are pale stones.
Her watery pale fingers
flutter with fin-like grace. They are hands
that quickly sorted laundry,
fried a chicken, built

a friendship. No one
can see scars or drops of blood
to show what these hands felt when her life
exploded, where each attempt
blew up in her face.

Over and over
she sucks her lips to taste skin,
relaxes, sucks again. The lamplight
gleams a white point in the white
of her staring eye.

Adolescence

Alison Seevak

The last time anyone
gave me the perfect present
I was thirteen,
and my mother climbed
into one of my dreams,
brought back a pair of earrings
she found there.
She handed me a small white box
and when I opened it
and saw them, carnelian,
curved like twin pears,
or maybe, the hips and breasts
I did not know what to do with,
I wondered if she had seen me
in her dark closet, pulling the cool silk
of her ruby negligee to my face.
Try them on, she said.
I lifted one to my ear,
but it slipped through my fingers,
then lay there on the tile floor,
sad, broken fish,
and I saw everything
coming towards me
that I did not want,
the salt I would have to taste,
the blood, the small ways
we would disappoint one another,
and I knew that sometimes
the fairy, the unhappy one
who has not been given a chair
at the birthday feast,
does not always stand over a cradle.
Sometimes she stands
next to a twin bed,
watches the girl curled into herself,
breathing, then casts her spell.

Maps

Kirsten Lillegard

I AM GOING to live with my cousin Sandy because I envy her biceps, ivory slopes dotted with caramel freckles. When I was a kid I licked a freckle, to see if it would taste like candy, grazed a dime-sized splash above her elbow with the tip of my tongue. Her arm flew back into my face so hard my brains sloshed and I fell back into the stall. The Alfalfa smelled sweet and the blood tasted salty pooling in behind my lower lip, and I went to Aunt Rudy and told on Sandy. She grabbed my chin, pulled it toward her cold eyes, examined my lip, then sent me upstairs to take a bath. You'll be okay, she said.

LESLIE STANDS outside my screen door. The orange porch light makes her face look swollen.

Hello, Sandy, she says calmly. Mind if I crash here for awhile?

She hops a little and readjusts her canvas backpack, the same one I bought her two years ago at an army surplus store. She had said she was going to leave Tacoma and walk to Beliz, to live in a Mayan ruin. I imagined her there, tying her hammock to fig trees, a bed with a view of a vine-covered temple.

My mother couldn't believe I'd helped her. You fool, she said. She's not going to Beliz. She's going to find a cliff and throw herself off it.

She had maps, I wanted to say, of Mexico. Beliz.

We found her sixty miles south of here on a roadside lookout, having a picnic of tuna and saltines. We took her back and my mother had her committed for the fourth time.

Leslie squints at me under the melon glow. I promise I won't be too obnoxious, she says. I'll cook. I'll make things nice.

I wonder if she's still taking the medication they gave her.

Leslie sits at the kitchen table with a stack of erasable bond paper fanned out like a hand of cards. She uses a ruler to draw horizontal lines across one sheet, then fills in the slots with half hour time markers. Most of the slots are empty. Monday at 3:30 reads Appointment with Shrinky-Dink. Tuesday at 9:00 P.M. is Weekly Floss, and Wednesday at 7:30 is Croatian Basketball—Channel 16.

It was my suggestion to make a schedule, since she was having problems keeping the appointments my mother claims she is legally required to attend. Sometimes that helps me, I said. Not just for remembering things, but it puts my mind at ease.

I don't know why, but I had imagined a leather-bound agenda, one with a plastic ruler and paper thin calculator.

Leslie pulls the pencil along with excruciating slowness, then tries to erase a dip at the end where the ruler tilted and the pencil went with it. The eraser leaves an oily smudge. Fuck! she shouts, then wipes the paper off the table, sends it swinging back and forth to the floor, where a pile of half-finished schedules is growing. She grabs her hair with both hands, holds it at the temples. Her eyes are scrunched and dry.

Is this my fault?

SANDY LEAVES at night, later than I dare go outside myself. I'm afraid of the dark now, especially where it intersects with hard places, with sidewalks, parking garages, bridge supports. As she leaves I watch from my upstairs window, watch her straight shoulders traced with orange light floating down the steps.

I know what happens next. She drives to the airport, eases the thick headphones onto her ears and positions herself in front of jets full of Japanese business men doped up on motion sickness pills. She'll stand there for hours, pulling the jets into herself with perfectly aligned forearms: this way, this way. At four in the morning, after hours of breathing jet fumes, she'll drive to the river, unlock the boathouse, and together with one other woman and two men, hoist a long slender boat off its wooden rest. They'll carry it to the dock on their shoulders, roll it down to their knees, place it gently on the water. They'll step into the boat, crouching, tie in their feet, tipping side to side, push off from the dock, still tipping, then in long balanced strokes row themselves out across the water into the uneven darkness. They will pull until mist rises from their shoulders, until their tummies are weak and their legs ache, and at least one of the men will confuse this ache with desire for Sandy, with the hope that her car will break down, or she will, so he can take her home.

SATURDAY I WAKE at two in the afternoon. I stumble into the kitchen and find Leslie in the corner, on the floor, head by her knees. Blackout, I think, or even worse. But then she turns to me and smiles, a rag in one hand and a bottle of cleaner in the other.

Good morning to you, she says in a bad British accent. I say, did you have a good row this morning?

It was fine.

Jolly good.

She turns back to the base board and begins scrubbing it. This is a project my mother always suggested to us when we claimed we had nothing to do. She would scrape her finger along the crevice and show us the block of dirt under her nail. What about this? she'd say. How can you stand it?

I move to the counter and fill a cup with coffee. I open the sugar jar but then drop it when I see something inside, either a long worm or centipede. It thuds to the floor without breaking, sending out a wave of sugar, the dark pod riding on top. A vanilla bean.

Leslie scrambles to the jar and sets it upright on the floor. Don't worry, she says. You didn't mean to do it. She sweeps the spilled sugar onto a piece of paper with her fingers. Then she lifts it and drizzles the crystals—hairs and dust and all—back into the jar.

Leslie, I protest.

What? she says, peering up at me like a dog who has just let her bladder go.

Never mind.

She stands with the jar, scoops out a small spoonful of sugar, plops it in my coffee, stirs, removes the spoon, licks it thoroughly, then drops it back in the jar. The vanilla bean will make your coffee taste yummy, she says.

I take a seat at the table and she asks me if she can borrow my bike, to buy some tomato plants and green peppers. We need a garden, she says.

I didn't know you did that kind of thing.

Well, I don't. I want to learn how. That's the whole idea, silly-willy.

Oh. Yeah sure. Hey, did you look into that job at the library? I had imagined her behind a long mahogany counter, stamping books, wearing a cardigan. Chatting up old men and little kids.

She sighs and takes a seat at the table, places her palms on top of it. Her thumbs tremble. They do that most of the time.

No, she says quietly. I don't want to work at the library.

Libraries are for nerds. Why are you trying to find me a job?

I just thought—I stop myself because the truth is hard to admit:

I thought you needed a life. That's the truth. Instead I say: Don't you need some money?

No. I get crazy checks from Uncle Sam. Once a month.

Oh. That's too bad. That's good. I see. So that's it. How do you feel about that? Are you crazy?

Any response I think of sounds ridiculous to me.

Leslie was thirteen when she came to stay with us. I didn't know my Aunt Becky had killed herself, because Mother didn't say anything at first and Leslie acted like she was joining us for a merry holiday. When she arrived, she gave me a hug and asked me if I wanted to hear a song she and her friend Tammy had recorded. I can sound just like a black girl when I sing, she had said.

It was only after she had gone to bed that Mother told me about Aunt Becky.

She didn't even leave a note, she said into the kitchen table. Her hands were laid out on its surface, touching at the fingertips, and her forehead was resting on top of her knuckles. In retrospect I feel sorry for my mother, who was coping with all of this a few months after her second husband left. But that wasn't how I felt at the time, watching her talk into the table and tell me that the world was coming apart at the seams. I was agitated, and scared, and I blamed her.

I found Leslie with some older guy named Dell, she said. Shit, Sandy, for all I know she could be pregnant. She's not like you. She has no direction.

That was back when I had everyone including myself convinced I was going to become a civil engineer. I like to figure out how things work, I had said to people who thought it a strange thing for a teenage girl to want. I went to college for one year—athletic scholarship—and then dropped out, realizing afterwards that I had no desire to know how things work, only that I wanted them to, always.

This was long before I had even heard of the term "bipolar."

Mother calls me at 10:30 exactly.
She's asleep, isn't she?
Hello to you too, I say.
So, how are you doing?
Just fine, how are you?
Cut the crap. How are you doing with Leslie?
I don't know. OK, I guess.
Isn't it funny how you start to feel like the crazy one?
I don't know.
Is she taking her meds? Mother asks.
I don't know. I don't even know what she's on.
Lithium.
They still give people Lithium?
Hey. She doesn't think about killing herself when she's on it.

This is bizarre to me, that a chemical can shut down one route of imagination, that the physical can reign in and control the emotional.

Sandy, she says. You've got to find out. If she's not taking it, she can't stay there with you. She'll have to come home.

I gulp and nod, as if Mother could see this. I know I should speak but my jaw gets too tight to open, and it feels like a slab of concrete is being eased down on the top of my head.

SANDY IS STARING out the window, stirring and stirring and stirring the sugar into her coffee, the spoon clinking. Sandy, I say. Did Aunt Rudy ask about my medication?

Yes.

What did you tell her?

I told her I didn't know.

Do you want to know? I say. She is staring out the kitchen window, stirring and stirring, staring at the half-diseased elm, at the cocker spaniel forever tied to his blue-roofed dog house, "Sparky" painted above the door. Hey, I say. Why don't you talk to me?

The stirring stops.

I don't know what to say, she replies. It seems like anything I do sets you off.

I think she's fooling herself. It's the old Don't Want to Make the Crazy Person Snap problem. She thinks she doesn't know what to say because I'm crazy, but what she doesn't realize is that she'd have this problem with anyone. Even if she took a liking to one of those lovely oarsmen, even if she brought him home and into her bed, even if he was the most understanding, most reasonable person on earth, she wouldn't know what to say to him. It would get to that point. She'd have him on her obligation list and then she'd freeze up, wouldn't have one damn thing to say, not leave, not stay. Poor dear.

THIS MORNING THE WIND SLAPS our backs. We pull against it, pull in higher than usual so the oar blades will stay buried under the choppy water. The whole row is Hellish, like my body is no good, like it could be blown out of the boat and into a tree, snag on a branch.

I look over my shoulder to spot the bridge, make sure we are pointed straight. We're angled a little to starboard so I take an extra hard stroke and even us out. The next stroke sends us under the bridge (always an act of faith), and the wind stops altogether, and the oars banging in their locks make echoes. The mildew, the water forcing quivering gold shadows on the walls—it makes me want to stay here, in the quiet, rancid safety under the concrete. But we're out of it in two strokes, and the wind is back, filling my ears and mouth, and after two more strokes I can see the top of the bridge, and there of all places is Leslie. She is waving at us with her whole body, her fingers getting tangled in her hair. She jumps in the air, claps wildly. Yeeeeeee—hah! she screams. Get on, little doggies!

When we are pulling the boat out of the river, I look around for Leslie. She is nowhere in sight, and this concerns me. She isn't home when I get there, either. I don't sleep. I sit in the rocking chair and wait for an hour. I think about everything that requires no intensity—where the wood in the rocking chair came from, what kind of man made it, where it will all go after I die, who will sit in it and what they will think about, if they will wonder where the wood came from, and then back to really wondering where the wood came from, who made it . . . .

Leslie appears, her face bright red, wisps of blonde hair stuck to her forehead.

Whoo-ee, she says. It feels so good to get exercise. I tell ya. You've inspired me. After I left the bridge I rode my bike all over the damn place.

She falls into the sofa, puts her feet on the coffee table. Her knees are trembling, her thighs covered with splotches of heat rash.

What's the matter, you look pissed, she says. Her breathing is beginning to slow, her stare becoming more focused.

Nothing's the matter, I say. I didn't know where you were.

Were you worried?

Well, I don't know.

I'm OK. I'm a big girl.

I say nothing, only nod, and this does it. Her eyes quiver, as if a spring behind her forehead is winding itself tighter. She says, voice thick, You don't trust me, do you?

I trust you.

No, you don't.

It's not like that. It's just . . . . I just want to know, that's all.

Know what?

This is worse than having teeth pulled. I want to know what you're doing, I say.

You mean am I taking my medication?

Well, yes. No, not necessarily. I mean . . .

You mean am I going to kill myself?

She's relentless. I take a deep breath and look down at my knees, as if they could help me. What to say? What not to say?

What's your plan, Leslie? That's what I want to know.

What in the Hell do you mean by that?

How long do you want to stay here, what are you going to do?

You want me to leave.

No. I just want to know—

131

Yeah. You want me to leave.

NO. Maybe she's right. I can't tell. I feel so disoriented. And exhausted.

Well, to tell you the truth, Sandy, I don't want to stay here any longer because I'm NOT COMFORTABLE here. She over articulates her words. She stands and strides dramatically toward the stairs. Something wells up inside me and before I know what's happening I'm on her, pulling her head down, locking it under my arm. She throws her fists around frantically, hitting me on my legs. An especially hard blow lands on my lower back and it pisses me off, so with one swift and strangely organized burst I force her down onto the stairs. I pull her wrists together and pin them behind her back, not caring how hard I squeeze. I flatten her out on the stairs then sit on her back. My senses don't catch up to me until I hear a pinched wheezing sound beneath me, like she's sucking air through a kinked hose. After a minute I stand and back up; she rolls over with a flushed face. She coughs a few times, wipes her mouth, looks at her hand, at a smear of blood, smiles at me.

I walk out into the kitchen, get a glass of water. By the time I return to the living room she's gone. I'm suddenly very tired; even my bones are weak, not just my head and eye lids. I finish my water then collapse into the sofa.

BLAMO! AND HERE I AM again, a seven-year-old on my back, smelling the alfalfa. My body tingles from the blow and I want to lie here, stare at the sky and drink in the yellow sun through my pores. I want to feel the ground heavy and wet underneath me, soft against my shoulder blades but hard enough to shatter small bones, toss brains in skulls, turn pink flesh purple.

My Shrinky-Dink would say I crave abuse because my mother abused me (though she didn't—only once, really). Sandy is a mother figure for you, she says, and you're trying to work out your mother issues through her.

Nice try, but No. Sandy is my cousin and I moved in with her because I want to have muscles like she has. But shrinky wouldn't understand that. Everything is mappable to her—families, machines, emotions. You start in one place and trace the road back to the blockage—a mother, a childhood blow, a chemical mishap—and then you exorcise it. You have the plugged up soul talk it out, or you dissolve the clot with Liquid Lithium Draino.

I wouldn't be able to explain the truth to her. I don't understand it myself.

So I focus on tomato plants. I don't understand them either but I think I can make them grow, or at least keep them alive. I roll over onto my stomach, pull myself up on my knees then go back to digging small holes in the ground with a miniature spade (perfect for this). I stick the cone shaped bottoms in the ground, being careful with the angel hair pasta roots, then fill the gaps with dirt clots.

I stay here until the sun sets, working slow, and then I see Sandy stagger out into the yard, barefooted. Her white shorts and tank top make her look billowy, small. She kneels down, close enough for me to see a red canal across her cheek left by the seam of a couch pillow.

I thought you were going, she says.

I didn't know where to go.

She fixes her eyes on my spade, as if she's trying to memorize it.

Then she looks up at the tops of the trees, and I look too. They have yellow-green shawls, sparkling.

There was a time when that didn't matter to you, she says, still looking at the trees, and I think it is amazing that she is speaking without thinking. I reach for her neck, kiss her high on her cheek by the ear. She doesn't wince, doesn't backhand me. I feel like I could sleep for a week, she says.

Yeah, but you won't, I say. You should, but you won't.

She reaches for the ground, fingers the grass blades, collects small pills of dirt under her nails and examines them. She stands, still looking at the ground, then drifts back into the house.

THE SIGHT OF HER with anything metal-edged, even a grapefruit spoon, still shakes me. The possibilities—of what could happen, of what won't happen, of how all that intersects with what I do—it's overwhelming.

But I can make her stay around, and I can make her take the pills. It's savage, I know, but it's all I have beside myself (and myself is not enough).

I PRESS the heel of my palm into the dirt surrounding the last tomato plant, the smallest one. It looks content to be there. Of course tomorrow it will have new needs—the insects to be picked off, the weeds to be pulled and smashed with dead grass, support trellises to be driven into the ground. It makes me dizzy to think of what they will require, of what the world requires. But for now I have the heel of my palms pressed hard into the ground, and my weight is here, on my hands, and the world spins faster (that's where the wind comes from, I always knew this) but my hands are still here, the earth's crust is hard and wet and for the moment I have no desire to be buried far below it, as I once did. I'm not sure why.

Grief Therapy

Jane Bailey

The mourning dove lights again on a branch
in the dead tree of your throat.
You ignore it, believing you know
what you've paid for, an expert infallible voice
unfolding like a brilliant scarf, tropical
birds and fruit falling out, orchids
audaciously blooming through grief
like pink and white vultures at a funeral.
Happiness! Happiness! their only cry.

Instead, you're back in the forest again,
speechless under a light that falls
like knives through a canopy of firs.
Two sisters, pleasure and pain
argue at the Y in the trail.
You scan the carpet for clues,
leaves and mosses, poison berries,
the secret footprints of explorers,
distractions that keep you occupied
with the fine art of postponement.

The sage won't give up any answers,
none you don't already know. She sits
in an ordinary chair, peeling an ordinary orange
expertly, like a child pulling petals
away from a flower, or plucking
the legs off a daddy longlegs,
dropping appendages into her lap
while the traffic outside on the busy street
goes on repeating the life that goes on
in fits and starts and turnings of wheels.
But then the sun starts throwing diamonds
from window to floor to your feet, and then
you speak, because you must
make sense of the repetition of light,
must name the aching bird in your throat
and talk about which way the wind blows today.

Press Conference

Trenton Hickman

Q: Why have the butterflies gone to Mexico?

A: It has nothing to do
with the cold, everything
to do with desire, their longing for passionfruit
blossoms, the angled waves of sea,
and tattered children playing baseball
with bottle tops.

Q: When will the butterflies return?

A: When men and women learn
to kiss openmouthed again. When
suburbanites rubberneck for Chilean grapes
and the sun distilled in their glowing
globes. When angry mobs
hang the inventor of the car alarm
high like a prizewinning trout.

Q: Of course, the butterfly problem is not nearly as frightening
as the decline in skyscrapers.

A: Look to the subterfuge of cockroaches
and termites. On this subject I will say no more.

Q: When will you climb down from your treehouse?

A: When will you let go of the grass
beneath your feet? You are long truant
in your companionship to the birds.

Before you were called
M.C.A. Shimabukuro

politically correct, you want to slice *geisha doll*, the boyfriend's
mother blurting out, smile earnest in her face. You don't know
what she means to say, what sometimes can spill from comers
cut in open mouths. This two bit agony of every word
follows to your college years. There, everyone yells
across the field. The latest headline: *P.C. Patrol, Nigger*
scrawled on seven doors and down the hall: *Do two
woman have to kiss where I eat my morning toast?* Two
years later, a classmate white tells you what he thinks of
oriental. Inside your head, you watch his mouth carve
the air with case. You want to know his traffic voice,
the slow slide of words you could slip into his hands
but all he does is talk and talk and talk and talk, so far
from where you stand.

Sleeping Brook

Edward W. Wood, Jr.

for H. John Wax

I

THEN, near the eastern edge of the continent
A nameless stream rose from crystal springs,
Wound gently through the wild forest
West of the great and unknown bay.

Clear and swift and cold,
The stream surged toward the marshes,
Split around green-lichened boulders,
White rivulets that frothed in summer sun.

Broad-trunked oaks and maples,
Rooted deep in mossy banks
Where ferns glistened cold and damp,
Towered high above the murmuring ripples.
And willows dusted the pools
That swirled at the stream's turning
With feathery patterns of sun and shade.

At dusk
Deer stepped, supple jointed, down those banks.
Small, soft animals,
Rabbit and chipmunk,
Crept silently through the ferns,
Drank at deers' feet,
Eyes vigilant for leap of wolf or fox,
Paws washed by wakes of otter
That swam through pools fired with evening flame.

Deep in clear water
Trout drifted to the surface,
Sucked in fluttering nymph,
Sank back to the bottom:
Fins gently brushed golden grains of sand.

THEN, this nation, this colossus,
This breeder of pollution,
This spoiler of the moon,
This land we call The United States of America,
Lay nameless and unknown to the west.

Only wandering tribes of Sioux and Cheyenne,
Fox and Arapaho,
Knew the land's clefted mountains, rolling plains,
Virgin forests and flat plateaus.

Folded deep in narrow valleys,
Hidden far in broken mesas,
Their rough camps conquered,
For an instant,
Brooding and wilderness.

But, with the seasons,
Time's steady pulse,
Wind and rain and sun bruised their shelters,
Tree and vine and shrub healed scars slashed into the soil.

For then man had not proclaimed himself
Master of creation:
Earth still mother,
Sky still Lord.

THEN, the land lay unbroken and uncorrupted,
ripening slowly under the summer's warming sky,
Dying each fall,
Reborn each spring.
Patterns of birth and life and death
Stretched across time,
Sprawled across a nameless continent.

> *Twisting back to that ancient moment*
> *When, from boiling sea*
> *A synthesis was made.*
> *A one-celled being that squirmed,*
> *Alive,*
> *Source of all mutants,*
> *Great dinosaur and tough crustacean,*
> *Species exploding out of species.*

Profusion unbelievable
Caressed and covered rock and stone
From one great ocean to the other,
Formed mountain, forest, field.

THEN, the land lay nameless to the west,
Virgin, muted, still,
Union of earth and sky, plant, bird, insect, animal,
Eons and millenniums tumbling through time
To the year of our Lord, 1637:

In May of that year a rough wagon drawn by a pair
of oxen bounced to the stream's shaded bank.
Children, all sizes and shapes, burst to the ground.
A chunky man and a slim woman, almost a child,
followed them. The children darted wildly to the
bushes; the woman walked swiftly to the stream;
the man stood by the wagon, gazed over water,
marsh, sloping hill.

"This be where Roger said," he called. "We
build our cabin here."

At dusk, when chores were done, the woman
always filled her buckets at the stream, took
a drink herself, shivering as spring water iced
her lips. She paused, heard rapids roar at her feet.
Setting sun angled through leaves above her
head; dust particles danced in its beams; a thrust
warbled, pressed its song deep into the evening sky.

Lord, she thought, but this earth is lovely, like
my youngest baby when he was born. 'Tis better
than the England we fled, the colony that expelled
us. Spirit has breathed upon this land, the mother
and the son I love so well.

She dropped her head and prayed: her prayer her
dream, her dream her prayer:

> *This great green loveliness, God's*
> *Gift to men and women. Aye. The*
> *Kingdom of Heaven, even the words*
> *have their own beauty. No more*
> *beatings, rapes, murders, quartered,*
> *drawn, and screaming flesh; no more*
> *wars, young men butchering each other*
> *for Church and State; no more soldiers'*
> *footsteps creaking in the night.*

"When I was a child, I spoke as a child,
I understood as a child, I thought as a
child. "Since Mary bore Jesus, men
have but killed and raped but here, here on
this new land, the Kingdom is at hand.

She sighed.

Her body slacked into the earth.

She slept.

Her husband found her at dark.

"Sleepin'!" he shook her shoulder. "No time to be sleepin', woman."

"Twas the stream," she mumbled. "It cast a spell on me."

"A spell?" he mocked. "Your only spell be dreamin', wife. Fix my food. Hush the child's cry. Bring the water."

He mentioned her spell again the next day and named the stream, "Sleeping Brook," a sly chuckle on his lips.

II

Now the hills and valleys were fielded and fenced.
Wheat thrived in the good black soil.
Hogs grew fat on corn.
Cattle lowed in pastures
While sheep cropped wild grasses.

Only the stream still ran
As it had when the land was fallow:
As clear, as swift, as cold,
The place where boys congregated after school,
Lovers wandered,
Philosophers pondered,
The place where women still gathered water,
Carried buckets to cabins
Built on shaded banks,
Hearth, a fire, a garden,
Perfume of baking bread mixed with wood smoke,
Soft murmurs at dusk,
A place of safety made by women,
Free of frontier's fear.

A place that held in its shaded green banks,
Shaded pools,
Pebbled depths,
Murmuring ripples,
A memory of all that once had been:
Already those virgin hills, great trees,

Vast herds of game nearly gone,
Almost myth.

The white man's world had spread from its birthplace
Upon the eastern shore
Like fire whipping wild grass:

Scorched the Native American:

In 1637 Puritans (loving God)

       Burnt a Pequot camp
       And Cotton Mather exclaimed:
       "On this day we have sent six hundred heathen to hell."
       In 1763 Lord Jeffrey Amherst (loving war)
       Distributed blankets and handkerchiefs
       From the smallpox hospital at Fort Pitt
       To nearby Indian tribes,
       Inventing biological warfare.
       In 1830 Congress passed the Indian Removal Act
       And Martin Van Buren exhorted how
       The handling of the Cherokee Tribe on the Trail of Tears
       Was "Directed by the best feelings of humanity."
       While in 1863 Kit Carson (western hero)
       Butchered Navajos.
       In 1864 Colonel Chivington (Methodist preacher)
       Destroyed Cheyennes at Sand Creek.

       Generals Sheridan and Sherman (heroes of the Civil War)
       Then initiated a twenty-year holocaust
       Against the American Indian,
       Ending in 1890 when General Nelson Miles
       (Leader of our Army in the Spanish-American War)
       And Captain "Black Jack" Pershing
       (General of our Army in France in 1918)
       Subdued the last warring tribe of Sioux,
       Final holocaust at Wounded Knee.

Abenaki Penobscot Pennacook Mohawk Onondaga Manhattan Iroquois
Tuscarora Oneida Cayuga Seneca Munsee Mahican Mohegan Wappinger
Nipmuk Massachuset Stockbridge Narraganset Delaware Nanticoke
Wampanoag Montauk Shinnecoc Unami Schaghticoke Susqehanna
Brothertown Paugussett Pequot Podunk Pisctaway Mattaponi Pamunkey
Monacan Powhatan Chickahominy Rappahannock Nansemond Meherrin
Tutelo, Saponi Koasati Cherokee Lumbee Catawba Cheraw Pamlico
Waccamaw Coharie Pedee Santee Edisto Cusabo Guale Etowah Yuchi
Creek Hitchiti Yamasee Yazoo Apalachicola Apalachee Seminole Timuca
Miccosukee Calusa Coushatta Mobile Alabama Choctaw Chicasaw
Biloxi Natchez Tunica Mississipian Shawnee Miami Potawatomi Erie
Adena Hopewell Kaskaskia Cahokia Illinois Peoria Winnebago,
Kickapoo Fox Sauk Menominee Dakota Iowa MissouriQuapaw Caddo
Hasinai Houma Kichai Chitimacha Oto Osage Omaha Kaw Tonkawa.
Waco Tawakoni Wichita Comanche Lipan Kiowa Apache Southern
Cheyenne Pawnee Ponca Arikara Mandan Northern Cheyenne Lakota
Hidasta Tonto Ute Arapaho Eastern Shoshone Western Shoshone
Northern Shoshone Bannock Crow Nakota Gros Ventre Piegan Salish
Flathead Coeur d'Alene Goshute Southern Paiute Cayuse Nez Perce San
Carlos Anasazai. Pueblo Jemez San Juan Santa Clara Zia Pojaque Santa
Ana Laguna Zuni Acoma Piro Mimbreno Mimbreno Apache Mogollon
Chiricahua Manso Ysleta de Sur Isleta Sandia San Felipe Santo Domingo
Tesuque Picurus Cochiti Jicarilla Tiwa Taos Tewa San Ildefonso Nambe
Towa Pecos Keres Tano Tompiro Mescalero Manso Sobaipuri Pima Zuni
Hohokam Hopi-Tewa Hopi Navajo Walapai Havasupai Apache Yavapai
White Mountain Maricopa Aravaipa Tohono O'odham Cocopa Yuma
Mohave Kumeyaay Cupeno Luiseno Cahuilla Tataviam Karankawa
Kitanemuk Gabrielino Chumash Serrano Halchidhoma Chemehuevi
Tubatulabel Yokuts Nomlaki Owens Valley Paiute Southern Paiute Mono
Salinan Costanoan Yahi Kawaiisu Esslenen Miwok Wappo Patwin Pomo
Sinkyone Washoe Mattole Maidu Cahto Yuki Chimariko Yana Wiyott
Wailaki Nongatl Wintun Bear River Lassik Atsugewi Lassik Hupa
Chilula Karok Huchnom Achumawi Yurok Whilkut Modoc Northern
Paiute Shasta Tolowa Tutuni Takelma Klamath Chastacosta Upper
Umpqua Coquille Coos Latgawa Kalapuya Siuslaw Cow Creek Band
Umpqua Aslea Yaquina Kuitsh Siletz Tillamok Wasco Nooksack
Kwalhioqua Muckleshoot Clatsop Chinook Stillaguamish Steilacoom
Coast Salish Swinomish Cowlitz Yakima Kootenais Klikitat Wishram
Chehalis Squaxin Island Twana Saanich Umatilla Wenatchee Kootenai
PalouseColville Sanpoli Nisqually Skokomish Klallam Puyallup
Duwamish Lake Chelan Wallawalla Hoth Quinault Snoqualme Tenino
Spokan Kalispel Snohomish Quileute Makah Skagit Sauk-
Suiattle Columbia Shoalwater Samish Lummi

Two hundred twenty-two Native American nations,
Two hundred twenty-two human patterns,
Ways of loving, hating, dying, living
Destroyed, demolished by white man's greed.

Now only memories of this former richness,
Once intimate to the nation's earth,
Survive, recalled for an instant in Pueblos,
Villages of a few privileged tribes,
Descendants of this honored past
Imprisoned on reservations,
Crushed in the ghettos of our great cities.

Three hundred and twelve tribes,
Ways of relating to the earth,
Experiments in living:

Never to return.

Never.

• • •

Like fire whipping through wild grass
Seared earth and sky, plant and animal.

> In 1822 William Ashley began the beaver slaughter.
> Until its ending in the 1830s,
> Millions of plews were shipped to Europe
> For the production of fur hats.
> In 1869 eleven million passenger pigeons
> Were killed in the State of Michigan in forty days.
> From 1850 to 1871
> An area larger than France, England, Scotland, Wales
> Was granted to the railroads.
> And careless loggers burnt
> As much as twenty-five million acres of forest a year.
> And in 1883 the last wild herd of Buffalo was destroyed.

Independence Chub Thicktail Chub Blackfin Cisco Deepwater CiscoLongjaw Cisco Grass Valley Speckled Dace Las Vegas Dace Amstad Gambusia Ash Meadows Killfish Pahrump Ranch Killfish Miller Lake Lamprey Smoky Madtorn. Clear Lake Minnow Blue Pike Monkey Springs Pupfish Shoshone Pupfish Tecopa Pupfish, Utah Lake Sculpin, Bluntnose Shiner Phantom Shiner Big Spring Spinedace Pahrangat Spinedace Harelip Sucker June Sucker Whiteline Top Minnow Alvord Cutthroat Silver Trout Yellowfin Cutthroat Trout Las Vegas Leopard Frog San Felipe Leopard Frog Heath Hen Carolina Parakeet Passenger Pigeon Dusky Seaside Sparrow Santa Barbara Song Sparrow Smyrna Seaside Sparrow Henslow's Texas Sparrow Bewick's San Clemente Wren Ivory Billed Woodpecker Bacham's Warbler California. Grizzly Bear Badland's Bighorn Sheep Woodland Caribou Penansco Chipmunk Wisconsin Cougar Eastern Elk Merriam's Elk Southern California Kit Fox Goff's Pocket Gopher Tacoma Pocket Gopher Sea Mink Anastasia Island Mouse Chadwick Beach Cotton Mouse Giant Deer Mouse Pallid Beach Mouse Steller's Sea Cow Caribbean Monk Seal Amargosa. Meadow Vole Gull Island Vole Louisiana Vole Atlantic Gray Whale Cascade Mountains Wolf Florida Red Wolf Kenai Wolf Mogollon Mountain Wolf Plains Wolf Southern Rocky Mountain Wolf Texas Gray Wolf Texas Red Wolf Bigger's Groundwater Planarian Flatworm Holsinger's Groundwater Planarian Flatworm Rubious Cave Amphipod Sooty Crayfish Hay's Spring Scud Pasadena Shrimp Duck River Beetle Mono Lake Beetle Nickajack Cave Beetle Tooth Cave Beetle, Valley Mydas Fly Volutine Fly Antioch Dunes Shieldback Katydid Diverse Mayfly Robust Mayfly Fort Ross Weevil Yorba. Linda Weevil Robert's Stonefly Atossa Butterfly Fender's Blue Butterfly Florida Butterfly Silverspot Butterfly Wood Nymph Butterfly Strobbeen's Butterfly Texas Tailed Blue Butterfly Wilamette Butterfly Blue Xerces Butterfly American Chestnut Moth Casebearer Chestnut Moth Ermine Chestnut Moth Leaf Miner Chestnut Moth Nepticulid Chestnut Moth Long-Horned Athens Caddisfly North Carolina Magnificent Snail Texas Magnificent Snail Fish Springs Marsh Snail Alabama. Magnificent Snail Coosa Live Bearing Snail Alabama River Snails, Avalon Snail Catenoid River Snail Longstreet Spring Snail Socorro Snail Alabama Virginia North Carolina Tennessee Kentucky Georgia Ohio River Mussels

One hundred and twenty-seven species of fish
And birds and animals,
Insects, snails, mussels,
Never to swim, fly, dart again.

Never to grace the earth again.

Never.

• • •

Like fire whipping through wild grass
Scarred the African American.

  In 1619 the first slave ship docked at Jamestown
  In 1664 Maryland passed a law declaring:
  "...people of color...(are)...slaves."

  Other Colonies quickly followed this precedent.

  In 1787 the Constitution accepted slavery.

  The Supreme Court enforced it.

  By 1800 ten million or so Africans
  Had been transported over the Middle Passage,
  Sold into slavery,
  Five hundred or so to the United States.

  One third died in quarters eighteen inches high.

  Families broken by slave owners,
  Children ripped from mothers,
  Husbands from wives.

  Rebellions failed as whip and garrote,
  Chain and fire mutilated flesh,
  Crippled soul.

Asantes and Fantes of the Ivory Coast,
Yorubas and Benins of Nigeria,
The Ibos of the Cameroons,
The whole people of Dahomey
And the many nations of the Congo.

Races, clans, tribes.
        A folk,
Which over millenniums
Formed its systems, economies,
Art, religions
To define and worship the mysteries of the earth.

Tribal ways of loving, hating, dying, living
Destroyed.

Demolished.

Never to grace earth again.

Never.

III

Virgin land, great forests, vast herds of game
Nearly gone,
Almost myths,
Union of earth and sky, plant and animal
But challenges to these men,
Not God-like forces to be feared.

From their European forefathers
They inherited minds of logic,
Created concepts, developed ideas,
Plans for conquest:

Plans that required,
Above all,
Hearts nourished by vision, courage, and desire.

> *The vision of a Jefferson,*
> *The man who wrote:*
> *"We hold these truths to be self-evident,"*
> *Authored the Declaration of Independence,*
> *Forged the Virginia and Kentucky resolutions,*
> *Sponsored The Bill Of Rights,*
> *Purchased the Louisiana Territory,*
> *Founded the University of Virginia,*
> *Designed Monticello.*

> *The vision of those who wrote and signed*
> *The Constitution,*
> *Frame for a government of democracy.*

> *The courage of the pioneer*
> *Who opened up the wilderness with axe and plow and gun.*

> *And the desire to possess and ravish*
> *Those resources,*
> *Spread over the land since the beginning of time,*
> *Reach a material security*
> *Greater than any foreign prince.*

With minds and hands and hearts
They conquered this land,
Formed a new nation upon it:
Four wars required:
Two against the old,
One for expansion,
One, most bitter of all among themselves.

THEN, the land was theirs,
Profusion from eastern to western shore
Lay beneath one flag
They could use it as they pleased.

THEN,
Then, Oh, then,
They plunged into an orgy of exploitation:

Cut trees,
Grew grain,
Raised cattle,
Mined metals,
Produced more THINGS
Than had ever been made in one place before.

Discovered they could better utilize these resources
With machines than with their hands.
Invented machines to do the work of a hundred men.

Machines to plow the land,
Machines to send their voices through a wire,
Machines to rush them over the ground.
Machines to make machines to make machines.

They congregated in the cities,
Lived by and for machines.
Machines brought in Europe's rejected,
Chewed them, spat them out,
Neither part of the old, nor the new
But with economic opportunities
Greater than those of a foreign prince.

Machines comforted
Machines warmed.

Machines created the modem way of life.

From BOSTON THROUGH PROVIDENCE HARTFORD
NEW HAVEN BRIDGEPORT NEW YORK NEWARK
CAMDEN PHILADELPHIA BALTIMORE WASHINGTON
lies the city of the machine, the great megalopolis: its
commercial heart thrives with new towers and jammed
streets and cars and pedestrians but out from this center,
cancering the city, spreads a sea of corruption, vacant
buildings, littered streets, the two decker tenements of
New England, fetid brownstones of New York, brick row
houses of Philadelphia and Baltimore, Washington, an
environment inhuman at its best and prison—like at its worst,
so hot in summer that one cannot breathe, so filled with
pollution in winter that one chokes, jammed with the
forgotten of urban society, blacks and Hispanics and
Native Americans, the homeless, the crazy, those
infected with AIDS, those wild with drugs, those wealthy
on drugs, people piled on people, filth on filth, women
unable to make homes for their children, violence their
only way of life.

IS THIS THE DREAM THE PRAYER THE WOMAN MADE ON
THE BANKS OF SLEEPING BROOK?

Out from dark ghettos lie shiny suburbs,
Wooden boxes set at right angles to the street,
Impermanent, unattached to earth,
Paint quick to peel, pavement to crack.

IS THIS THE DREAM?

Great planes pour black trails of smoke into skies once clear;
red and green and blue automobiles whiz by on eight-lane
Expressways.

THE DREAM OF JUSTICE, EQUALITY, AND FREEDOM?

At each cloverleaf motels offer the latest in loneliness.
Bulldozers devour the soil; chain saws snarl through old
oaks and maples and elms, a thousand families migrate
in a ceaseless search

IS THIS WHY JEFFERSON WROTE? LINCOLN DIED? OUR WARS
WERE WON?

IV

In 1962 the city and the machine reached the stream.
That year in most solemn ceremony,
Given on the bank where the woman once drew her water,
Prayed and dreamed, dreamed and prayed,
The State Highway Commission christened
The new Expressway as "The Sleeping Brook Extension,"
Continuation of I-95 across the land,
Extolling the contribution it must make
To a newer dream: economic growth.

Development companies bought the farms,
Sliced fields into city blocks,
Blocks into lots.
Contractors excavated basements,
Slopped cement into wooden forms,
Carpenters laid plates, joists, studs,
Nailed sheathing tight.
Plumbers piped homes;
Two and a half baths,
Dishwashers, laundry rooms,
Rec rooms.

Rooms for very function of the human body.

Split levels, ranches, fake colonials,
Circled curving streets,
Obliterated the land.

Managers, accountants, brokers, sales executives,
Descendants of those immigrants from Europe,
Migrated to Sleeping Brook to find their dream,
Fled the city and the blacks
Euphemistically named "them."

Weekends spent landscaping,
Barbecue pits, TV rooms, bedrooms for babies added,
PTA joined,
High taxes paid,
Good schools demanded,
TV watched
Thought shortened to half hour bits,
Women freed by the pill.

Husbands traveled on great jets,
O'Hare, Kennedy, Logan, San Francisco
Meetings, meetings, meetings,
All week Sleeping Brook and an oasis of women and children,
Wives bored with housekeeping,
Children frantic with activity.

Friday night martini time for daddy,
Saturday chores never finished,
Saturday night a dinner party.

Sunday prepare for Monday.

Women served by machines,
Their once honored role of place-maker
Given over to chauffeur.

They fled to a new discipline:
Career. BA, BS, MA, MS, PHD,
Sixty eighty hour work weeks,
Children left with strangers.

Consolation in the goods purchased
That brightened teeth,
Masked odors,
Shaped flesh into an image of marketability,
Little different from the toys
That ordered patterns of desire.

BIG THINGS
LITTLE THINGS
SHINY THINGS
DULL THINGS

      TELEVISIONSETSPILEDRUGSELECTRIC
      TOOTHBRUSHESCANOPENERSSHAVERS
      SAWSKNIVESSAUNASMICROWAVE
      OVENSGARAGESFILLEDWITHGASOLINE
      LAWNMOWERSGOLFCLUBSBRAKES
      HOESONETWOTHREECARSRECROOMS
      WITHPOOLTABLESSKATESTENNISRACKETS
      SKIISROLLERBLADES

      AND DOLLS THAT
             WET

            AND WHINED
            AND EVEN WHIMPERED

V

And when they hurried to the stream for solace
Orange rinds and oil slicks
Wheeled sluggishly in its torpid current.

"A menace to health,"
The Public Nurse cried.
"That dirty ol' stream 'll drown our kids,"
Mothers complained.
"Threatens development! Decreases Profit!"
The Chamber of Commerce intoned.

"And we certainly agree!"
The City Council pontificated
As it unanimously passed the Ordinance condemning
Sleeping Brook.

That autumn a construction crew
Lowered great concrete drains into the stream's bed,
Trapped soiled water,
Bulldozed gravel over the pipes.

> Where the stream had once rippled,
> So clear, so cold, so swift,
> Where the woman had once prayed and dreamed,
> Dreamed and prayed,
> Prayed and dreamed,
> Engineers added another lane
> To the Sleeping Brook extension.

> Rivers of BUICKSFORDSPLYMOUTHS
> VW'SHONDASTOYOTASMERCEDES
> VOLVOSSAABS

> Buried the cycle, balance, and unity
> That had prevailed since
> The beginning of time.

Oh, listen America in the night
And listen America in the silence
For deep, deep underground
The stream still whispers
Its sweet murmur to our wounded heart,
Cries for restitution of the dream...

> And the promises once made.

Another AIDS Poem or
Why do I have to write this
Qwo-Li/Paul Driskill

What makes me angry
is the resignation I
feel
It seems almost inevitable
I didn't know how to
respond when I learned
your most recent ex died
Noone knew he was sick
until the end
you said
If you knew you would have
used condoms

I don't know what to say
I don't know if it's more
dangerous to believe
slow painful death
is inevitable
or impossible
And I don't understand
how anyone our age
can believe either

We grew up
    came out
    fell in love
in the grip of this plague

I remember being
five six years old
talking about the disease
on the playground
When I was ten a
toe-headed boy named Rusty
told me faggots got it
That was the first time
I can remember hearing the

word
AIDS
and knowing I was
somehow connected to it

We know sex can kill us
and
We know it doesn't have to

When you moved to
San Francisco
I was happy for you
Hoped you would be safer
without cowboys sticking
guns in your face
You had left after that
The imagined smell of
gunpowder mixed with
your blood too frightening
You were learning to stay
alive
and I was grateful

But now the bullets
are a virus and you are
like a train out of control
I hoped you had learned
from our brothers

We have lost so many
If those who go before us
are anything
they are teachers
But we have already
learned too much
and you are
barely a man
No more teaching

I swallow
Hope somehow
you don't have it
that you will call us

joyful
that the test
came back negative

Part of me knows
there will be
no
celebration

Part of me knows
we will be doing dishes
or reading
or not paying attention
to life
when the phone rings
squeals   screech
like a train
halting in the darkness

Part of me knows
we will not know
you're sick
until the end
And I'm angry
at my own
resignation
somehow knowing
we will lose you

Wild Indians

Qwo-Li/Paul Driskill

Yes you could say I am wild
I don't like flower gardens
to be kept up
Don't like TV lies
and I would scalp you in a second

Yes I'm wild
I can't find God in white-walled churches
Don't like the pope
and would scalp him in a blink

I'm wild
Don't like cages
Can't walk on a leash
and never eat the food you leave out

Wild as hell
means you should treasure that scalp of yours
cuz I've got some dancing to do
and that scalp might be just what I need

Song of Removal
Quo-Li/Paul Driskill

Walk down sidewalk
thump feet on concrete
concrete on bones
Walk into libraries built on sacred languages illegally destroyed
Our Words gone
We are still being removed

Big Mountain chanting New Echota
Wounded Knee chanting Tellico
Peabody Western Coal burning Dineh
University of British Colombia poisoning Gros Ventre
Broken Hill Propriety Co. Ltd. wearing bones on wedding rings
Joined forever with death
And we are still being removed

And this white girl who lives on the stolen lands of the Southern Ute and the Dineh
    says *People on the east coast think we're still fighting the Indians*
as if they are not still fighting us
As if their ranch homes are not built on burial mounds
As if we are not still being removed

And 1838 chants 1996
and 1492 chants 1997
and Clinton chants Jackson
and we are still being removed

And I hear white folks say
I didn't kill the Indians
Didn't put them on reservations
Why should I be responsible
not seeing that when the government
wants our land they
remove us
remove us
remove us
remove us
and if we resist we are killed
and reservations are death camps

and Arizona chants Ontario
and Oaxaca chants Tahlequah
and San Francisco chants Cape Town
and we are still being removed

In Denver walk by Indians
Old men sitting on concrete
sitting on bones
sitting in a circle
passing beer in a circle
listening to sacred chants on a portable radio in a circle
dying in a circle

and Budweiser chants Columbus
and AIDS chants smallpox
and senators chant murderers
and we are still being removed

And this white college student says to me
says to me
I hate it when Hispanics won't speak English
This is our country

But it is not your country
Never will be your country
and the Xicano and the Xicana
shall speak whatever they choose
shall keep alive their ancestors
shall keep living
and I wonder why you don't speak Cheyenne

And while Disney paints Pocahontas the great white wet dream
while Russell Means sells out
military occupation of our homes persists
We are still being removed

And we shall be removed
and shall resist
and they shall kill us
but we shall not die

and our tongues shall be stolen
but we shall take them back
and we shall lift our elders off the concrete
and they shall weep in our arms
and we shall weep with them
and we shall stomp on concrete
and it shall crumble

and we shall drum on monuments
and monuments shall fall
and we shall find the bones of our people
and bones shall dance

and in the North borders shall vanish
and in the South borders shall vanish
and in the East oceans shall rejoice
and in the West oceans shall rejoice

and they shall remove us no more
but we shall always remember

we shall sing of removals
we shall sing of removals
we shall sing of removals
we shall sing of removals

and the Ancestors shall sing
and the People shall sing
and the Animals shall sing
and the Earth shall sing

and mothers chant children
and fathers chant children
and Sun chants Moon
and Sky chants Earth

and we are still being removed

Milagro

Patrick Lawler

    •

When I'm in Mexico,
Mickey Mantle
is dying of cancer.
I once burned
his baseball cards
in a shoebox—
a symbolic gesture
of leaving innocence
behind

    •

The seas are rough around Cancun.
Black flags on all the beaches.

        •

Everyday I go looking for a milagro,
miniature figures: body parts, inner
organs, animals. They are offered
to a saint to commemorate
a miracle or to ask the saint's intercession.

    •

How do you say:

            "I am an American,

        and I am prepared

to buy everything you have"?

        •

I'm going to go swimming with the dolphins.
I'm going to go diving into the strange—as if words
were a species, as if desire were a species, as if pain
                were a species.

•

        I have this dream about
parachutists
            in bright colored jump suits
            failing through the sky.

•

This is the week when we celebrate
dropping the bomb on Hiroshima.
There will be the usual parades:
shadow floats, balloons filled with tears
and helium carried by men and women
            with melted hands.

        •

        On the way to Tulum,
        I dive into a cenote,
        a hole into an underground
        river, a lavish mouth,
        a fantastic eye filled
        with holy water and forgiveness.

    •

Everyday I go looking for a milagro,
tittle medals made of tin or silver or gold—
wax or wood or bone.
If you have a headache,
the milagro will be in the shape of a head.
If your heart is hurt,
it will be in the shape of a heart.
You pin them on a saint
and everything is made better.

                •

            How do you say:
            "I am an American,
            and I will sell you
            everything
            you will never need"?

•

Mickey Mantle, I am afraid.
I am afraid of the catacombs of sleep
where. parachutists keep falling.
I am afraid I will not find the appropriate milagro.
Mickey Mantle, I am afraid of your death.

•

It is 8:15 a.m. August 6, 1945.
A six-year-old boy waits
on the platform of the Hiroshima Station.
He waits for a train that vanishes as it arrives.

> •
>
> I have this dream about parachutists—
> 1000s of them in brilliant yellows,
> whites, and oranges dropping out of the
>   sky
> in the field next to the house
> I grew up in as a child.
> They are on a secret mission.

> •
>
> A woman rubs my hair and says it will cost
> a certain amount of pesos for the room,
> a certain amount of pesos for her body.
>   She offers me the cenote.
> The delicious waters of her skin.

> •
>
> A Mexican friend and his wife feed me
> in a bungalow of sticks and tar paper.
> *La casa de mis sueños*. They are proud.
> She is pregnant. I am American.

•

I needed someone else other than my father
to be my father. Mickey Mantle
stumbles around the bases.
        The ball will never land.

•

        I go looking for a milagro for Mickey Mantle—
        something in the shape of lungs or wings.

     •

      Fifty years ago we set the sky on fire.
      Robert Lewis, the co-pilot
      of the Enola Gay,   writes in his
            journal,
      "My God, what have we done?"

              •

              I look for
              milagros
              with
              melted
              hands

  •

It is 1961 and I am dying.
My eyes don't need me any longer.
It is 1995 and the parachutists
come and announce
I've been dead a long time.

        •

        I want to give   my Mexican friend
        a milagro   the size   of a fetus.

     •

The sea's shoulders are collapsing
under the pinned moon.
One hundred fifty thousand people
come out of the sea waving black flags.

           •

          How do you say:
           "I am an
          American"?

•

In Hiroshima they will float
brightly colored umbrellas and lanterns
on Hiroshima's seven rivers
oo remember the dead, to remember those
who drowned trying to cool
their burning bodies.

•

Tonight, there will be an aluminum moon
pinned to the sky.
I won't go swimming with the dolphins.
It's 1995,   and America
will put Mickle Mantle in a shoebox.

Of Her I Sing

Mary Chi-Whi Kim

Gang-raped at 16 in Nashville, Tennessee,
Jenna manned an Auto Works counter
in Columbus, three years later.
She leaned towards me across Formica,
her words a husky rush,
"Hannah, you know,
after the hysterectomy,
I didn't want, didn't think...
Then I met him down
at Radio Shack.
Our wedding's in August."

Of her I sing, daughter of napalm,
of the Mekong and one U.S. Marine.
She chose alabaster silk
and bird of paradise
for her own summer day.

In the air around Marissa
bristled a veil of thorns,
mantled in ice. Her voice
drew a wire between us.
Adopted by a U.S. Sergeant
who incested her for 15 years,
she taught me the samba
behind the counter
of Sana Furs and Leather.
We sold skins together.

Of her I sing, daughter of the DMZ,
of Seoul City and an unknown john.
We dance till dawn
at Mean Mr. Mustards,
a bar on High Street.

My colleague Alisa wore
a blue-black sheet of hair;
in her dorm room
overlooking Harvard Square,
she wrestled and lost against her first date.
Born in Cincinnati, she hammers
nails with Jimmy Carter,
building houses for the homeless
with Habitat for Humanity.

Of her I sing, daughter of the bomb,
of Nagasaki and a Baptist minister.
Holding my niece, her godchild
at the christening, she wears
red plaid flannel, blue jeans,
and black army boots.

Of her I sing.
Hear the thunder of our feet
stomping pavement,
making slippers of blood blisters
as we march along
Pennsylvania Avenue.
Crushing cherry blossoms
beneath our heels, we map out
a Yellow River Brick Road,
with our fists raised
in blasts of peony.
Our throats are alive
with unbidden music,
our anthem ringing
Of Her I Sing.

The Missing Arm of the Father
(after Picasso's "The Fisherman")

Ray Gonzalez

Naked woman and child
on the beach,
the boy with hands

outstretched to the sky,
father cut-off
by Picasso's knife,

the fish erased with
the left arm that couldn't
reach wife and son,

give them what
the air once held.
Broken canvas as if

the man with one arm
was the right male,
provider of invisible fish.

Father of the one arm.
Father of the torn canvas.
When Picasso died, he kept both arms.

White sand, pink bodies,
huge mother holding
her son to the father

as if her husband's arm
and the fish are still
suspended above them.

Son of the one-armed father
and the hanging fish
Son of the mourning mother.

Her hunger will not change.
The fish must be there
even if Picasso took

the arm and fish away,
isolated the man
to give him time to heal,

leaving the mother
and son alone
to bury hope in the sand

I Painted the House Myself

Jeffrey Franklin

As sleep is a form of work, so I
am the dull but diligent overachiever,
just trying to get it down in black
                         and white.
If I could, I'd lift from the myriad array
of postage-stamp-sized samples
                      the one named
Fiery Coral or *Bishop's Purple* or *Lime
Sherbet* and stoically say,
This one, fourteen gallons, please.
                          But, as it is,
innocuous *Basswood*, neither light nor dark,
neither brown nor gray, serving a certain
oyster logic—
                drab camouflage
for a lustrous opaline interior life—
must do.
              I'd thought *Sans Souci*
was the name of a raunchy bar on 9th
until I crossed the Potsdam Bridge, its
checkpoint guardhouse guarding unmanned
a country whose national color had been
                          Drab,
and found the Great Frederick's palace:
the cavernous main salon's ceiling and walls
inlaid with sea shells in numbers
rivaling the infinite,
               huge swirls
of pearly conchs, Persian labyrinths knit
of a thousand pink cockles, edged
with lavender winkles.
               For wainscot,
a band of geodes (grapefruit-sized and split
to show the amethyst sea-urchin cores)
and giant quartz crystals like milky shafts
of sunlight in sea water.

One waltzing brush
would leave the evening gown in tatters.
This I imagined
                    my lustrous and opaline
(if fretful and sedulous) interior life—
brunching on caviar as the Red Army crosses
the lawn, la la—
                    for nothing eggs
the mind to sleights and high-wire antics
like ceaseless painting.
                    I was in trouble, I knew,
when first I savored the whiff of a freshly
opened gallon: that new-car-smell laced
with the Jersey Turnpike
                    and brain damage.
It's not for nothing that painters
drink.
          Far below, soaked t-shirt pressed
to the baking sandpaper of asphalt shingles, lies
my body, but I'm
                    up here,
floating among the feathery leaf tips,
a giddy bouquet of champagne bubbles,
where a sea breeze borne from a hundred miles
brushes the tree tops with
                    Golden Sunshine, and,
hovering here beside me, a hummingbird
decked out in *Chromium Madder-Orange* ascot
and plush *Tawny Sienna* waistcoat.
                    I have
counterbalanced the can in the left hand
with the extended right leg
                    at the top
of the extension ladder and mouthed
the instant convert's last-ditch prayer
that the tremor—whether in leg,
                    ladder footing,
or the earth itself—would not
                    come again.

I have earned the wages of the sins of commission
in the unwiped
                    drip, in the freckling
fantail splatter on glass, and suffered, too,
the sins of omission
in the discrete recesses left unpainted
(the soffit's armpit, the stairway's crotch)
                                        not to mention
the neglected brush, its bristles now set
in a permanent rictus.
                        I have bowed, at last,
to the steady practice and the modest reward
of the sure hand and the brush's mastery
and ridden the rolling paint bead's surge
down the line between putty and glass
and known
              the wave's curl—inevitable!—
the surfer riding its crest beachward,
the two
          one.
I have come in the end to a kind of surrender,
the sheer repetition like the mother's heartbeat
heard from within, so that even in sleep
I keep on painting, my dream-arm flapping
like the one
                good wing, and me sentenced to wander
the countless
                other rooms at *Sans Souci*—
long stripped by museums or The People's Army,
where gray shadows peel from the ghosts
of paintings, and ceilings recede in cobweb clouds
of bygone, imperial mutterings—
desperately in search of a little
                              color.

Two Bad Bulls
Ann Barrett

"Two bad bulls can't reign in the same pen." Tony's words roll out heavy with Jamaican accent. He tosses his head back and peers at me from under the visor of his baseball cap. I can tell by the smug look on his face that he thinks he has stifled me, forcing an early end to our argument. I don't give in that easily.

"What is that supposed to mean?" I ask, feigning innocence.

Tony sucks his teeth in a long, drawn-out hiss. "Come on, Annie. You know perfectly well what I am talking about."

Tony is not much for words. He was born and raised in Jamaica. Jamaicans are thinkers; something about the incredible beauty and energy of the island encourages contemplation. As a rule, Jamaicans think that Americans "chat too much." Tony says, "Empty barrel makes the most noise." Being married to me, however, has given Tony a greater appreciation of the power words possess. I am American, and I am extremely verbal.

When my husband and I argue, I often employ an extensive arsenal of literate weaponry, bombarding him with highfalutin accusations and insults. I like to experiment with my words, like Saddam experiments with chemicals, occasionally producing a combination so potent it knocks the wind right out of Tony. When this happens, he usually resorts to one of his heavy West-Indian wisdoms in a desperate attempt to tip the scales in his favor.

Don't misunderstand me; Tony is not ignorant. Watch him play a game of Scrabble and witness genius. He can take the word "the" and make a fifty-point play. Tony's wisdom runs deep. It doesn't flaunt itself in gaudy costume, dressed up in polysyllabic words. No hint of it is hidden among the stack of Archie comics piled on his bedside table. And if you measured his intellectual prowess by his ability to converse, an otherwise tall Tony would come up short. Tony's sagacity shows in his way of being, in the meditative and calculating way he makes his decisions and moves through life. He is never impulsive. He plans and projects, considering every possible consequence and result before taking action. His patience is infinite; he rarely loses his temper. Tony is the anti-Ann.

The house we inherited from my mother in Miami is a perfect example of the dynamics between Tony and me. It was a crazy structure, full of all the character that only my mother could appreciate: lots of little rooms, one running into another, many of them added on over the years;

different sized windows; different sized doors; sloping ceilings, which in some places didn't allow enough room to stand; sloping floors, all pitching toward the center of the house; four bathrooms, not one single shower; a floating staircase landing in the middle of a bedroom; exposed pipes and wires webbing across the ceiling; no air conditioning; no screens for the windows; a septic tank directly under the living room; sealed off doors that wanted to be reopened; a floor of white-glazed wall tile that encouraged dangerous living when wet—just some of the things that gave it its appeal. So, when my mother passed away and left her house to Tony and me, it was no wonder we thought we had inherited a treasure.

During the five years my mother owned the house, she made only two changes; at my four-year-old daughter's request, she built a swimming pool in the front yard, and, of her own initiative, she installed a bidet in the guest bathroom. My kids were fascinated by this piece of plumbing, occasionally turning it on full force to admire the fountain of water that blasted into the air. I always knew when they had played with it by the trail of grubby footprints streaked across the tile floor, or by their screams of anguish as they slipped and landed on the glassy, ceramic surface.

Preparing to move in, Tony and I decided to be prudent and address the practicalities of family living before we attempted any cosmetic changes. The tile would have to go. We needed to convert one of the claw-foot tubs into a shower, and we either had to condemn the septic tank or seal-off two more doors leading to the living room. The leaking roof demanded attention, and a new footer was necessary under the center of the house. No big deal.

Decorating was another issue. Once we removed the white tile and replaced it with oak, the house took on a majestic air; it became a palace of secret chambers, European boudoirs, and architectural originality. I immediately began covering the white walls with my brother's artwork— huge, colorful canvases inches thick with acrylic paint, violent images of political upheaval with busy patterns of people and movement.

"What's that supposed to be?" Tony asked, pointing at one of the paintings.

"People, Tony. Obviously."

"Doesn't look like people to me."

Tony is not big on artwork. His idea of fine art is the carvings for sale in the Jamaican crafts market—old men smoking pipes, their skin tones matching the color of the wood they are carved from, their awkward postures accommodating the irregular twists and angles of natural tree growth, or generic landscapes depicting painfully realistic scenes of tropical tranquillity, also sold in the crafts market.

Feeling left out of the nesting process, Tony took his biggest crafts market carving, a four foot high crooked and bent old man leaning over his scythe—a laborer—and put it in the living room. Weathered by the sun, the wood was split in several places and, because of the unlucky existence of a knot on the bottom, the base was uneven and the statue rocked back and forth, threatening to fall over.

"That looks like people."

"Tony, the base of that is wobbly and if one of the kids bumps into it, they're liable to get killed."

I had scattered a wide assortment of rugs across the floors, making a special effort to ensure no two were alike in color, texture or size. Tony pulled one over and wedged its corner under the statue's base for balance. Tony doesn't like rugs, either. "Rugs are stupid." They make more work out of housecleaning and "mash up" the beautiful wood floors.

After hanging an unstretched canvas above the front door—a ragged-edged painting of a Rastafarian smoking a pipe—Tony went outside, relinquishing the rest of the decorating to me. I waited until he moved away from the house, and then I took down the picture. Maybe it would work in the baby's room.

Tony decided to attack the yard, planting bananas, mangos, plantains and limes. And then, to give his garden ethnic distinction, he planted callaloo, a Jamaican version of spinach, and Scotch Bonnet pepper, the seeds of which he managed to smuggle from Jamaica in the toe of his shoe. Soon, the bananas and the plantains began to do their thing, sending up shoots in every direction and spreading outside the bounds of the neat pile of stones encircling them. Then, the callaloo went to seed, its offspring floating on the wind like dandelion seeds to the far reaches of the yard. When Tony was finished, there wasn't a foot of unused space left. The grapefruit tree my mother had planted during her short-lived spurt of gardening energy stopped growing, silently protesting the presumption of its new neighbors.

Now, I'm not much of a gardener, which is why I let Tony have his way with the landscaping. Dealing with the tropical vegetation seemed to ease Tony's longing for home, and I figured if he was busy in the yard, he would leave my domestic endeavors alone. Occasionally, Tony invited me to join him, but I was too involved with what I was doing, and it seemed like he offered out of courtesy rather than a genuine desire for my input.

Tony often took breaks from his hard labor in the yard, coming into the house to get something to drink. He clomped through the living room in his steel-toed work boots, marking each step he took with a pile of caked earth.

"Tony!" I whined.

"What?" Following my angry gesture, Tony looked back at his mess. "Thank god, we got rid of that tile," he said with satisfaction. He walked past me into the kitchen, leaving the dirt behind him.

Excited by my decorating efforts, I ignored Tony's thoughtlessness and dragged him from room to room, attempting to elicit some favorable response.

"That's nice." He said as he picked the grime out from under his fingernails. "I have to get a load of topsoil. Do you mind if they dump it in the driveway? Just until I get a chance to move it."

Avoiding his question, I asked, "Do you think that painting looks okay over there?"

"You know I don't have any feeling about art, but if you're gonna cover these beautiful floors, why not carpet it so that all the rooms match?"

"Never mind." I sensed the beginning of a struggle in which I had much to lose. A lack of appreciative feedback seemed like a small price to pay compared to wall-to-wall carpet. Besides, I didn't really want his opinion; I only wanted him to think I did.

One day, when Tony and the kids were gone, I decided to venture out into the yard and take advantage of the solitude. Instead of offering the moment of relaxation and solace I hoped for, I became distracted by the stray callaloo growing around the base of my favorite coconut tree. I began to pull the scraggly, bug-chewed weeds when I noticed several dried fronds hanging loosely from the tree.

Seized with a fit of ambition, I went into the garage to find a pair of clippers. After an unsuccessful and aggravated search through a massive collection of junk Tony had salvaged from the renovations, I gave up and resumed my weeding. In the middle of a flower bed, I encountered an unusually large weed that wouldn't give when I tugged on its stem. I took a stick and wedged it into the ground, levering the plant, roots and all, out of the dirt. Satisfied, I tossed it to the side.

Then, I discovered the clippers. They were covered with rust and lying in the grass. When I lifted them, they left behind a perfect, yellow impression. I picked up a container of engine oil lying on the side of the garage and dripped some onto the clipper blades.

Now, I was on a roll. Sweat trickled down the bridge of my nose, dropping onto my cheeks and making tracks through the fine layer of garden grime that covered my face. What a beautiful sound those clippers made as the blades slid past each other and closed with a click. And how satisfying to slice through a stem and watch a dead frond fall to the ground. Now I knew why Tony loved this work. When I was finished, a huge pile of debris gave testimony to my efforts.

Later, after picking up the kids, I sat at my desk and watched Tony pull into the yard. He moved slowly, unhitching the trailer full of lawn equipment. Having realized his landscaping talents in our yard, he was now in the business of doing others', his reputation based on his ability to create a "natural look." He turned on the sprinklers and launched into his evening ritual—communing with the flowers. I held my breath. He must have been really tired because he didn't seem to notice how good the yard looked.

Tony moved over to the bed where the giant weed had been, standing with his hands on his hips. I smiled. He couldn't miss it now. He stood there, motionless, for several minutes and turned toward the house, his eyes squinting against the late afternoon sun. When he turned back toward the road, he spotted the pile of trash. His hand fluttered up to his brow and then dropped back to his side. He walked over to the pile and studied it for a moment before tentatively sifting through it. What was he looking for, I wondered. Finally, he pulled a stem of withered leaves out of the heap, shaking it lightly in front of him. He looked toward the house again. Something was wrong; I could tell by the look on his face. He put the branch down on the picnic table and continued moving around the yard. The kids soon realized he was home and joined him outside, and I went into the kitchen to prepare dinner.

Through the thick steam wafting up from a pot of boiling pasta, Tony appeared to me. "Hi." He waved the shriveled weed. "How was your day?"

"Fine. What's that?" I asked.

"It was my pepper plant." He answered mournfully. "What happened here today?"

"What do you mean, what happened here today?" Oh, god, his pepper plant, I thought. All the glory of my gardening accomplishments, like steam from the boiling pot, disintegrated around me. "I did a little work in the yard, that's all. How was I supposed to know that was a pepper plant? It didn't have any peppers on it."

Feeling like an idiot, I muscled up for an argument, but it never came. Tony looked at his murdered plant one final time before shoving it into the garbage. "Oh well. Maybe I can get some seeds from the peppers I picked off yesterday." He opened the cupboard and pulled out a bowl full of red, green and gold Scotch Bonnet peppers.

"I'm sorry," I relented. "I didn't realize what it was. It was growing in the middle of a bed of Impatiens. What's a pepper plant doing in the middle of a bed of Impatiens?"

"They both need the same kind of light," he sighed. "I know. You were only trying to help. Well, I'm gonna get cleaned up for dinner. Call me when it's ready." He shuffled out of the kitchen.

I felt terrible. Although I eventually ended up enjoying myself, I had started the yard work aggravated at Tony, aggravated by his style, by the design, or rather lack of design of his garden. I pulled those first few weeds maliciously, in spite of Tony, but by the time I reached the bed of Impatiens, my anger had dissolved in a wash of sweat and fatigue. I never meant to kill his pepper plant.

At dinner, Tony returned to his jolly self; all was forgiven. I smiled at him from across the table, thankful for his easy nature and feeling even more guilty than before. His generosity amazed me. If it had been my pepper plant, I would still be grumbling about it today. The kids teased me about it but backed off in a hurry when they saw me grimace.

About a week later, at dinner time, Tony pushed away from the table and leaned way back in his chair. Balancing the chair on two legs, he looked around the room, letting his eyes pass over two paintings before stopping on the blank wall beyond.

"This place needs some color."

"What do you mean?" I asked.

"Everything is white. Thank god we got rid of that tile."

"But, Tony, art looks good on white walls," I said as I focused on the vibrant colors in the two abstracts.

"Art," Tony snorted.

Well, here it was. This was the payback. I didn't argue; I decided to try the Tony strategy. Stay calm, cooperate. Maybe if he noticed I wasn't threatened, he would lose his steam.

"What color were you thinking of?" I asked. Visions of Tony's mother's pool-blue house nestled among flaming red, pink, and orange Bougainvillaea flashed through my mind.

"Oh, I don't know, something cool. Green, maybe."

Close enough. Green, aqua, pool-blue—they were all the same.

"Where? In here?" I searched the rug for a trace of green, but what caught my attention was the magenta. "I know! Let's compromise. Since you're the one who wants color, and you like things to match, how about if we skip green and go with a bright pink." I carefully avoided the word "magenta," trying not to offend Tony's sensibilities. "It would draw out the color in the rug."

Mistake. Tony looked down at the rug and curled his lip back. "How about if we skip the rug?"

"Oh, Tony. Come on. Be fair."

What we ended up with in the dining room was "raspberry." I giggled as I dragged the roller, dripping with magenta paint, across the bright white wall. If worse came to worse, we could always paint over it.

Tony worked on the opposite side of the room. Neither one of us dared say anything. I watched the sun wash across one of the finished walls, filling the room with a warm glow. It really was beautiful.

"Tony, how about peach in the bedroom?"

He cocked his eyebrow and studied me for a moment. "Forget the bedroom. We need to decide whether to do the living room in this same color." Tony pointed to a wall connecting the two rooms. "If we don't, half of the wall will be white and half will be…magenta."

"Raspberry. Oh, leave it. We'll just make sure to give it a straight edge. Maybe put a piece of trim there or something." I laughed. "All over a pepper plant."

"That's not true." Tony looked down and tried not to smile.

The kids decided what color to paint their own rooms, and Tony and I divided up the rest. When we were finished painting, only the kitchen remained white. My five-year-old proudly announced to his teachers and friends, "We live in a rainbow house," and he was right.

Each room was dressed in a different shade, one more brilliant than the other. Every time I passed from one room to the next, I had to stop and catch my breath. The color added excitement and surprise to our lives and became a symbol, reflecting the eclectic nature of our family. It was easy to tell where I had prevailed because, inevitably, the walls picked up a shade from whatever rug was spread across the floor. Tony's rooms were equally distinguishable. His were the ones without any rugs.

Art by Amos Miller
Copyright © Amos Miller 2001

The Gold Rain Tree (Excerpted Novel)
Mary Sharratt

Set in Minneapolis and St. Paul and spanning the years 1911-1918, the novel concerns Kathrin, a young German immigrant who works in the flour mills until an enigmatic older woman hires her to translate fairy tales. The heroine is drawn into a mysterious new world as the tales begin to assume a reality of their own.

I had never met a woman like Mrs. Waverly, could never decide which facet of her impressed me the most—her elegance, her generosity, her wealth or her formidable intelligence. Despite her warmth, I was in awe of her. She seemed aloof, not to me personally, but to the world in general, as if she did not inhabit the same earth as the rest of us. "She has something up her sleeve," my cousin Lotte had told me, conjuring up an image of Mrs. Waverly concealing her secrets like jewels in the folds of her white muslin dress. She was a sorceress of some sort. Not an evil sorceress. Her secrets were not of the malevolent kind. But she was one of those people who could hide whole worlds behind gentle manners and an ordered life. I wondered if I would stay in her house long enough to find out what any of her secrets were.

When I came home from church, she was in the garden, crouching in the black earth like a peasant. She wore what were probably her oldest clothes, heavy brown cotton that would not easily show stains. Her sleeves were rolled up above her elbows, exposing her arms, ivory pale in the sunlight but less delicate, more muscled than I would have imagined. She was planting seedlings, digging holes with her trowel, putting the naked little plants in and patting the soil around their roots. Though I was standing only a few feet away, she seemed not to notice me. She was singing something under her breath, something sad. Something private, I thought, overcome by a sudden sense of shame. What was I thinking of, intruding on her solitude? Perhaps I wasn't allowed in the garden without her permission. I was about to creep back to the house when she turned and saw me. Her face froze. She didn't scream but dropped her trowel, which fell noiselessly into the earth. Her face and even her arms were blazing red. She was as flustered as I was.

"You gave me a fright," she said. "I didn't expect you back until evening."

"I'm sorry. I did not mean to disturb you."

"I was dreaming again," she said before I could retreat. "You caught me in the middle of a daydream." She brushed the soil off her hands. "And yourself?" she asked, her equanimity returning. "How was church? Did you have a nice chat with your cousin?"

I murmured something polite and vague.

"Your dress is lovely, Kathrin." She had never called me by my first name before. "Turn around. Let me see the back."

Feeling a bit silly, I spun around in a circle. The wind lifted my skirt, making it flare out around my calves.

"That's my favorite color," she said. "Blue like moonlight. Is it new?"

"Yes. I bought it yesterday."

"It suits you." Mrs. Waverly picked up her trowel again. "I'm nearly finished here. After I get cleaned up, we can have an early dinner. You're too thin, Kathrin. You need to eat more. Put some color in your face." She smiled at me before digging another hole, patting in another seedling. As I walked back to the house, my ears were ringing. The way she had spoken to me, more like a mother than an employer. Calling me by my first name.

Since it was so mild, Mrs. Waverly decided we could eat at the wicker table on the back porch. She opened a bottle of white wine, and when she poured it into the glasses, it glowed golden in the evening light, sparkling with a luminosity of its own. This was how I always imagined a magic potion would look. It was as if I had never left the mill—I felt like a barefoot unwashed mill girl who had wandered into a palace by mistake. I'd never drunk good wine before, ever. Sometimes my mother had made elderflower cordial, and I'd had the odd teaspoon of rum in my tea to warm up in winter and the weekly mouthful of sour communion wine, but never anything like this. "Cheers," she said, clinking glasses with me. I took my first sip. It tasted as golden as it looked. It burned inside my mouth.

She took my plate and piled it with asparagus, potatoes, chicken, and salad greens. The food tasted of spring, a distillation of the flowering apple and pear trees, the last daffodils and the first irises, and the other flowers I couldn't even name. Back at the mill, whole springs had passed without my noticing much more than an absence of snow and a gradual accumulation of warmth, but now the season was unfolding around me everywhere I looked, and the chicken was the most tender I had ever tasted. I took this in with a wonderment so keen, it bordered on pain, for I was afraid to trust any of it. Where was the hitch? What would move a lady like Mrs. Waverly to be so kind to someone like me? Why was she serving me this grand meal? She could have let me take my dinner in the kitchen with the maid. Not that I wasn't humbled by her goodness, but I knew she was concealing something from me, just I was struggling to conceal my hunger and uncertainty from her.

I forced myself to eat the chicken with the silver knife and fork, tried to wield them as deftly as she did, though I really wanted to pick up the whole chicken breast in my hands and gnaw the flesh off the bones like the farmer's daughter I was. With one false move, one display of peasant coarseness, I would make the whole illusion shatter like a broken mirror. For this had to be an illusion, a spell, a dream. Despite her talk of helping me get a steady office job when the translations were finished, my secret fear was that sooner or later I would wake up and find myself back in the boarding house beside my cousin. That I would wake up hungrier and more desolate than I had ever been.

"Tell me about yourself, Kathrin," she said. "I don't even know what part of Germany you're from."

I set my silverware down, took another burning sip of wine. "My village was in the Black Forest, which is in the province of Baden." Using my best English and trying to banish my accent. "My valley is called the Höllental. In English the name would be Hell Valley." Then I cursed myself for being so uncouth. Hell is a bad word in English. "The nearest city is Freiburg," I added quickly. "There is a university there."

"Ah, yes." Mrs. Waverly nodded. "I was in Freiburg once. A long time ago. My husband had friends there, also professors of ethnology. Höllental, you say?" She copied my pronunciation. "I'm surprised Arthur didn't take me there. It would be just the sort of place that would intrigue him. He was fascinated by the Black Forest, all the customs and so forth. Like those wooden masks they wear for carnival. I thought they looked a bit like African masks. Do you have them in your valley, too?"

"Yes," I said as diplomatically as I could. I never liked those masks. Our carnival in the Black Forest is not some lighthearted affair with paper hats and confetti but something raw and very old. We don't even call it Karnival or Fasching like they do elsewhere in Germany, because it is no carnival in that sense. We call it Fastnet, for those are the nights before Lent begins, and our masks are not meant to be funny or quaint but to terrify. "It is mostly the men who wear the masks," I told her. "They march at night with torches through the valley." When I was a child, those processions gave me nightmares. I thought the men with their masks lit up in the torchlight were evil spirits, the bogeymen my mother was always warning me about. "On the Tuesday before Lent begins, they march into the village square and make a big fire. Then they burn a witch."

Mrs. Waverly set down her glass, splashing some wine on her hand.

"Not a real witch," I explained. The way I talked, she must think I had sprung from a race of philistines. "A big doll made of straw." I paused before going on. "But long ago they burned real witches. Well, not witches," I amended, lest she think I was superstitious, "but people... women they thought were witches. Not far from my valley is another valley called the Hexental, the valley of witches."

"I've read about the witch burnings," she said, cutting her asparagus into smaller and smaller pieces. She seemed to spend more time slicing her food than eating it and had barely touched anything on her plate. "I think that if I had lived back then, they would have probably burned me." From the tone of her voice, it didn't sound like she was joking.

Picking up my knife and fork, I sliced one of the new potatoes into quarters, raised the fork to my mouth. Yes, she is a sorceress, I thought as I chewed and swallowed. She admits it herself. Maybe that was why I had never met a woman like her before. In my part of the world, they had been burned long ago.

"Tell me some more about the Höllental," she said.

"Once... one hundred years ago, Goethe came to our village. He spent the night in our inn." I didn't want her to think we were completely uncivilized. "And before that, the Austrian princess Marie Antoinette traveled through the Höllental on the way to Paris to marry the French king. She came through our valley with a train of fifty coaches."

"Marie Antoinette?" Mrs. Waverly was amused.

"Yes. In those days there were no proper roads in our valley, but the people had to build one just for her."

She laughed. "Oh, yes. I'm sure they did. Traveling through the Höllental on her way to be married. That's what I call tempting fate." She broke off, shaking her head. "It's such a pity my husband never met you, Kathrin. He would have had all sorts of questions to ask you. Well, tell me something else but not about carnival or anyone famous. Tell me something about your valley that you loved."

Something that I loved? What kind of question was that? I had to think a long while before I could answer her. "On the first day of summer, the longest day of the year, we rolled wheels down a hill into the mill stream. Burning wheels. They were on fire. They rolled and burned all the way down the hill, and then they fell into the water."

"We call them Catherine wheels," said Mrs. Waverly. "After the wheel St. Catherine was martyred on. Actually the custom predates St. Catherine. It's a pagan survival. Sun worship," she said, between sips of the shining wine. For a moment, she was silent. I used the lull in our conversation to finish my chicken, but even after cleaning my plate, I was still hungry enough to eat everything left in the serving dishes and the food on her plate that she had sliced with such care. But then, as if reading my mind, she started to eat. She finally seemed to have found her appetite.

"Tell me about your family," she said a few minutes later. "Do you have any brothers and sisters back home?"

That's when I dropped my knife and fork. What an ugly clatter they made as they fell against the polished oak porch. I leapt out of my chair, nearly knocking it over, and knelt to pick them up, wiping them on the damask napkin, making an ugly brown mark on the cloth. Kneeling on her porch with a stained napkin in my hand. How was she to know that my brother and my sisters were long dead?

"Sit down, Kathrin. It's all right," she said. "I'll get you some clean silverware." She disappeared through the screen door into the kitchen. As I returned to my chair, I felt a dangerous prickling behind my eyes. She came out again, handed me a new knife and fork, a clean napkin, then sat down like nothing had happened.

"I have two brothers and a sister," Mrs. Waverly said. "Older than me. I'm the youngest. Next Saturday you'll meet them. They're coming by with their children. I have nineteen nieces and nephews, if you can believe that. Kathrin, your plate's empty." She took it from me and filled it again, a generous helping of everything. Then she looked at me the same way she had when she'd asked me to tell her about something from home that I loved. "Do you get homesick?"

"No. Never." I ate my food, so I wouldn't have to say anything else. She hadn't meant to wound me, but it was a pointless question, like asking me if I miss my dead parents when I can't even remember my mother's face. I took a sip of the wine, an awkward sip, some of it spilling over my lip and down my chin. I wiped it away with the clean napkin, grateful that at least the pale wine wouldn't leave a stain, but the wine clouded my vision, making everything shadowy and dim. I bit my lip hard to steady myself.

"I remember Freiburg as a very pleasant place," she said, her voice drawing me out of the valley of my thoughts, back into the wicker chair in the sunlit garden. "Much prettier, I think, than Heidelberg, where all the Americans go. I had a hard time with the language, though. I learned French in school and Russian at home—my great grandmother was born in St. Petersburg—but German was difficult for me. Arthur, of course, spoke excellent German. Languages were his specialty."

She didn't speak of him the way most wives speak of their husbands, living or deceased. Not with the usual mixture of affection and good-natured griping, but with a distant sort of reverence, the way my uncle spoke of Schiller and Heinrich Heine. It's because he was a genius, I told myself. No ordinary man.

"He was a great professor, your husband," I said shyly. "Mr. Jelinek said he was brilliant."

"Yes," she said, glancing across the garden. "He was very intelligent, and he didn't mock me for being so bookish." She was silent for a moment. "After he died, it took me a year before I could pick up a scholarly book again without being reminded of him, of what I had lost." Her eyes were somewhere else, seeing things I couldn't see, seeing things I couldn't even comprehend. For the first time, I had an inkling of what John had meant when he'd said, "You can tell she's lonely, all right." I began to sense her loneliness. The sadness she kept hidden.

"You know," she said, still gazing at the flowers and trees, "too many men just want a wife for a piece of decoration." She turned to me with a half smile. "You're at the age where you have to keep that in mind, Kathrin. I'll give you the same advice I give my nieces." She used a sisterly tone. "Before you settle on a man, make sure he loves you for more than your pretty face."

Before either of us could think what to say next, Franny came out with a wheel of soft white cheese on a silver tray and a basket of freshly washed peaches, droplets of water still clinging to their skin. The peaches looked too perfect to eat. Mrs. Waverly picked up a silver knife and began to cut the cheese into wedges like a pie.

"When I went abroad for the first time, I was a grown woman, twenty-one years old, with a husband to do the translating for me, but even so, I was petrified. The way I looked and talked and dressed, everyone knew I was a foreigner. I felt like a gawky young girl at her first dance. I keep thinking how brave you were, Kathrin, coming here when you were sixteen, all by yourself, learning the language from scratch, speaking it so well after only two years. I envy your courage." She spoke so sincerely, I was at a loss. I could not believe a woman like her would see anything enviable in a person like me. I wasn't brave, I was desperate, I wanted to tell her, but, of course, I didn't. That would have been rude.

"Here, try a peach," she said. "They're from the hothouse, but nice enough, I think." She reached across the table to hand me one. The fruit was heavy and moist in my palm.

"Thank you," I said and bit into it, my teeth sinking through the fuzz on the firm skin and into the sweet flesh. I thought of the old stories of the gods eating nectar. This was nectar, this fruit, this kindness. I smiled at the woman sitting across from me. I could smell her faint perfume.

"My great-grandmother came over from St. Petersburg when she was fifteen." Mrs. Waverly held out the silver tray, so I could take a piece of cheese. Velvety on my tongue, tasting like raw almonds and wild mushrooms, the kind my mother and I used to pick in the forest every fall. "She came here alone, just like you. She arrived in New York and found work at a furrier's, fourteen hours a day. She was a wife and mother at sixteen, a grandmother by the time she was my age, and through her years of having babies, she kept working at the furrier's because she had to, just to feed them. She saw to it that her daughters went to school and married well, and they saw to it that their children did even better." Mrs. Waverly stopped short, biting into a wedge of cheese.

"My father had a Russian name. Andresky. But he changed it to Andrews. That was my maiden name. Violet Andrews. When I was a girl, my father wanted us to speak only English, but my great-granny was living with us then, and she ignored the rule. She was over ninety and so ornery, nobody dared to cross her. She sat me on her lap and told me story after story in Russian. That's how I learned the language and how I came to love fairy tales, even before I met my husband."

Her eyes were so far away, you would think she could see across the ocean. As distant as they had been when I surprised her in the garden. Not wanting to intrude on her thoughts, I looked across the lawn, drenched in sunlight, dappled in shadow. My eyes came to rest on a delicate tree covered in pendulous gold flowers, shimmering in the sun, so radiant, it seemed to crackle, dancing and shifting like a beautiful ghost. "What is the English name for that tree?" I finally asked her. "In German we call it Goldregen. The flowers are like gold rain."

"The English name is laburnum," Mrs. Waverly said. "Untranslated from the Latin. Quite unpoetic, I'm afraid." We lapsed into silence, staring at the tree. I took a long sip of wine, let the gold burn inside me.

By day I sat in the sonorous dining room, translating for hours, getting ink stains on my fingers and cuffs. I practiced my typing, learning to pick out the letters by touch, practicing at least an hour a day. At the end of each session, my wrists ached and my fingers were like lead, but I kept telling myself that typing was the most important skill I would take with me from this job. If I could type well, I would never have to go back to the mill.

Our real life took place in the evenings, during the long meals we shared on the back porch. Sometimes we sat talking and sipping wine until the sun set and the moths came out. Those evenings we recited the fairy tales we had translated that day. I told her the German tales, and she told me the Russian tales. Those May nights are fixed in my memory like an engraving. Watching the sky darken to indigo, waiting for the first stars to appear, and listening to her stories. There wasn't enough light to make out her face, but her voice was an entity of its own. The tales emerged from the darkness. She told me the story of Marussia who had the misfortune to marry a vampire, and of the Firebird who carried the water of life that could make the dead rise again. But the story I remember most vividly is the tale of the girl who walked into the thick of the forest to the sorceress's house. The story that was to become my story, shaping my life like a prophecy. "Once there was a girl who lost her mother."

I shivered as she said this, pressing my hands together in my lap and leaning forward to inhale the lilacs in their crystal vase, white lilacs, ghostly in the sputtering candlelight.

"The girl's name was Wassalissa."

A name like music. I could see her. A skinny girl with long plaits. A girl who was always hungry.

"Her dying mother gave her a magical doll that would look after her always. 'Remember to keep her secret,' said the mother. 'No one must know you have her. Listen to what she tells you, and remember, above all, to feed her.' As soon as she had passed the doll into her daughter's hands, she laid her head back on the pillow and breathed her last breath.

"Wassalissa mourned her mother. So did her father, but not for long. Before the year of mourning had ended, he brought home a new bride, a handsome but spiteful widow with a mean-hearted daughter. As suddenly as he married, he went away on a long journey, leaving Wassalissa alone with her new stepmother, who made her do all the work while her own daughter sat idle. She was jealous of Wassalissa's beauty and wanted to break her with toil, make her hands rough and her face coarse, but the girl had her mother's blessing. She labored without complaint and only grew more beautiful. The stepmother plotted and plotted. Finally she moved the family to a cabin at the edge of a dense wild forest."

I was back in the Höllental. It was November, and the thin strip of sky we could see from the bottom of the valley was black, moonless, but full of stars.

"That forest was the home of the sorceress Baba Yaga who ate human flesh and flew around in a cauldron shaped like a mortar, using a pestle for an oar, sweeping away her tracks with a broom made of dead man's hair. The stepmother sent Wassalissa into Baba Yaga's forest to gather firewood, yet the girl always came back unharmed because the doll and her mother's blessing protected her. Finally the stepmother took the most desperate measure of all. She let the hearth fire go out. She let the fire go out in December, just before the winter solstice, the darkest night of the year. Without fire they would perish. The stepmother accused Wassalissa of letting the fire go out. She thrust the girl out the door in the middle of the night in the freezing cold. 'Go to Baba Yaga and ask her for fire! Don't come back until you have a burning torch.'

"So Wassalissa set off at midnight through the forest of twisted trees. There was no moon. Thick clouds hid the stars, so dark it was. But the doll guided her on her way. Gradually the darkness began to pass. A man rode by on a white horse, and it was dawn. Then a man rode past on a red horse, and the sun began to rise. Wassalissa walked the whole day until she came to a clearing, and the doll said, 'There!' In the middle of the clearing was a house set on hen's feet, dancing round and round in a circle."

It was too dark for Mrs. Waverly to see that I was crying. I would have died of shame had she seen my tears, but it was my mother's house that danced in that clearing.

"The house was surrounded by a burning hedge of bare branches, and atop each naked branch was a flaming skull."

I saw this, as sharp and clear as if it were taking place in front of me. Except the skulls were our wooden Fastnet masks.

"Wassalissa wanted to run into the forest and hide, but then a black rider swept up on a black horse. He called out a charm to the hen-footed house, which immediately stopped its dancing and lowered its door to the ground. The door was made of dead man's bones. The door latch was a human collarbone. The lock was a grinning skull. The rider jumped off his horse, opened the door and disappeared. Then it was night, the darkest night of the year. Her doll whispered, 'Go!' So Wassalissa stepped inside the strange hovel, and there was Baba Yaga herself."

The pictures inside my head began to diverge more and more from the story she was telling me. She was describing what a hideous hag Baba Yaga was, her wart crusted nose touching her greasy chin, but the sorceress I saw was not grotesque. An older woman, yes. Twice as old as me with some gray in her hair, but not ugly. She looked like Mrs. Waverly.

"'Well, my daughter,' said the Yaga. 'Who are you and what do you seek?'

"'Lady, I have come, because we have no fire in our house.'

"'You let the fire go out? That was a very foolish thing to do. For foolish acts, you must pay. You'll get your fire, but not for nothing. First you must do the tasks I set for you. To start with, you can get my dinner.'

"Wassalissa ran to the oven and took out dish after dish, a feast for at least a dozen people, but the hag ate everything herself, only leaving a crust of bread for the girl. 'Tomorrow when I go out you must clean the house, make my dinner, sweep the yard, then wash the laundry in the river and hang it up to dry. Then you must go to the grain shed and separate the mildewed corn from the good corn. When you're finished with that, you'll find a pile of dirty poppy seeds. You must separate the seeds from the dirt. If you do not finish your work before I come home tomorrow night,' said the Yaga, 'I will feast on you and suck the marrow from your bones.'

"A little while later, the sorceress fell snoring into bed. Wassalissa offered the doll her crust of bread and told her about the work she had to do the next day. The girl trembled, but her doll whispered, 'All will be well. Have you already forgotten your mother's blessing?'

"The next morning, Baba Yaga whistled for her mortar, pestle and broom, and they flew up to the door. She stepped into her mortar and was gone. Wassalissa was about to start her work, but it was already done. The doll had done it for her while she was sleeping. The only thing left to do was make dinner. When Baba Yaga returned that night, she could find no fault in Wassalissa's work. 'You did well,' she growled. Then she called her servants to come and grind the corn. Three pairs of hands appeared out of nowhere and did their task. They pressed the oil out of the poppy seeds. The sorceress made bread with the ground corn. She drank down the poppy seed oil and ate the dinner Wassalissa had prepared. The girl stood beside her without making any noise.

"'What's the matter with you?' asked the hag. 'Can't you speak?'

"'If you will allow, Lady, I would like to ask you some questions.'

"'Ask what you like, but remember, too much knowledge makes a person old.'

"'I only want to know about the riders,' said Wassalissa

"'Why, that's simple,' said the hag. 'The white rider is my day. The red rider is my sun. The black rider is my night.' Wassalissa nodded but kept silent. 'Don't you want to know anything more?' asked Baba Yaga.

"'No, Lady. You said yourself that knowing too much makes you old before your time.'

"'A wise answer, my dear. Well, now I shall ask you some questions. How did you manage to do all that work?'

"'I have my mother's blessing,' said Wassalissa.

"'Get out right away!' sputtered the hag. 'I will have no blessings in this house.' She chased Wassalissa out the door, took a flaming skull down from her hedge, stuck it on a stick and thrust it in her hand. 'Here is your fire. Now, go! Right away! Before I change my mind and eat you!' So Wassalissa rushed off through the forest, her doll pointing out the way."

I was that girl, and I was running. I could feel the hard pumping of my lungs, the sparks glancing off my face. I was holding the fire in my hand.

"She arrived home by evening the next day. The flaming skull looked so fearsome, she wanted to bury it in the snow, but the doll whispered, 'Keep it!' So she went into the dark house and gave the fire to her stepmother. The woman used the skull to light the hearth. Then she tried to extinguish the skull itself, but it would not go out. It burned and burned, its eyes boring into Wassalissa's stepmother and stepsister the whole night through. By morning they were burnt to cinders. When day came, Wassalissa buried the skull. But that is not the end of her story."

Mrs. Waverly paused for a least a minute. I sat very still in my chair and waited for her to go on.

"Orphaned again, she walked into town to look for shelter. A kind old seamstress took her in. Wassalissa spun thread for her new mistress, and the thread she spun was fine and soft as human hair. It was too fine to weave, but the doll gave her a magical machine in place of a loom. This machine produced the finest cloth there ever was. Wassalissa gave it to the old woman and told her to sell it and keep the money. The seamstress brought it to the royal court and showed it to the king. When he asked how much she wanted for it, she told him it was a gift. It was priceless! No money on earth could pay for such exquisite handiwork. The king thanked her, gave her gifts in return and sent her on her way. He wanted to have a shirt made from the cloth, but there wasn't a tailor in the realm who could cut and sew such marvelous fabric without ruining it. Finally he went to the seamstress's house. 'Old woman, since you have woven such fine cloth, you alone can sew it.' But the seamstress told him that the cloth was the work of a beautiful young girl. 'Then let her make me a shirt,' said the king.

"Wassalissa didn't make one shirt. She made a dozen, which she gave to the old woman to present to the royal court. When the old woman returned from her errand, she told Wassalissa to comb her hair, put on her best dress and wait by the window. The king was very curious to meet the young woman who wove such beautiful cloth. He sent a servant to bring her to the palace, and as soon as he laid eyes on her, he fell in love."

Mrs. Waverly's voice was curiously cool and ironic as she said this.

"He took her hands, set her on the throne and made her his wife. Wassalissa's father came back from his long journey in time for their wedding. Wassalissa was married in the grandest style with silk and jewels, but that is not the end of her story."

Mrs. Waverly paused for at least two minutes, sipping from her wine glass and resting her voice.

"Wassalissa," she said softly, pronouncing each syllable like a separate word. Waa-saa-liss-saa. "Wassalissa was a good and loyal wife. She bore her husband seven sons and seven daughters. She lived long, outliving her husband, but through her years of marriage and her years of widowhood, she kept her doll with her, treasured in secret."

Her voice rose a little when she said the word secret.

"She kept her doll until she was a white haired crone. She kept her doll and her secret of fetching fire on the darkest night with her until the end of her days."

Her tale finished, she drained her glass of wine. I drank down the last few swallows of mine. This time the wine was red. Red wine grown cold in the darkness. I shivered. My blouse was too thin. I could tell that she was chilly, too. She kept rubbing her arms to keep warm. We should go inside now, I thought. It was late, and tomorrow was an early day. Yet neither of us could move. I stared at the gibbous moon, emerging from the inky clouds the wind was pushing across the sky, the wind that made the trees creak like dancing skeletons.

Then I opened my mouth, and the most incongruous sentence came out. "Mrs. Waverly, why do you like fairy tales so much? They are for children."

It took her a while to come up with an answer. In the darkness I could not see the expression on her face, had no way of knowing whether I had offended her or not. I was mortified for having spoken so carelessly. It was the wine. I should never be allowed to drink another drop. As I was about to apologize, she spoke.

"Come up to the study, Kathrin. I have something to show you."

On the one of the window sills in her study was a Russian doll made of brightly painted wood, cylindrical in shape, scarlet and gold with a white face, black eyes and hair. "Here, Kathrin." She placed the doll in my hands. "Open her up and see what's inside."

I pulled the doll apart to find a smaller, slightly different doll. This opened to a smaller doll and a smaller doll still, a progression of ever shrinking dolls, until I came to the core, holding the ninth doll, no larger than a glass marble, in the palm of my hand.

"When you look at her on the outside, you think she's simple and crude. But she's not. It's the same with fairy tales."

"Were these your great-grandmother's?" I began to put the dolls back together again, one inside the other.

"Yes. One of the few things she took with her when she came to this country."

That night I dreamt of the dolls, dreamt that my skin was also made of brightly painted wood, falling off in layers and layers until I had a different body, a different face from the one I had always known. The tales enveloped me like a cloak, and I entered them, a little farther, a little deeper each day. They became a part of me, layers and layers inside me. The tales would become my secret treasure. I knew I was living under a spell but no longer resisted it. Like a wave, it swept me off the shore, drawing me into another element.

Enter Usher, Daydreaming
Edward Bartók-Baratta

If the curtain were only
about to rise,
we could dress
in monkey skins.
You could grow so well
into your skin
to become real monkey,
and I, indefatigable,
could say things like
"Not so fast, buster,"
in my screeching
monkey tongue.

I would learn
to put up with you,
your screams
and crazy haircut.
We could meet
evenings at the water hole
to discuss
major monkey tragedies:
a chimp
squeezed to death
by a boa constrictor
in the rain forest.

If the sun were only
about to rise tonight
rather than set
behind this ancient mask,
concession girl, hair
in a bun
you could undo
these small knotted hands.

As You Eat Eggs
Edward Bartók-Baratta

The hard rain comes, and ants stretch themselves,
they lie prone over the holes of their home—

the egg-shaped dome risen from the earth,
pine needles they collect one at a time.

Lettuce leaves fall under the sun at noon,
large bees come knocking at the cabin window.

The fly has had his seven weeks of life,
then dies trapped between the screen and the wood.

Far north from war, the secluded forest,
a small brown spider walks across the page.

Bombs are dropping on someone else's home.
The eggs of their misfortune are hatching.

Ioanna
Edward Bartók-Baratta

A fruit, a berry, a beautiful animal
in the sun: a woman, with her arms behind
her back, her hands folded, and her face pushed up

to take in the sky and the rain. Bring in
the moon, too, on a blue velvet carpet of sky.
Let snow fall, let angels descend, let all

our countries meet. We are driven by buckets
of weather (how we love what is haphazard!)
in a downtown café, where she walks through

the doorway to serve a platter of squid, light
in her olive face so Mediterranean
I could drown there and never regret it. Now

to fumble for a clean corner of a napkin,
to transcribe the syllables of her name,
printed so carefully on my check, a sound

that crawls like a lizard into my palm:
Ioanna, rub your thighs, your belly, your
sun-backed neck, over the hot stones of my fingers.

Morning

John Willson

There, again, piercing the chatter of other birds,
a long, single whistle, like a referee's whistle
stopping play, the bird itself hidden by salal
and the shadows of madonna and fir. An arrow
of sound shot back to an alpine dawn: sunlight

through tent fabric turned my hands
blue as the water where I swam until my eyes
opened to the same whistle. Creature that stays
from sight, how do you range from a mountain
down to this sea-level hawking
of crows, the finch's gossip?
Again, your pure syllable

taut as a tent-line from apex to ground.
Did you see the flap open, watch me crawl
out, scoop water to my face,
scratch my chin when glasses
turned a white blob into a goat
above the pass? First-Thing-in-the-Morning,
I have never seen the color of your soft
throat, but with a wingbat's ease

You shuttle me across the distance, pump
thin air into my lungs, turn me
toward the dwarf lupine by my boot.
Though you remain anonymous as a painter
of ancient caves, I salute you with a cup of tea
and I would welcome your call as the signal,
the last sound before leaving the flesh, the whistle
bearing me into the wild blue.

Stories II

Allison Graboski

Like sheer folds of tissue paper or the stain of flower petals, the stories your mother told you were too beautiful. Her words sketched your world, cut rock and gauze, with only one flaw: the world she prepared you for was not this one. It was some other world she told you about, some world only she could see veiled and shimmering beneath the dirt.

Your mother knew the secrets of the landscape.
Though it seemed arid   a wasteland   it was not
Beneath the piles of drab gray stone there lay buried an ocean

Before she died, there wasn't time for her to tell you everything. Quick breaths pass out of body; and hands
once brown   grow blue with cold

From where she stood, you were so far away—the space between you thick like glass, or an emptiness. You watched as the rain weathered her body, eroding her like a pile of sand. And slowly, over time, the enclosures that seemed tireless dissolved into fissures and fractures, cracking the landscape that kept everything else at a distance.

From where she stood, it was the space that enveloped her she tried to warn you about It's cold, she said. Cold and fast-running like Alpine snowmelt. Dark like black ink filling in the cracks of the skin. If you're not careful, she said, it will sweep you away. These words reached you, if at all, in a hush.

Before she died, your mother told you the secret of the tides. The ocean is ruled by the masses of two bodies. The gravity of the sun works against the pull of the moon to create neap, tides. The pull of the sun piled on top of the pull of the moon creates spring tides. You cannot be exactly sure what she means—if spring is a season or a sharp uncoiling - but what you do know is this: as though by the arms of a woman, dogged and tender, water is dragged across the bottom of the sea.

She told you the secrets of the landscape knowing full well the world would evaporate and leave behind its only residue. As she spoke, your brown hands grew sticky with salt. Staring at them you believed, as did she, in some impending change: that the next morning you would only be a skeleton with no need of flesh, that your vision would be filled with the shadowy outline of the mountains against the sky, barely flooded with light.

Just before dawn, she called you to the edge of the crevice where the smell of saltwater was strong. She motioned and you knelt beside her. Though you were not afraid of spiders, you were afraid of the edge.

The ocean is not to drown in, she said. Saltwater is denser than freshwater. You can float with almost no effort at all.

After a long drawn-out pause, these three actions she said to take:
Refuse. Contact. Swim.

Hoodlum Birds

J. Eugene Gloria

The fearless blackbirds see me again
at the footpath beside the tall grasses
sprouting like unruly morning hair.
They caw and caw like vulgar boys
on street corners making love to girls
with their *hey mama,*
this and their *hey mama that.*
But these gang of birds are much too slick.
They are my *homeys* of the air
with their mousse-backed hair, black coats
like the petty hoods who smoke
and joke about each other's mothers,
virginal sisters, and the subtle art of revenge.
These blackbirds couldn't care less
for my uneaten celery sticks
I laud the roadside with. Small gestures,
I know, my ineffective hosannas.
They call to each other, shrill and terrible
as if naming all my daily trespasses.
But they let me pass, and then, flit away.
They won't mess with me this time—
they know where I live.

Truths in Tibet
Stephanie Griest

I could feel Tibet before I stepped foot on its dusty soil. As our plane swept over its landing strip, cradled between mountains, my heart crept into my throat. I was nearing delirium by the time we landed, partly from elevation, partly from altitude. Sand dunes are considered hills in my hometown in South Texas, so Lhasa—all 3,600 meters of her—was going to be a challenge, though not the only one.

Tibet was the culmination of a year spent on a Henry Luce Scholarship, where I taught Western media concepts to a staff of Chinese journalists at a state-run newspaper, *China Daily,* in Beijing. It was the most unsettling year of my life. Everything I once understood was questioned: my beliefs, my culture, my religion, my profession—not only by the Chinese, but by myself. A year of long walks and longer talks with confidants, scribbling in a half dozen journals and dancing enabled me to wipe away a few strands of confusion, but many more remained. Including Tibet.

My life had reached a crossroads, and I did not know which path to travel upon next. My fellowship—and funds—would run out within the month, and for the first time in my life, I had no plan. It was terrifying and exhilarating all at once. Should I stick to my earlier idea of freelancing across Asia until my laptop was stolen or I got a tapeworm? Return to America and get a real job? Run away to Istanbul and become a professional belly dancer? My mind seemed so clouded, I felt incapable of thinking clearly. Spending a year at a propaganda-saturated newspaper had not helped.

I had heard Tibet described as a center of energy, an oasis. I was drawn into it, and decided that before I left China, I must experience it fully. Alone. So I went.

But first I had to get over my altitude sickness. I was nauseous and dizzy by the time my bus rolled into Lhasa, a sweaty two and a half hour journey from the airport. My hostel room was on the fifth floor, and there were no elevators. Seven stairs up, I was panting. At two floors, I had to stop to catch my breath. When I reached the third floor, I let my backpack fall from my shoulders to the cracked floor and I collapsed on top of it. I wanted to ask for a room on a lower floor—or even better, an oxygen tank—but that would entail climbing down all those stairs. The sun had shifted by the time I made it to my room and flung myself onto the bed.

I did not move for two days and may never have again had it not been for the kindness of a hotel attendant, who filled my thermos twice a day with salty yak tea seasoned with little black hairs.

Memory immediately took root during my first encounter with Jokhang Temple, which stands in Lhasa's bustling center. I watched in awe as worshippers took one step, raised their arms high above their heads, clasped them together, then swooped them forward, like a diver might before entering the sea. Their bodies formed a full prostration: Head, shoulders, knees, and toes embraced the dusty pavement. That position of complete submission was held for half a second, before they picked themselves up, took a second step and repeated the process. They slowly inched, in a clockwise direction, around the sprawling temple.

My attention was quickly diverted when I saw a man—perhaps in his fifties—enter the holy grounds. He looked as if he had not showered or slept in a month, and a large sack was slung across a drooping shoulder. I was not the only one who noticed him. A toothless grin spread across his windburned cheeks, and he let the beggars grab his bag. A scuffle thus ensued which reminded me of children darting for candy once a piñata has been struck. But rather than licorice and lollipops, the bag was full of something the size and shape of bowling balls that were brown in color and grainy in texture.

I crept a little closer and was greeted by a haggard old woman. I was overwhelmed with a desire to read the story of her life by tracing contours on her face with my hands. If wrinkles are our trees' rings, she has lived a long one. She offered me her ball graciously. It appeared edible, so I put my hands on top of it to break some off, but all I got were flakes beneath my fingernails. It was quite solid. The woman was watching me so expectantly, I felt I should show appreciation, so I put my fingers in my mouth, made a sucking noise and smiled before shuffling off with her manna. My eyes returned to the pilgrim who had brought the bread. His alms dispersed, he tossed the bag aside and began a slow progression of prostrations around the temple.

The Jokhang Temple reminded me of the Shrine of the Virgin of Guadalupe in Mexico City—"La Villa"—where the devout cross the holy grounds on their knees. I remember how transfixed I was by that sight: Hundreds of older women wrapped in shawls, their rosaries wound through their fingers, sobbing as blood seeped through their skirts as they hobbled on their knees. But though the Tibetans threw themselves upon the rough pavement over and again, I saw no wincing, scratches, or blood.

Tibetans are no stranger to pain, and in fact—they seemed to transcend it. Their entire past century has been scarred by violence. Their spiritual leader, the Dalai Lama, was forced into exile in 1959; his Potala

Palace is now a museum that raises money for a government many Tibetans despise. Lhasa, the spiritual and political capitol of what has become a province of China, is visibly divided between the Tibetan's old town—marked with temples and crowded outdoor markets—and the Chinese's thriving city of appliance stores, karaoke bars and Internet cafés. Police patrol the holy grounds; guards pace through the streets. During a 5-day journey that culminated at the luscious Nemstvo River, my travel group stumbled across a military convoy of some 50 jeeps, and the vast countryside was momentarily speckled with yaks, rocks, and soldiers.

But outside occasional acts of resistance, the Tibetans seemed to have meditated their reality as they rotated their prayer wheels in one hand and a string of Buddhist beads in the other.

I was determined not to jump to the quick and easy conclusion most Westerners share, that the Tibetans are the oppressed and the Chinese are the oppressors. I tried to keep my Chinese friend's passionate perspective in mind as I observed all that surrounded me. "The Dalai Lama made all the Tibetans serfs in their own land," one journalist colleague told me. "We liberated them from their oppressors, just like Mao Zedong liberated us from the emperor," another said. A lawyer friend insisted, "Just look at all we have done for Tibet. We gave them roads, cars, Internet. They were living in the Dark Ages and we brought them into modernity."

My Chinese friends often recited an old proverb to me: When you go to the forest, don't look at the trees. There is no room for dissent in a country with one billion inhabitants, they would argue. They seemed incapable of caring less for the province that, with help of Hollywood, had captured the heart of my own country. And so I spent weeks traveling through Tibet's mountains and rivers, its valleys and villages, trying to draw my own conclusions. But I felt as though I understood less when I arrived.

My last full day in Tibet, I rose with the sun, rented a rickety old bicycle and pedaled to a small monestary on the outskirts of a neighboring town. I lost a wheel along the way, and got lost twice. The monastery seemed devoid of tourists, for which I was grateful. The corridors of the temple were dark only a hint of incense lingered in the musty air. I noticed a monk sitting near the sole window, his face illuminated by a thin stream of sunlight. I greeted him in Mandarin, but he responded in English and stood up politely. I asked him about a particular Buddhisatva whose mural covered a great part of one wall. He described her significance in proud detail, and then started on the story of another.

I had made a friend.

The tour that thus ensued took hours, as my monk wanted me to appreciate everything from the workmanship to the spiritual meaning behind each icon. He shared a lunch of bread, yogurt, and milk tea with me on a terrace that overlooked the village and the mountains that embraced us. He was curious about my own background. I rarely admitted I was journalist in China, as I was under stern restrictions not to write or print during my tenure with *China Daily.* I had also learned that many Chinese are intimidated by the media. But I did not want to withhold the truth from him. He was momentarily shaken, but he held his composure and murmured that he had never spoken with an American journalist before. He seemed to let that piece of information tumble about in his mind for a while, Then in a low voice, he asked if I understood what the Chinese had done to his ancient land.

My stomach tightened. I has a thousand questions. Practicing religion in an officially atheist country must be like trying to conduct journalism in a government that outlawed free press. But what would happen if our conversation was overheard? Chinese have been known to pose as Tibetan monks; what if one was listening? It seemed to great a risk—for both our sakes, but especially his. So I changed the subject abruptly to linguistics. "Do you speak Mandarin?" "I can, but I don't," he said carefully, then switched the discussion again. He had an English class to teach and needed to go.

I took that as a polite invitation to continue my day alone, and stood up to leave. "No," he said, and smiled. "I want you to come too."

The only light source in the classroom was the sun. The floor was dirt and the walls were wooden, but there was a blackboard with some chalk that looked like lava rocks. About 20 monks, ranging in age from 5 to 25, filed in. They were animated and lively in their dark red cloaks, but they stopped short when they saw me. I greeted them in English, which was terribly funny to them. They were called to a stern attention by their teacher, who motioned for them to open their aging workbooks. No time was wasted: He immediately began leading the class in a discussion of the colors, which were recited as a chant. "Red, green, yellow, orange, blue. Red, green, yellow, orange, blue." The little monks repeated it in unison.

I couldn't help but wonder if the monks even knew what the words represented beyond some bizarre, foreign mantra when the teacher began a new color scheme. "Pink, purple, black, white, brown." He pronounce the latter hesitantly as "brune" and glanced my way for help. I corrected his pronunciation and stole a look at the littlest monk, who giggled and turned his head away shyly, but not before he stole my heart. Then the teacher asked the class a question in Tebetan. Laughter ensued, but there seemed to be a consensus to whatever question he had posed. He looked at me, smiled, and handed me his workbook. "Will you lead the class?" he asked.

It was a request that did not need repeating. I bolted up and headed toward the front of the class. Twenty pairs of thoroughly amused eyes greeted me. I pointed to my shirt. "Black!" I enunciated carefully. They looked surprised. "Black!" I repeated. Whispers, a cough, silence. Then, from the corner, a monk whose years were maybe half my own decided to take the lead. "Blllek," he mouthed. "Good!" I cried. Confidence wa won. "Blllek!" the other mons chimed in.

I had become a teacher.

It was nearing dusk by the time I parted from my monk. My eyes moistened as I said good-bye to him, and before I ever stepped on Tibetan soil. "I'm so confused," I told him. "I don't know who or what to believe in all of this, and how can I be a journalist if I cannot...."

He interrupted by placing a hand on my shoulder. "There are many ways to look. Trust what you see," he said quietly. And then he turned and walked away, his red robe flowing behind him.

Travelling West (São Paulo)
Neil Leadbeater

(i) The Mythographers

Hearing the news at midnight, he knows he is far from sleep. They have set him so many tasks and sensitivities run deep. He resolves to keep all promises and absolve himself from wrong; remembers the kindness of friends who came to his aid with gifts: a bow, some arrows, a sword and a shield—all of them now in the room beside him in the Hotel Amazonas where the Avenida Vieira da Carvalho meets the Praça da República in the City of São Paulo at the centre of the map. At dawn he will search for Megara. Some say he killed her at Hera's behest, his children also, travelling west, the glow all gone from their smiles.

(ii) The Snake Institute

In the vivaria, the fork-tongued snakes can kill outright if the whim should suddenly take them. Their elongated limbless bodies loop into circuits, fold over fold like figures of 8, coiled to spring at a motion. Each is a Hydra with the venom of 50 from the swamps of the Argos marshes.

(iii) The Pursuit of Hinds

A whole year he pursues them, escaping the city onward and upward into the Serra do Mar. His bearings are browse lines, parings of bark, roerings round the margins. Stalking outdoors or crouched in hides, he maps the slots of hooves hard on the heels of the hinds; notes the change of coats through seasons: soft blue-gray to glossy red and keeps downwind to log all tracks, 16 meters in a single spring—all of the hinds Megara.

(iv) November Roads

Here, under southern skies, the year already late, he recalls one winter the passage of time that plied like tides between them. And looks down November roads, the straight stands of Lawson cypress locking his vision into a lifelong memory of 'loss. Today, as the bright sun roars through the vibrant ease of summer, myth transcends all time. He knows he could be in any clime at the close of another year. Her voice, bright with the rhythm of waves, rounds like the sea in his ear.

(v) First Orchestration on the Rua 7 de Maio

At dawn, the girl of his dreams leaves home. The doors all close before him. A succession of footfalls dies down the road. The cadence of her voice is lost in the harmony of women for ever. If he could only discover her scent he would journey the world just to glimpse her.

(vi) Arcadian Birds

To the people of this city he sends down birds: a flock of doves from the weed seeds of stubble fields exchanging land for land. Exemplars of innocence, birds with no blemish, spirits that have no bile. Their bodies, ripped like pillows, discharge their autumn down. Dustshadows from the powder quilts work their way on the wind. Five-, three- and two-note rhythms fall from the sky in song. All the world is at peace today. The urge to let it stay that way has never been so strong.

(vii) On Seeing a Grecian Urn

Of all the treasures in the world's embrace, this funerary urn has pride of place. What feat of strength is played out on its form? What plight of circumstance? What man? What beast? What synergy of forces? Its stalwart, tensile strength holds him to attention. A prerecorded message politely breaks the tension: THE MUSEUM WILL BE CLOSING IN TEN MINUTES. He stumbles into the street, rubbing the sight from his eyes. The blood of a bull streams down the steps by his side. Here where the old vies with the new, he cannot tell them apart: sometimes it seems so real to him; at others, merely art.

(viii) On Looking into the Greek Myths

He conjures her name from the page. The belief that she once belonged is taken straight out of the text. All his life he has walked beside Megara. In the index, between MEDUSA and MELEAGER, there is a void that he cannot bear. The compilers have left unrecognized the burden of his despair. He closes the book as he closes his life. Heads west, like the rest, out of Eden.

(ix) Jardins

Seeing the name for the first time, he pictures the golden blossoms of the Ipê tree; the magnificent branches of the Jacaranda; imagined beds aflame with blooms, their sword-like leaves thrust like rapiers in the close-knit, monocot borders. A glance at the guidebook disrupts the dream. Page by page, the buildings of Cerqueira César, Jardim Europa and Jardim America come into view—a cluster of districts whose names are as beautiful as the names of plants- the domain of high-class restaurants, luxury hotels, shops and bars: a place where the women turn to the name of Megara. Calling her name, she moves towards him with the look of a total stranger. The flower of her innocence, devoured by cities, crosses his path like a shade.

(x) Elysian Fields

From the drab monotony of dormitory slums he dreams of Elysian fields, Today he will drive shambling herds through vistas of ancient land. At noon, where the curled croziers of fertile fronds shield the earth from the sun, he will rest beneath their canopy to seize all the shade that he can. At other times, he will drive them on, taking shelter in makeshift shacks to still the passage of rain. Hail, flung from the fists of the gods, will fall to the open plain. HIS BRIEF IS COUNTING IN CATTLE: AGAIN AND AGAIN AND AGAIN. Here, at the close of the year, sleep locks the mind. Only the myths remain.

(xi) Travelling West

You will all of you notice this propensity to travel west.

Arriving at the airport, Heracles, first time in a month, first time ever, hurries west. At Ibirapuera Park, the daughters of evening rest in the dark. Implacable Hera plucks the lyre—her sisters almost dreaming. Haracles holds the world. Atlas, relieved of his burden, plucks the apples of gold, Beguiled by deceit, he takes back the globe; the promise of an instant eternal lie when the moment of truth unfolds. Heracles holds his prize. He has traded the world for apples and possession makes him wise. All his life he has sought to delight in the smooth roundness of apples swelling before his eyes. He labors on (eleven down...one to go...). First time in a month, first time ever, he hurries through the suburbs—the Garden of Europe and the Garden of America- fast-forward to sundown. Journeying the stations at midnight there is no going back at the border. In the vast empty frame of the Roosevelt Terminal the vanishing taillights of westbound trains, dark olive and linear black, roar like bullets down the level track. None going east ever.

(xii) The Alsatians

Riding the metro (5:00 a.m. to midnight) they guard the ground with purpose. Their wolf-like look and defensive gait is the straight edge of the law. The lairs of the living and the lairs of the dead verge at the charge of their roar. He has trained them to obey all signals. At Ana Rosa and Liberdade, when the figure of a woman follows behind him, he knows he is not alone. Her shadow, ghosting the pavement, falls at his back like a stone.

Will-o'-the-Wisp

Katherine Smith

Swerving
around a bird that pecks a luscious-looking rotten apple
in the middle of the right lane. I wish I knew

an answer better than silence to the dazzle of these redbuds,
azaleas, pools of water. My meditation
is a strange plume in the brilliance of spring, the surprise

of fluttering leaves on uncut timber in the backwoods
spangled by my thoughtfulness
like the red squirrel whose dazzling guts sparkle on the road like rubies.

The squirrel vanishes like fallen leaves, like my own loves,
like my daughter's childhood, which I love, like all the life I'll ever know,
too briefly to answer. I think that I know nothing,

that my knowledge
is no different from the flaming azalea bushes
among the redbuds and dogwoods, that all I ever want life to know

I'd be able to say that swiftly. This morning my daughter
woke before me and came to sit in the dark
of the room where I was still sleeping.

When I opened my eyes, she was sitting on the white sofa
looking straight at me, waiting. As if wanting more from me
than breakfast or cartoons, her face was lit up

and the life in her blue eyes
was a blessing like fire on water
coming toward me from the shadows.

The Woman Who Loved Maps
Lyn Lifshin

Not for accuracy, she is tired of facts and distance,
longitude, unless it's carved out in aquamarine
and violet. She doesn't want carefully engineered, exact
miles, doesn't want to leave the draped rooms the old
parchment and linen's spread out in, throws out her Triple

A map, her Frommer's, her Michelin, doesn't want the
careful blotches, the interstates but loves those old
picture maps where flying monsters with lavender wings
inhabit islands mysterious as Rorschachs or hieroglyphs
almost too devastating to read, wants what shimmers and

intoxicates like velvets and old Persian rugs. It's too
exhausting to pack and unpack, she doesn't want to find her
self stranded in Istanbul or Tangiers in the rain and
no taxi. It's easier she tells herself, to love maps than
men who'll roll away from the pillow, whispering "for her

own good," or "it wasn't you, it was me." She wants to run
her fingers over their pale tourmaline and rusts old as tea
pots from Persia, the oldest Venetian glass. She doesn't
want exact latitudes but what is mysterious as a room behind
drawn lace, lips she won't have to do laundry for, aches for a

country in the shape of a fly blue fish washed with lemon,
something she can date with one glance, something from
the 15th century. Not what folds up, can split, along
the crease, wants what she can lie smooth in a locked flat drawer
or roll up to have there in the dark just for her

Hairbrush

Leonard Gontarek

Things are left on beaches. A kid's
shovel. A read paperback. Necklace.
The bottom of a bikini. Tape player.
Change. Things are left on dressers.
Change. An earring. Spoon. Note
scrawled on a receipt. A hairbrush.
I remember each hairbrush
I've owned. I remember each
I've given as a gift. Which is not
many. I gave a brush to my
mother in a dream. She said
she already had one. She did not
seem in a good mood to begin
with. She had, perhaps, a hangover.
See how dreams are freighted with
sorrow and useless worries. She
had beautiful hair and I wanted
to give her a brush. I leave it
on this beach.

Bang You're Dead, Trip Around the World
Nikki Moustaki

See a wet street with no end to it, the city's guesswork,
something always to be said (or unsaid) something to buy
(something to return). See me, at dusk:

green raincoat, carrying my tub of warm yogurt
home again, one I've carried to work three days now,
still it returns, uneaten. (*Listen*, the city says, *Bang*)

what the woman said as we crossed 9th Ave in the rain,
that moment where New York takes a moment (breathes
on your neck), says, *Listen, I'm just like you.*

See the woman talking to herself in the handball court
on the corner next to the loony bin. In this rain
it's hard to pick her out among the other bodies.

I feel them on my lips. *Bang you're dead, trip around the world.*
How can I listen on this avenue of strangers kissing,
sidewalks burning under all those feet (*Trip around the world*)

not today (*bang*) (*you're dead*) soaked through the shoes,
Hefty bag gown flickering red-gold-green, *Bang*,
I look toward traffic and step off the curb, *You're dead*—

sometimes you hear what it says, sometimes you're lucky
enough; she might look like something that didn't matter anymore.
She might look like a fork in the river and you without oars.

Mojave

Nikki Moustaki

Not the desert, but a little town fifty earth-wrenched
miles north of L.A. where our trip broke
for the third time in three weeks; the first cleft
happened in the High Sierras after four or six
martinis and Rebecca insisting on curling
her eyelashes for the fifth time that evening—
not the rustling Aspens nor the promise
of juniper and gin stopped my protest—
or the juniper and gin protesting right along;
the second sever came in Sparks, Nevada,
where I learned, according to Rebecca,
that deer are the main cause of highway deaths
in the United States, as we pulled over
with the other tourists to watch a crowd of elk
cross the highway, and Rebecca refused to leave the car.

Oh, I'm not blameless or always right:
there was the night outside Tahoe City
where I opened the "curse gates"
after a debacled rafting trip down the two-inch-deep
Truckee River where I drank too much Zinfandel
out of a five-liter cardboard box and referred
to Rebecca with the verve of Midwestern fraternity boys—
she cursed me for three hundred miles
and I cursed her back, not so much as I felt like cursing,
but for the joy and irresponsibility of napalming the road,
each word a bullet in the head of friendship,
and didn't friendship deserve it.

So we entered Mojave, almost to L.A.
but too hungry to make it. A pan-faced,
ruddy-skinned woman staring at the display
window of the attached mini-mart of the Mobile Station
turned to me and said, with the torpidity of someone
sedated or possessed: *That's a nice snake tee-shirt,*

at which I studied the display window too,
silk-screened boa wrapping an anonymous tree limb,
and it *was* a nice snake tee-shirt, at which I went inside

to get Rebecca, who waited by the toilet door
with three other women who screamed and pounded
the locked porthole to God
knows-what-or-whom, yammering a language
I've never heard, a carnival ride for the inner ear,
and how glad I wasn't the one behind that metal door.

We pre-paid for gas. I asked the woman
behind the counter for directions to decent food—
she had the largest face I've ever seen on a human,
flat as Florida and wide as Texas, something like hair
on top, what you'd find inside an old homemade pillow,
coarse and stiff as a receding friendship.

Before that night I thought bears only came down
from the mountains for rancid meat and greasy
McDonald's bags, but a monster loped
by the window then, sniffed at our rental car,
and for a moment I could hear my heart knocking in my chest—
everyone's heart, louder than the beer cooler,
louder than the thumping of a steel door
by three women speaking in tongues.

Louder than I supposed this woman
behind the counter could scream if that bear
came through the window, through the nice
snake tee-shirt and into our laps—
all of us breathing so loud I could hear
the villi in this woman's lungs waving like those palm trees
in Malibu we never got to see because Rebecca
wanted to find the HOMES OF THE STARS,
and I sat in the train station for ten hours
so I wouldn't have to go.

I pointed to the bear and the woman
behind the counter said, with a rumbling sound
only derived from the most numb of Mojavians: *Restaurant?*
The bear stood. Bigger than our economy-rate rental
by almost twice,
Restaurant? she said again.

Yes, I said, Restaurant. A place where there is food.

Food? she said.
The stuff you *eat*, I said. The bear looked around.
It could hear our hearts beating, too. Our spleens spleening.
The woman-who-admired-the-snake-tee-shirt
stepped behind me, another heart pounding in my ears,
another gray handful of future's soil,
another consumer of Slim Jims, spicy,
which is what she plopped on the counter,
and pointed to the bear.
There's a bear out there, she said.

The mini-mart woman turned her huge face
to the window. *He won't hurt nothing*,
at which the bear placed his paw through a car window,
not ours, stuffed his head through the hole,
pulled something out—upholstery, a large carton—
I couldn't tell, then sat down to rip it apart.

Snake tee-shirt woman turned to me, pointed a plastic-sheathed
Slim Jim back the way we came: *Down there is the Jimmy's,
the Denny's, and the Dairy Queen.*
Mini-mart woman pulled a hand gun
from beneath the counter, opened the glass door, shot
into the dusk over the deep canyon Rebecca and I
were afraid of on the drive here, the obvious
faults dividing the earth like laugh lines, instability and chaos.
The bear flinched with the bang
and took off toward the canyon, Mini-mart woman replacing
the gun with a clunk, ringing up the Slim Jims, taking the money.

Rebecca and I had filet "minion," two eggs, hashbrowns,
toast, jam, and orange juice for $5.99 at Jimmy's,
where Christmas lights staple-gunned to the walls
sparkled and blinked out memories of Christmases past,
and I stared at Rebecca chewing, swallowing, watching
silently our friendship squashed like the road beneath rented tires,
each silent second a forgotten day in the last years where Rebecca
and I shared a friendship closer than two fried yolks on a platter.

Cheap aluminum knives clanked
plastic plates, a prayer to August's passing into fall, an irritating
rattle to include the bear and us, tough steak,
damn good eggs, and the pale, bear-struck looking waitress
at Jimmy's taking our orders and collecting the bill
without uttering a single word.

Mosaic: Istanbul

Roy Jacobstein

1. *In Transit*

Next to me, on a black chair curved
like a scimitar, comes a pulse of *cheeps*

from an unaccompanied shopping bag.
Men from villages pace the *Room*

For Waiting: knit skullcaps, worn
worry beads, scarved wives wobbling

two steps behind. In crisp fatigues
the shade of late autumn, a bullet-eyed

soldier sifts the news for rumors of coup.
Döner kebap rotates slowly on a spit.

Hair cropped, dyed blonde, a city woman
returns to her bag, cracks a sunflower

seed, extracts its tiny striated kernel
and slides it down into the mesh cage.

2. *Beyond*

      the smoke-smeared window,
there where Asia starts, *Sahil Yolu,*
    the shore road. Oily
tanker spume streaks the Marmara Sea,
       minarets poise
upward into the heart
  of afternoon, rockets waiting
      for countdown. People everywhere—
families in outdoor tea houses,
  men fishing from quays,
    no one alone.

3. *Dancing Bear*

On the cobblestone path
between Hagia Sophia
and Topkapi Palace
a brown bear shuffles
behind a young Gypsy.

The Levantine sun glints
off the bear's brass nose
ring and summons
two clots of tourists
back from guidebook

tales of old Stamboul.
The bear does not
look left or right
just follows the leather
wherever it leads.

4. *Roses*

Every year the roses return,
climbing the stone wall

to the Palace, peeking in,
as if this is the year

foretold in the coffee grounds
when the *harem* will walk again

beneath the arch of the sacred gate,
one of their number plucked

by the Sultan.

5. *In The Courtyard of the Green House*

Half an hour since my lover left—
thirty revolutions of the second hand—
already her *Parting*
is the price of meeting
has drowned in the iron fountain,
her curled lashes and laugh
lines as vanished as the scene
in sepia on this souvenir postcard:

a middle-aged man, caught midstride,
midair, exits a wooden streetcar
into whirling snow.

6. *These Little Flies*

that careless or in heat
I swat
from the hairs
of my forearms
are a tune
someone's mother hummed
in a kitchen long ago
to her son
as he clung to her leg
and she peeled potatoes
and the little flies
tasted first the salt
of his naked skin
and then the fried potatoes
and then the steak
before they all took
leave.

7. *Lineage*

Look into the face of this Hereke,
says Kashif of *Kashif's Carpets.*

Fingers pulling wool through loom,
strand by coarse strand, bowed head
scarved in modesty, two tendrils of hair
escaping down the damp brow, inward-
turning eye squinting into winter light,
just one last swath to weave
beneath her mother's anxious gaze
before the middlemen arrive...

*The slender stalks and pale leaves are trees
of life, the blue-black center holds the sea,
the carmine border speaks of blood.*

8. *Infidel in the Calligraphy Shop*

This land: its eggplant, its noses,
the caress of its lilting tongue
in which my mother's name means *mother*,

and in every public place a picture
of *The Father of the Turks*, as in this shop
where the tourist can buy her name

rendered in the classical Islamic hand
he amputated and dumped with the fez
and dervish onto the Ottoman slag heap,

the sinuous letters flowing right to left
made to spell *Linda* or *Margaret* or *Anne*.
Or if she prefers old standards,

she can have *Inshallah—God Willing—*
black ink massed as a closed tulip,
or simply *Allah*, the ancient script

seeming to these eyes to resemble—
it must be said—a wriggling snake.

9. *A Far Cry From Home*

Five times a day, dark to dark, bursting
beyond its static, the muezzin's amplified call
arcs over tourist and Turk alike.

The rhythm of sands, of hawks and wells,
reverberates like blood in a three-chambered heart,
enters my arteries, murmurs

Even the now cannot be known.

I lay down my pen, remove my watch,
rise with the gulls to the minaret,
bend my wings to Mecca,

submit.

Tourniquet
Roy Jacobstein

It's like puncturing a tire on the turnpike of conversation—
that swerve, the slamming of brakes, those surprised exhalations

that invariably occur whenever I tell people at a dinner party
I was once a contestant on *Jeopardy*. Everyone wants to know

what the suave emcee's *really* like, what I won, how it feels
to be on national TV. I tell them a lot doesn't meet the eye—

it's not how fast you buzz in, it's how *well*, how exactly
you can mesh your synapses to those of the unseen aide

who waits off-stage for the guy with the caked-on makeup—
Alex, the emcee—to finish reading. The moment he does,

the unseen aide turns on the red lights bordering the game board
in the studio, which means *Time To Buzz In*. Buzz in too soon,

you're frozen out. Someone else will be telling Alex & America
for $400 the capital of Myanmar, formerly Burma, is Rangoon.

But here's the catch: your handlers, simultaneously earnest yet
distant & slick—it's *Hollywood* after all—warned: "Don't wait

to see the lights go on, it'll be *too late*. You must *anticipate*,
& buzz in *just before* they light up." That's why you see all

the new contestants pushing pushing pushing, just as I did,
pushing down on that blocky buzzer like it's a failing heart,

or they're a clerk in some classic Western (*Stagecoach*, say,
starring John Wayne, nominated Best Picture, 1939, lost

to *Gone With the Wind*). Yes, it's all in the timing, so if you too
go up against a returning champion, know this: you can win

only five times, & they shoot five shows a day. It's tough
standing up there & you'll be fresh, the champ more & more

fatigued, which almost levels the hill. Except this time, *this* story,
it's a new week. He's the 4-time champ with the winning grin,

the rested Monday morning eyes—not the blonde reporter
from Tuscaloosa & definitely not you, flown in from the East

Coast 38 hours ago, frantically depressing your buzzer. It's him,
the Physics Professor from USC, him & his 240 previous dates

with that buzzer. He's mastered its every subtlety, he's perfect,
it's a goddam *artform* how coolly he trips it a split nanosecond

after the unseen aide flips the unseen switch ON—so he's the one
telling us all the truth about the world's *Seven Ancient Wonders*,

how Babylon was home to the fabled Hanging Gardens, how those
ruins of the Temple of Artemis can be found at Ephesus, how, yes,

it's Mausolus who was entombed in the now-vanished Mausoleum
at Halicarnassus. When that category—*your* category, the one you

studied again just last night—appeared on the studio game board,
no one watching could glean anything from that blank screen,

that vacant field, your face. Your impassive face is an accurate
mirror: you are preternaturally calm, you feel iron toothpicks

are needed to prop open your eyelids, this metallic taste rims
your buccal mucosa—all after-effects of the sleeping pill

you took too late, late last night, when jet lag wouldn't let go.
Dalmane, 30 mg., that capsule the lovely blue of a robin's egg,

but it isn't so lovely now, isn't being counteracted fast enough
by the 10 mg. Ritalin tab you took on waking. Black coffee

wasn't an analeptic either, afraid as you were to drink it lest
its diuretic action lead to a bursting bladder & your bolting,

mid-query, from the lectern. Well, at least your face won't
give anything away, not shame, anger, rue: your hit of fame

isn't up yet & in that light olive Italian suit you're damned
well gonna look good. So the fact you knew all those seven

ancient fucking wonders, the modern ones too, their countries,
rivers, years of triumph & decline will go unregistered out there

in the variegated rooms of TV-land, in the one room that matters
most, out there at William Beaumont Hospital, where your mother,

who had the answer for everything Alex could ask, lies pretzeled
in a metal bed, no longer knowing *Who was Dr. William Beaumont.*

You know. Too bad *History of Medicine* isn't one of your categories.
Too bad, because they introduced you as the physician you were,

making it all the more memorable, all the more perfect, for all
those viewers at home when the Doc gets *First Aid* as a subject

in *Double Jeopardy* & actually manages to buzz in successfully—
by now he's buzzing in on everything, insanely, beating on that

black buzzer like some medieval pilgrim flagellating the Devil
right on out of himself, buzzing in on every subject: *Toothpaste*

*[What is Apana, Crest, Gleam, Tom's of Maine?], Flying Rodents,
The Comedian As The Letter C*—& this rare time, when Alex says

Roy, the Doc has 10 seconds to squint down a long corridor, out to
where the board is situated in the studio, past *What is Cincinnati,*

past *What is Syracuse*, 1/93rd the distance to the klieg-lit Sun
[What is one million miles?]. Ten brief ticking seconds: his time

to siphon the correct answer up from the viscous soup of his brain,
by now the Ritalin's kicked in, vision's tunneling down, the only

word he can discern, believe me, the *only* one, is *EXTREMITY,*
the extremely annoying theme song is a thong of ringing gongs,

he hasn't heard a word Alex has said, listening not his forte
even in the best of times and this damn near the worst [*What is*

*A Tale Of Two Cities? Who was Charles Dickens? What are Paris
& London*] & America—*Christ, the entire Anglophone universe*—

the 30,000,000 home viewers, the Doc's earnest & not yet slick or
distant son, home keeping faith (*Great job, Dad, you got 14 right!*),

the studio audience, the unctuous emcee, the Doc's sexy girlfriend
sitting out there in the audience, counting on a chunk of his winnings

the size of the Lone Star State—all of them are out there waiting,
humming that infernal song, *dee-dee, dee-dee...First Aid...Extremity...*

four seconds...must guess...must be *broken*...two seconds...one...
What, Alex,...is a splint? ...No, I'm afraid that's wrong, says

the smirking orange-cheeked prick above the mix of laughs & groans
in the studio, & immediately Professor's telling us all what we need

to treat that bleeding extremity is a *tourniquet*, phrasing his answer
carefully in the form of a question so he gets 800 bucks more,

& the only broken thing here is my chance of ever being a 5-time
champion, of coming back to win the *Tournament of Champions*

& going on to *Super Jeopardy* & taking First Prize, like that guy
who lives with my cousin—he sure did, Bruce won that 250K,

quit his job, wrote his book [*What is The Life Of Lola Montez?*],
& in the *New York Times Book Review* the reviewer noted

with favor Bruce's "wry & most unusual acknowledgment,"
wherein he thanked, besides the usual sorts—family, mentor, lover,

deity—the producers of *Jeopardy* & undoubtedly Alex Himself,
"for giving me the freedom to write this book," but all I'll get

is a vicious lawsuit slapped on me for telling you any of this,
especially since I vaguely recall—this all happened, understand,

more than seven years ago—signing papers promising to eschew
revealing the inner workings of *America's Favorite Game Show*.

Eh bien, let's not pay that no never mind, let's just try to tie up
the loose ends, for though such neat closure is often frowned

upon in contemporary poetics since it projects the illusion
of certainty & finality in a provisional world, isn't it in fact

what we're all interested in, the ongoing thing, what happens
later to our characters? So: Mom died soon thereafter; Son went

the way of sons; Alex & The Show still rule the early evening
airwaves. Sexy Girlfriend? Lost to follow-up, but I *can* tell you

we drove out to Malibu later that day &, facing west, watching
the surfers curl & crash & the sky turn purple, we split up,

without a tourniquet or a splint, without accepting the All-
Expenses-Paid-Trip-For-Two, Coach Class, to Hilton Head,

South Carolina, though I did receive a year's supply of free
hair care products, value $317, & was careful to declare it

miscellaneous income on my Federal Income Tax return.

Slit-Eyed Sparrow
Jean Hanson

It is a morning unlike the others. I've dressed, stocked my handbag, scribbled my shopping lists. I'm not exactly all right, but I'm better than yesterday. I feel buoyant, behaving like those who are of the world. Before I leave, I stare at my eyes a little too long in the bathroom mirror, noticing my permanent squint. It's as if I've been living at high altitude in ceaseless sunshine.

In the car, I concentrate on inserting the key in the ignition. I drive so infrequently these days; perhaps it's natural to have forgotten how to turn on the headlights or activate the windshield wipers or start the car.

The Audi chugs to life, I shift into reverse to back out of the garage, my back tires roll smoothly to the threshold of the driveway, and that's when trouble arises. The car strains, and there is a sound of grating, piercing intensity. I have a tendency to ride the clutch, I know, so I let up on it and instead infuse a healthy shot of gas. Still, the car barely moves, the racket continues, and I become conscious of a 'ding ding ding,' a warning that signifies seat belts unfastened or a trunk lid left open. Confusion, annoyance, a pause, and then I turn left and gasp: I haven't closed the driver's side door and it's being peeled from the car by the front garage wall. Like the contortions of a gymnast at her most grotesque, the hinges of the door are bent unnaturally back, almost to the front fender; now, even the garage wall looks ready to give way.

This is why most of the time, I stay inside. I lower the blinds, I lock the doors. I keep the answering machine on and the television off. I make my house as soothing as a vat of cotton balls. Yet I've broken half the crystal and left the stove on all night. I've misplaced things: knives tossed in garbage cans, hairbrushes in the refrigerator, credit cards in my underwear drawer. The other day I poured cottage cheese into the coffee grinder. My legs are bruised from ankle to thigh, as if I have a bleeding disorder. It is clear: I can no longer live out there in the world, so I exist here, inside. And it is no sanctuary.

My malady is not dramatic, neither life threatening nor uncommon. I have headaches, migraine headaches that, for the last two years, have escalated to such frequency that when I wake without one, I am stunned, distrustful. On those rare mornings, I send consciousness searching like a beacon, seeking to illuminate pain as if the day cannot proceed without it.

I once heard a radio interview with a neurologist who said he regarded his migraines as a gift. It was a privilege in his profession to be able to experience the symptoms of so many other diseases without suffering the long-term debilitating effects of them. I, too, had always been tolerant, rationalizing that if I had to suffer these bouts, at least I was among the percentage who experienced aura—the neurologic high jinks that accompany classic migraines: bright flashes, tunnel vision, aphasia, the world sometimes broken into stained-glass mosaics. I even read about the history and culture of migraine; it had intellectual interest. And I appreciated the humor of, for example, trying to pay for a purchase with a tape measure; attempting to drink from a glass and missing my mouth; hearing the phone ring and opening the front door. We're amusing, we madcap migraineurs.

It's no longer funny. Today I look back on once-a-week headaches with nostalgia—as if they were visits from a tiresome, though well meaning relative. Because now, my life is completely circumscribed by them.

A few weeks ago, I noticed a juvenile sparrow sitting on the ground below our tube feeder. She had strange eyes, narrowed into slits, and unkempt little feathers atop her head. All around, grackles were maneuvering for position, threatening each other and not allowing smaller birds to land. The yard was a tornado of wings, fluttering birds, jockeying for food, jostling for space, yet no one bothered this puffed bird; instead, they behaved as if she were encircled by an invisible margin. Outside her boundary, beating feathers, life; inside, dead space, a perimeter of silence.

I still venture out on good days, doing errands as if preparing for the Flood, but usually, it is only through the grace of my husband that I leave my house. He does a fine job of backing the car from the garage, and when we walk, his hand grazes my elbow as if my arm is a rudder, and he is steering me, his unseaworthy boat.

When one suffers frequent migraines, neurologists trot out daily preventive pharmaceuticals, drugs originally designed to treat other ailments but found, coincidentally, to suppress headaches. I have taken them all: prescriptions that in other doses treat hypertension, depression, seizure disorders. Sometimes, during a trial of medications, I am briefly free of migraines.

Suddenly, I'll sail through several days, feeling graced, empowered, lightened. So this is how it is for others, I think, those who live out in the world. How easy everything is. How simple to exit the house leaving behind self-injectors, painkillers, antinausea capsules, pieces of paper with your phone number in case you get sick and can't remember it.

During these respites, I plan trips to places far away; sometimes I even take them. I venture to bookstores, libraries, coffee shops. And I just drive around. Everything amazes me. Whole subdivisions have sprung up, as startling as the first drifts of crocus in spring. All this before even a week of health has passed.

And then, like a clever vandal only temporarily stymied by a change in locks, migraine finds its entry. I awake unbalanced. It's just one migraine, I say, that's all; it doesn't mean anything. Then two. No cause for alarm. Then three, four, five and so on, until migraine has broken through the latest chemical front. A few weeks or a few months later, after another respite or not, I'll fail the latest drug trial. Over and over. Status migrainosus.

The regional specialist I finally visited pulled out a paper. It was rumpled, as though it had been grasped and re-grasped by many others. The chart formed a hill: frequency of headache by age. There I was, just over forty, on the woebegone crest of this statistical summit. You are legion, it told me.

I stared at the chart, superimposing its bell upon the arc of my life and on the lives of those others who had clutched it. We'd all, I figured, been getting along rather well until now, dealing with our benign but troublesome affliction. All through our twenties and thirties we'd endured these vascular volcanoes. Most of us had husbands or wives (long-suffering ones), children, jobs, lives. We greeted one another throughout the years, whispering passwords: saltines and Coca-Cola, three Excedrin, strong coffee and a handful of aspirin, codeine in any form. We coveted offices with incandescent lighting and locking doors (just an hour or two with the lights off, please). We wore dark sunglasses and knew instinctively to avoid red wine. We were survivors, serotonin warriors. And for all those years we hadn't even had the benefit of the new migraine panacea—the designer drug, Imitrex, that works on the brain's synaptic receptors to interrupt the headache. Like a miracle, the injections work. Unkindly, they are expensive, cannot be used daily, and have side effects. For many, like me, Imitrex is an elixir hoarded for special occasions or the most brutal headaches.

Where were all the other forty-somethings, I wondered? Were they all looking forward to old age? How were they coping? Had they lost their jobs?

I heard my neighbor to the south is ill, but for all I know, she may not exist. People come and go from her house, but in the months I've lived here, I've never caught a glimpse of her. Like her, I am invisible, a shadow behind window blinds; if I'm a real person, I surely must be a diminished one. And what of others—people with crippling arthritis, spastic colitis, chronic fatigue syndrome, or end-stage cancer—ailments that keep them locked away? We are all simply absent, like the *desparacido* of Argentina.

It's characteristic of those with migraines, and indeed all 'invisible' disabilities, to feel guilty. It's easier to blame oneself, I suppose, when there's nothing to bandage. If you still retain the foolish confidence to make plans, you'll look unreliable. You will ask forgiveness, as if you have a choice instead of a disorder. Because your friends are kind and concerned, they'll inquire about your health. You'll be quick to answer. They're asking, after all, the only question you *can* address, for it is the state of your body (not your mind or heart) that consumes you. Later, you'll regret being a bore, but it will be too late. Soon, you will be identified not by who you are or what you do, but by the disease you have. The UPS man, seeing you stagger to the door holding your head, takes a giant step back.

All those years, I believed, against logic, that if I were stronger or more determined, more organized or more chaste, I'd have overcome my migraines. Having headaches, then, was proof of what I knew: I wasn't good enough. I got what I deserved.

Once or twice a week, I agreed to give up the muddled complexity of life for something stark, simple, and clarifying: pain. Afterwards, I felt refreshed, as though I'd undergone an ancient cleansing ritual. Some people confess, some do penance, and others atone with good deeds. Me? I had migraines, surely payment to the gods for something.

This reasoning sustained me when headaches were few. But now the metaphor troubles me with its extension: Are my flaws so irredeemable that I've been imprisoned in my own house? Am I so beyond redemption that my own body has become a penitentiary?

When I was a child, I had a cousin (distant in relation and proximity) with leukemia. She was a lovely, round little girl with golden curls and storybook cherry cheeks. I met her only once, but we began a correspondence that lasted the few years she had left to live.

Her letters were mundane, the musings of an ordinary child, but my mother updated me on the drama of her condition. During this particular month, she'd say, Kay was well enough to go to school. Later, Kay took lessons at home. Finally, she could not leave her bed; even the vibration of her mother's steps caused pain. I kept picturing the healthy, rotund Kay I'd met. Surely, this leukemia, this poison, could not reside within her; therefore it must be with*out*—encircling Kay, drawing an ever tighter noose, keeping her first from kickball after school, then from classes, coming nearer and nearer, confining her to her house, limiting her to bed, until finally this diminishing perimeter had squeezed the very life from her.

What if I were to say that my chronic illness does not arise from within? What if I were to believe that disease is only a boundary, a flexible one that exists outside me? Sometimes it veers closer, this boundary, forming a taut circle that sends me to bed. Later it loosens and I carefully unload the dishwasher, finish my freelance jobs, read the newspaper. Occasionally, it stretches like a giant rubber band, extending miles. Then I move with abandon and marvel at how lovely the world is, a world I vow never to take for granted again.

Here, I suppose, is the appropriate place to be upbeat, to make my metaphor auspicious, to predict that one day my pliable band of a boundary will stretch until it breaks. I won't do so, however. I am too experienced, too weary, by now, to expect this to happen—though not, I suspect, too bereft to hope it will.

After late-summer quiet, birds have again begun pressuring my feeders. They fly together in argumentative groups, competitive and uneasy, anticipating, some of them, a long migration. I watch closely, hoping to catch a glimpse of that slit-eyed sparrow I worried over weeks ago. But she has disappeared. Has she forsaken the fury of their wings for a restful branch where she can sit undisturbed? Or is she now so much a part of their noisy flock that I can no longer distinguish her at all?

Roala

Jacqueline Lyons

Basotho women bind a forest
of branches together, draw
the ends up into a taut canoe,
lift the bundle onto their heads
and walk, small moving forests,
footprints pressed deep.
What bones, what viscera
belong to women who
with this weight on their skulls
turn to answer my greeting,
branches dipping slightly
like a giant compass needle,
the women smiling and blinking
while the wood shifts,
changes the skin on their faces.
Bucket of water on the head,
baby on the back, sack of
maize meal across their shoulders—
these women add burdens
like accessories.
I wonder what bargain they have
struck with gravity, what visits
by their mothers to witchdoctors
to makes their spines
grow up straight, what charms
they have tucked in the blankets
wrapped around their waists.
The woman from the egg circle
picks her way over rocks,
feet slipped into shoes
with squashed down heels,
balancing an open tray of eggs
on her head, thirty brown curves
calm and breakable
above her red headscarf;
and the *shebeen* woman under

a crate of beer, brown bottles
clinking as she walks toward men
who wait in their chairs, wait
never worrying she might trip
on some stone she cannot
look down to see because she
is a woman.

Taj Mahal

George Moore

As we are told, this is but one white marble tomb
and was to have had a brother, black as Ganges' bottom
where the Shah himself would come at last to rest, asleep
in eternities with his lost bride. Like other black-and-whites,
other mirrors, this never came to pass. There stands
but one, almost smallish domed vault for the manner of the dead
in a city where they park the streets. At the edge of nowhere,
where the buses wait, after their heavy, oiled trek
across an endless Pradesh state, this tiny antique
monument, one suspects, was a Mogul center of the earth.
To eat at stalls, asafoetida, saffron, flies waved off
by fruit vendors, and the permeating smell of rice
is prelude to the shoeless walk along the shallow pool
toward death. Or no, not toward but through, two kinds
of death at play between the whiteness of the Indian sun
and the mud and tin of suburbs, feet the color of clay
pounding the earth to remember. Inside, sounds ring clear
as if in a stone bell; and at the edge of turbidity, the Yamuna
drifting downward. Alone, for this is always how we end,
I watch the suddenness of so many bodies moving outward
toward other purposes. Days, we guess, small quests,
all rooted to the spot by something that cannot fade,
but vanishes, as my face did, that sunburnt singularity
that none a moment later would remember, none had seen.
Few look beyond the marbled entrance to the tomb
for more than a visitation. But eyes within look out
like untethered lanterns in the trough of an inky sea.

Gypsy Robbery, New Delhi, 1994

Melissa Stein

i. Strangled battering of wings,

                                  ii. *Gather me up,*

collapsing tents of crimson,

                            alien sisters. Winding braids

translucent green: these women

                      like blackened ropes, bangles cuffing

around me sudden as water, forced

                    your wrists, anklet-jingle of glass

current drawing faster than I wanted to go.

                      crushed underfoot. I'll give you

Who can beat off a homing flock,

              what you want. I know the diamonds slide

a rising tide? I fell to moths and they rose,

               around your eyes, those fine threads

bearing away my false moon.

        in your saris flashing all the kindness of knives.

In Autumn

Melissa Stein

Some of you are born with alibis, we can see it
in your eyes. Among you rock-a-bye babies, we can sense it
there behind locker doors, ratcheted into pencil sharpeners,
wired through stuttering wall-clocks. Don't think we don't know
the apple on the teacher's desk is poisoned. Hall pass dusted with acid.
Inhale, exhale: breathing fear. Waiting.

Will you come near? through a corridor constricted with fumes.
If only to try to hear through this canny blur, the neon-rimmed noise.
If only to take my hand and, your fingers pressing my bones together
till they click, tell me to be careful here. To watch for arms kept
behind the back, bulging pockets. Clumsy elbows. Reinforced
smiles. Sprung shadows. Swinging doors.

Swaddled in lies, cheating even the silence—
and still, you remind us of ourselves,
enough to hope: love, yes, there's always
love. You—sum, division of us, running off
to school, razors stitched in your skin.
Switchblades tucked under your tongues.

Holding

Melissa Stein

Those close to me go gray. But I'm
watching the fog cotton the hills,
swallow seagulls; the wind's pale
do-si-do with the treetops of the eucalyptus.
Little things. The cilantro seedling
choked by its own soil, windowsill's
persisting trail of ants, the clinging
ivy's tiny suctioned feet. Grizzled
wing of a crow that lands on the C
of the balcony. It takes so much
to pull together this fabric, maintain
all its spidered trap lines. Who has time
to notice shadowed gestures, new terrain
etched in the mirror? What we love is near
enough. We focus on the hills.

Sonnet

Joy Arbor-Karnes

I want to be a cherry so he can
swallow me down. Sweet meat will fall away
and I'll lodge in his chest, let him carry
me to work: computers, meetings, phone calls.
Shaking with the great foghorn of his voice,
I'll hear him as I've never heard him—sure
and decisive, making everything right,
while I live in the harbor of his ribs.

My runaway loneliness will finally
be subsumed into the subway rattle
of blood commuting the long distance
around his body. I'll concern myself
with his heart's doors, and consistent breathing,
each gasp squeezing everything out of me.

Why She Returned

Lisa Shaw Black

I imagine she wanted to learn the word *no*,
look into the eyes of an angel and spit—
forget the good-girl stain that spreads
irretrievably to the edges of a narrow mattress;
the twisted *yes* that rides an arched back
buckled with favor. My Lord!
There are consequences unconceived
in the garden rushes, the lily's stone-white face.
How to descend from the altar's final prayer
and rise, on these pitted feet, to pray
for the grasp of *no*—the sight of wingless men.
To stand in a forest of dogwood and bleed
from memory's wound the sweet denial.
No Daniel memorandum to fulfill and more
a small patch of earth to dig and seed.

I imagine she wanted to taste the fruit,
wine soaked and deserted on the table;
drink the unclaimed goblet
left warming in the scarlet dawn.

Hills

Philip Ramp

The heaps of hills stretched out in unfolding sequence
in this early yet almost dark-defying light
could be the burial mounds of local gods or giants—
or just accumulated centuries of mythic sight.

On a wet day when the rain stops and the storm curdles, the hills can soar
like a meditation finding substance, finding out what thinking's for.

Sometimes I make them ripple through the imperfections of the glass
or try to catch the beat of their long pulse hidden in the heat,
even when they've whitened into sky as part of summer's disappearing feat.

I suppose it's more memories I'm seeing than anything that's there
a way of setting shape on distance, a hard edge to a dusky glow
but whatever, strong enough to contain and keep the fire burning, far below.

Senses
Philip Ramp

Our senses get overloaded with the feats of our prodigious genes
which are a fire raging through the wilderness of evolution and of dream
consuming what we have become with what we might have been.

Oh the morning was upon me, light flinging form and color in my eyes
and I decided my contract with the millennia had better be revised.
For one: the inevitability of the falling sky should not be idealized.

And a chill came from the garden with a hint of buried coin
the thrill of sequestered treasure, the sensual facet of purloin
or of time and space from their secret place turning their focus on the groin

and my skin seemed like a message woven of something not yet said
or rather an elaborate linkage of nutrients on which the future must be fed
yet all the while my senses keep insisting it's but a home for the living dead.

Emily Dickinson and Van Morrison Meet at an Artists' Café

Richard Robbins

"Wild Nights—Wild Nights!"
—E.D.

"The wild night is calling."
—V.M.

She never had a thing for eating out
but comes here just the same for coffee
and the corner window's view, two flights up,
of ghosts and angels crossing dirty snow.
She writes quatrains on the coaster
and has room to spare.

The cowboy sits behind her scatting Bach
and Lightning Hopkins at the same time.
His body rocks, his eyes and fingers roll
in opposite directions. Then he sees
her writing, bent into small word,
and hears the sacred

hum of hymns coming his way, electric
and slow as steam. Faint hairs on her neck
sing only to him. She looks at the words,
looks out at the angel dark. He wants to
pull her to her feet, dance mad steps
throughout the quiet room.

She knows he's watching her and feels the chair
and table float, the oak floor suddenly
black water, the spirits growing their fins.
He pulls her like tide, pushes with his eyes
like wind until she turns around,
abandoning port,

sashaying toward his arms and slow twirling
moves made of grief and joy—skin and soul
one again in this impossible place
among the outer islands, too distant
to care about who stares at them
or how they'll get home.

Cat Facts

Marjorie Carlson Davis

More cats fall out of New York City apartment windows on Saturday nights than any other night of the week. Renee doesn't know where she learned this, but she wonders if the same is true for Chicago, where she lives. On summer nights, she finds herself glancing up at cats lounging in open windows, imagining a furry body hurtling through the air, tail first, then head first, finally landing on its feet to trot off down some dark alley. She knows cats only usually land on their feet, not always. She has also learned that the salicylic acid in one adult aspirin can kill a cat, and this she believes is fact because Simon, the veterinarian she is involved with, explained it to her.

It is Saturday night when Renee unlocks Simon's apartment, bracing herself for his cats, a tomcat with a missing ear named Van Gogh, and two Siamese, their whining a constant headache. Simon's practice is devoted entirely to felines. Small and lithe, he is catlike himself, eyes slanted, head triangular, and he walks on the balls of his feet, springing like a cat. Sometimes she wonders why she is involved with him, given her history with cats, but then she remembers the first time she saw him with one of his patients.

One Friday afternoon Renee sat in Simon's reception area waiting for him to complete his last appointment. An egg-shaped woman with amazingly small feet teetered into his office, holding a cat carrier. Though the box was small, the animal inside hurled itself against the sides with such fury that the woman almost lost her balance. Simon met the woman in the waiting room and opened the carrier. Renee held her breath, imagining a baby tiger or lion hurtling out of the box with teeth bared; she imagined bites, and missing fingers, and blood. Instead Simon pulled out a snarling ball of white fur, so small it could have been a kitten. Wrapping his arms around the cat's body, he circled its head with one hand, stroking from mouth to ears, instantly calming it. Renee recalled stories of St. Francis of Assisi, who could calm animals with just a touch or a few words; she wanted someone to touch her like that, to calm her so effortlessly.

She knows she is not the only one to feel this way about Simon. Simon's clients, cat owners and mostly women, call him Dr. Cat and seem in awe of his knowledge, batting their eyes and listening intently to his lectures. They fawn over their pets, as if they think they can win Dr. Cat's favor by demonstrating passion for cats. Their behavior irritates Renee, but she knows she feigns an interest in Simon's cats only when he is home. When she is alone, she keeps far away from them.

Renee doesn't exactly hate cats, but an encounter with one takes her back to her childhood on the farm. The youngest of four children, she was the only girl and tiny, an anomaly in a family of tall, big-boned people. According to her brothers, she had been nicknamed "Runt" because their father held her up as an infant and joked, "What's this? Should we drown her with the barn kittens?" Renee has never asked her parents if that is true, but she does know her father regularly drowned barn kittens. One of her few childhood memories is seeing her father set down a bowl of milk for a cat, plucking the newborns out from under her while she drank and stuffing them into a plastic bag. Renee followed him down to the creek, hiding in the weeds to watch. She has nightmares about it still: the bag thrashing underwater; blind, mewling kittens clawing at black plastic. What kind of man could drown kittens? she has often wondered.

Most of Renee's childhood memories are vague and shadowy. When she tries to recall a specific moment, it surfaces slowly and out of focus, as if her mind is nearsighted and in need of glasses. What she does remember is that her childhood seemed to be a time of perpetual fear. She remembers her brothers pushing her down in their rambunctious play, her big-hipped mother knocking into her as she bustled around the kitchen, her father staring past her as if she didn't exist. Even the farm cats seemed mean and conniving, skulking in the fields, then hurtling out of weeds and pouncing on her ankles, biting with malicious intent. She felt more connection with the field mice that the cats teased mercilessly before eating. She cried whenever she came across a half-eaten mouse, wishing it could have found some defense against the cats. She buried the bones under the willow by the creek, fashioning a miniature cemetery out of smooth, round stones.

Renee tried to stay out of her family's way to avoid harm, yet at the same time, she hoped to be noticed and valued. At mealtime, food disappeared, gobbled up by her hungry brothers and father before she got her helping. Her mother often looked blindly over Renee's head and bellowed for her. Oh, Renee," she would say, finally noticing her small daughter, "I didn't see you there. You need to speak up."

Renee felt lost in her family, a pinprick of light in the vastness of the universe. Though she did well in school, her family didn't value academics, didn't find the scholastic awards she won particularly noteworthy. Sometimes she made up stories to get attention. Barn cats became men sneaking around the school yard, following her home.

Renee balances grocery bags on one knee to close the door, and cats instantly surround her, meowing and rubbing against her legs. She fumbles in the bag for treats, knowing Simon won't approve. He likes the cats to stick to their regular diets. Strange foods cause urinary infections and digestive troubles, he has told her. Educated advice rather than fact, she decides.

"This will be our secret." She tosses out a liver treat to Van Gogh, who pounces on it and carries it to a corner. She throws out more for the Siamese. Tonight Simon has been called in for an emergency, and Renee plans to make him dinner—a vegetable curry. She sets down the bags and glances at his spotless kitchen. Clean spice bottles are alphabetically arranged. Empty white counters gleam, an incriminating reminder of her own kitchen where dishes crust in the sink, sauces spatter the walls. Simon is the most fastidious man she has ever met.

She remembered an early dinner date when he took her to an Italian restaurant, rich with the smell of cream and oregano. Renee imagined seafood alfredo. She could almost taste the buttery crab. Then she noticed Simon studying the menu, his mouth in an unbecoming pout.

"They've changed this place," he said. "It used to be great for vegetarians. Look at this, everything loaded with meat and cream. My god, they're serving veal now. I can't eat here." He threw down the menu.

Veal, Renee thought, flesh of a young calf. Her father had raised calves for veal. Simon chastised the waiter, and they made a dramatic exit, ending up at a vegetarian café, where he talked for the next hour about the horrors of meat. She realized he'd assumed she was vegetarian too. She created a story of her transformation: a pig she'd hand fed who ended up on the dinner table. Simon listened, touching her hand in empathy. They slept together that night, his soft hands exploring her body. Afterwards she dreamed she was a cat on an operating table and that St. Francis, draped in white robes, was her veterinarian.

Once Renee made up her stories about the strange man, her family paid more attention to her, for a time. Against Renee's protests, her mother called the school to alert the principal. "He hadn't heard any other reports of men bothering young girls, but he was concerned," she reported. Even Renee's father got involved by summoning the police. Renee remembered her stomach churning when the police officer entered their living room to take down the official report. Her eyes straying to the black gun attached to his belt, she answered his questions with stammered yesses and nos, elaborating as little as possible, even though she had begun to believe her stories. She liked her brothers' mumbled threats: If any pervert even looked at their little sister, they'd pulverize him. After a few days the questions began, "So where was this man, Rennie?" "Why did he single you out?" Then the lecture by her parents: "We're disappointed in you. This is a serious thing to lie about." Her family noticed her even less after that, so she became more cautious; little lies were safer. Kids at school teasing her. Sudden headaches. At least her mother would give her a look of concern, a pat on the head, a few aspirin.

The air is thick with a yellowish, cumin-scented haze when Simon arrives home. Renee finishes chopping vegetables while he greets the cats. When he finally kisses her, she smells antiseptic and cat piss. Simon reaches for a broccoli flowerette, but pauses, hand hovering midair. "Washed yet?" She nods. He studies the broccoli; then rinses it. She shakes her head, amazed anew at his fastidiousness.

"You wouldn't believe what the emergency was tonight," Simon says, munching on the broccoli. Renee smiles. Something small, no doubt. Dr. Cat's clients will call him for anything.

"A hair ball."

"What?"

"A giant hair ball. You know, when a cat grooms itself, hair collects in the digestive tract." Renee nods. Yes, he's told her this before. "Ms. Lopez's cat had the biggest hair ball I've ever seen in my life."

Simon wipes at something on her cheek. "How about a shower?" he asks.

"For you or me."

"For both of us."

She follows him into the bedroom. "I'll just watch."

"Fine with me," he says. "I always was an exhibitionist."

He places his shoes neatly in his closet, hangs his tie on the rack, and drops his dirty clothes in the hamper. You're too careful to be an exhibitionist, she thinks, but she enjoys watching him anyway. She likes his small, lean form. The ropy muscles across his back. He disappears into the bathroom. Then she hears a shout.

"What the hell...."

In the bathroom Simon balances on one foot while he inspects a foul brownish smear on the bottom of the other. The room smells of liver. Renee looks around the immaculate bathroom and spots foamy vomit by the shower door.

"One of the cats vomited. You didn't give them anything unusual, did you?" Simon looks sternly at Renee. She feels like a child scolded by a parent, yet she can't take Simon seriously while he stands on one foot, his penis dangling like a tail.

"Of course not, why would you think that?"

"Well, this smells like liver." He narrows his eyes. "You know what I've told you about the cats' diet."

He's no longer St. Francis of Assisi, her robed savior; he's Dr. Cat about to lecture her on cat care. If he were a cat, she thinks, his ears would be slicked back against his head.

"Isn't that strange," she comments, not a question. "You know, I better finish dinner."

In the kitchen she discovers a pinch of turmeric on the countertop, but when she wipes it away, an orangy stain mars the pristine surface. She scrubs fruitlessly, then covers the spot with a dishtowel.

Her first year in the city, Renee felt the same way she had as a child, perpetually frightened. The roar of traffic, push of bodies overwhelmed her. Though she wasn't sure why, she gravitated to large men, men like her brothers, like the football players she dated in school. They guided her through crowds, large palms sweaty on her back. Large men were attracted to Renee. She thought her smallness made them feel superior, as if they needed someone to protect, like cavemen. For a while she desired their need so much that she tolerated them and their lovemaking, these men who pumped themselves into her like they were performing an athletic event. She put up with their size, their arrogance, until her disgust became greater than her need.

At the beginning Simon seemed different. For one thing, he was smaller. For another, he played chess and tennis in college, not football. He came into the brokerage wanting information about socially responsible investments, and Renee met with him several times, looking over his finances and discussing those companies that were both a wise investment and ethical. She remembers that he listened closely on the first visit, his eyes roving the small office, taking in details. On the second visit, he seemed to trust her. She liked that. Most men didn't believe she knew what she was doing. They had a condescending attitude, nodding when she offered advice; then asking questions that demonstrated they planned to do the opposite. What else Renee liked about Simon was his singlemindedness; his gentleness; and his way of making love to her, differently than other men had, soft, slow, and gentle, the way he touched his patients.

At dinner Simon compliments her curry and then launches into his cat stories. He is thinking of writing a book filled with amusing anecdotes interspersed with medical advice—Dr. Cat, a combination James Herriott and Dr. Spock for felines. Renee stifles a yawn, tries to look interested.

Much later after dinner, Simon and Renee lie in bed while his cats prowl the apartment. Simon has been all over her body with his hands and his tongue, yet she feels disconnected. Even during lovemaking she feels dishonest, a fake.

"Did you know cats see six times better at night than humans do?" Simon mumbles sleepily. "Their eyes have extra reflecting cells, which absorb light." Renee imagines the cats, their eyes reflecting moonlight. Cruel yellow orbs, condemning her. She thinks Simon believes she is like the other women he has dated, vegetarians, cat lovers, Dr. Cat's fan club, a woman fascinated by his cat trivia, cat facts. She knows she has made herself over to fit into his neat, fussy life, and, for the first time, she no longer wants to lie, to concoct these versions of herself.

One of the Siamese howls, and Renee sits up, restless. She looks at Simon curled childlike on his side, one hand tucked underneath his head, snoring softly, almost purring. He has told her that a purr does not always mean contentment: sometimes injured cats purr to soothe a possible attacker. Suddenly, deeply hungry, Renee rises, dresses, and slips out of Simon's apartment, into the cold air. On the corner, a diner is open, aglow with artificial lights. Before she met Simon, after abandoning the large men, she ate many late meals in diners. Greasy hamburgers, chicken fried steak. The heavy food satisfied her. She liked the anonymity of diners, where people knew nothing about her, where she didn't have to make anything up.

Renee slides into a vinyl booth. By the row of windows, an elderly man stares blankly at his reflection and picks his large, reddened nose. At the counter, a policeman leans over his coffee cup; his shoulders form a saggy letter M. The night's specials are scribbled on the chalkboard: split pea soup, liver and onions, cherry pie a la mode.

Simon told her that cats are the most carnivorous animals of all, that they can't extract enough nourishment from vegetables. Their teeth are designed for ripping flesh. Renee orders the liver and onions, and when it arrives, she picks up a piece of meat with her hands and bites into it.

Pelvic Poetry

Kathleen Serocki

okay
I'll be the one to do it
kill Elvis
pull the rhinestone studded lid down

put a stake through the sightings, songs, apparitions
the eternally grasping impersonations
endless jokes, ubiquitous photos and plastotica
such swelling cosmic clutter
articles of underwear madly flung across the stage
vats of black hair dye, pompadour gel
enough of the migrations to the motherland
their crutches and wheelchairs hoisted from its gates

and so many trying to snatch at
that elusive white polyester sleeve
masses of fans in formations
watch him midair
though bellied and bleached
white bell-bottomed suit
white pointy collars
like a moth
madly fluttering across the stage
every time the light came on
in each movement a sad appetite for light

I roll out a white stone
draw a straight pin through styrofoam walls
releasing its little dry pointed cry
still bloating though dead and transfixed
an undisguised double cheeseburger
glows pinkly under a red transparency
a conspiracy of heat lamps

For the Mother of My Korean Daughters
Joanna C. Scott

In the high cold mountains below Seoul,
I knelt for dinner with a woman
fragile as a traditional Korean doll—
the same white face, hair twisted at her nape,
fixed with a carved jade dragon pin,

the same hot-pink high-breasted gown
called *hanbok*. She smiled a tiny painted smile
and ate daintily. Noone introduced us
and after a while I said, *What should I call you?*
but she didn't understand, and when

it was translated, she held her hand
in front of her teeth and dipped her head.
Then her husband answered for her.
Korean wife have no name, he said,
and he said it proudly, *When son is born*,

she is called 'Mother of...' and he spoke
the name of his son like an invocation.
I saw the painted mouth smile, the white line
of her parting bow before him, and even though
this happened more than ten years ago,

I sometimes think about her. And I think about
the mother of my Korean son and daughters,
not, perhaps, a modern woman either.
I wonder, *What, now, is her name?*
Is she called "Mother of Lost Son?"

Sometimes, in the summer, I want to speak
urgently to her, I want to tell her
that her two daughters are tiny colored birds
who fly in and out the windows of my house,
their voices twigs of bright red berries

broken off and carried in their mouths
like gifts. I want to tell her they are carp,
who all summer long gather small bright
pieces fallen off the sun and store them
in the secret chambers of their bodies,

and when winter lays its cold stiff form
across the pond, they burn like twin stars underneath.
I want to tell her that for each of her two daughters
I have planted in the yard a gingko tree,
and when they all are grown, trees and daughters,

I will cut down the trees and make two boxes,
one for each, I will inlay them with jade and beaten gold
and carve them with fine detailed carving.
I will carve the frozen mountains of Korea,
the hot wind blowing from the north,

five darting birds for freedom,
five twigs of berries to keep their bellies full,
five swirled carp for their imagination,
five seated Buddhas for reflection,
five dragons to stand guard.

All these will be in sets of five
so there will be one for Sun Ok, one for Sun Young,
one for their Korean mother,
one for every mother who has given up a child,
and for the child, one more.

Forbidden Fruit

Joanna C. Scott

for Gran

Elsie May, old,
took to her bed and ate bananas,
left them in a soft accusing trail
bedroom to bath
on an unplottable internal schedule.

She abandoned moderation,
all consideration
of those who came behind her
cleaning up.
Warned, she demanded,

insisted as she'd never done before.
Refused, she called the Chinese greengrocer
who brought green-fingered hands,
left them to yellow at her door.
She crept to them like Eve to apples,

crept back to bed to wallow in her sin.
Perhaps she had determined that
she'd cleaned up for so many
for so long herself,
a little cleaning up was due to her.

Due or not, she no longer cared
for family opinions,
had completely shed
the guilt of motherhood.
Now she cared only for smooth golden skin,

smooth sliding on her tongue
and in her throat,
the sweet dense slipping
of her final
scatalogical remark on life.

Under the Scorpion's Heart
Margot Schilpp

What you were reaching for
was a handle, a brick,

or a gun, so you didn't notice
the sky darken to black canvas.

You didn't notice the rain.
You sat on the steps

and let the light obscure you.
There are places

you'll remember as kindling,
where centrifugal force

drives everything from the center,
and nothing you've ever heard

is true. What if the mud dries
to mirage, and there is no door

by which to leave?
The surf entangles

the logic of the sun,
but sadness is no answer.

Take into your mouth
the constellations of lemons,

and as feathers presume water
and wind, make up your mind to rise.

For Protection Against Faeries: A List
Angela Regas

Bread

Running water

A crucifix or cross
Faeries do not have souls. Their bodies are hollow
where the soul might otherwise reside. The intimate places.
Their hands, their eyes, the soft pulse
at the bottom of their throats,
are all hollow.

It is not a fear of God that keeps the faerie away,
but a fear of human faith.
Faith strong enough to fill them
until they are crushed by their own weight
into a leaf, a branch,
a smooth, tiny pebble—

sometimes still warm under our feet.

The Bible

Iron

Daisy chains

Clothes turned inside out
The insides of faeries
are made of the same smooth, weightless silk
as the outsides. Peach and lavender.
The insides of people are dusty
with misplaced love affairs
and undigested anger.
Quirks that collect over the years,
seeping out through our pores
and coating the insides of our clothes.

Stones with holes

A twig of broom

Ancient churchyard mold

Flax on the floor
>Once, seven swans became seven men
>as their sister pulled seven shirts of raw flax
>over their feathers. The flax caught
>in their skins, pulling away their down and faerie spells.
>Flax will pierce through the delights
>and illusions that dust the tracks of faeries
>and shine in the eyes of sleepwalkers. Flax will pierce
>through the smiles and gestures that cover the paths
>of the people these manners protect.

Shoes placed with toes pointing away from the bed

A sock under the bed

A knife under the pillow
>Also good for protection against robbers, murderers
>and in-laws.

St. John's wort

Bells

Rowan and red thread
>Sometimes mothers will send their children out
>with red ribbons tied around their chests.
>The ribbons bind the children's ribs
>close to their hearts, for the hearts of children
>are wild, and prone to wander.
>Will-o-the-wisps are the flying hearts of children
>that escaped these cages of ribbon and bone.
>They float along the edge of your eyes,
>hoping to tempt your heart away
>so they may steal your body and live again.

Salt

Holy prayers

Horseshoes

Pageants
Linda Tomol Pennisi

I keep searching for religion, but the closest
I come is O'Keeffe's lilies, or my dwarf
half cousin, Mary, stepping from death into the porch light's
yellow semi-circle in a dream,

Don't be afraid. I'll stay with you, she says.
For a while, I'm comforted. But when my throat
closes off and I try to cry, *Mary!*
the name gets stuck, weighted

with pageants and powder-blue shawls,
and the rubber doll I pretended was Jesus,
swaddling it in last years musty blanket
near where my breasts hadn't begun to bloom.

Chosen to play Mary, my daughter, six then,
broke down on her way up the aisle.
The cardboard donkey she held like a skirt
around her, clumsy. A throng of angels

awaiting their cue. In the vestibule
she clung to my legs before leaving
for Bethlehem, the donkey slid to the floor
as she tried to escape it. *You can do it,*

I urged her into a sanctuary of expectant
faces. The congregation smiled, laughed
even, as she silently wept on her way toward the town.
It was too much for her. Every day for a month

when she went off to school, she cried,
as if every journey were that difficult journey,
that half-smiling donkey still on her hips, and she losing
control of where it might take her.

The Front Row

Linda Tomol Pennisi

Each Sunday, behind
a drape the color of wine
they sit, only shoulders and faces
visible to the congregation.
Eyes on the preacher,
the sopranos pass time
passing their hands along
each other's hands and forearms,
barely touching,
a drizzle of fingertips
calling sensation up
to the surface like new grass.
Their way of getting through it—
the long unraveling of rights
and wrongs, of Christ
doing this and doing that.
They perk up, sometimes,
with word of Eve's labor pains
or one of the Marys, quivery
when he talks of the serpent
or angel. In the feel
of another girl's flesh,
they are learning themselves.
They take turns—five minutes
touching, five
being touched.

Normal: A Surgical Lovesong

Elisabeth Murawski

The lamp's
frayed cord. Wet
skin. The shock
enough to knock
the baby out and blow

a fuse. Where
did she go?
Was there a bear
or owl to guide?
An arrow

to annihilate?
The mother smears lard
on rye bread.
Sprinkles it
with sugar. The two

oldest siblings
sail records
a half inch thick
from the attic.
The father, drunk,

snores loudly
on the couch. King,
his vicious
German Shepherd, lies
pagan and alert

at his stocking feet.
The baby finds her thumb.
Her eyelids flutter.
She drifts
within reach.

Of a Feather

Elisabeth Murawski

You bend forward
as you speak of China sky,
the moon torn from clouds.

Your dark eyes
do not follow me,
hold the warmth I want

hostage.
I who would fly beside you
like a crane

am the common shell
you will never pick up
on the beach.

I work the rim
of your indifference.
I'm just a woman

hiding stretchmarks,
undressing
in the dark.

The Confession

Elisabeth Murawski

"I have committed love," the woman says.
"For that," the priest replies, "I gave Degas
a hundred rosaries!" Then, with a guess,

he condemns: "The way you look at him in bed!
No man deserves such worshipping!"
Behind his eyes he sees backstage with Degas

ballerinas adjusting their straps, poised
for the overture. Says, "Do not come down
from your cross. Stones will be bread

soon enough." The tiny grille slides
shut. She lifts the heavy velvet curtain
to face an empty church. Then kneels,

connected once again to the wheat, suffering
her familiar. Who can change the holding
pattern in her knees, her throat's

long memory? Christ's robe of red
stained glass spills rays of carmine light
on her shoulders. A grief at bay

knocks at the gate. She turns to meet
the flood. She is a bubble riding a wave.
Pollen on a bee's wing. She begins to ask

"What is this?" and the words are a gong
vibrating the first sound, penetrating
further and deeper than any angel's dart.

The sun beneath her heart has always known
what her body knows. And then she does
what she does. Equal to the sparrow. Inviolate.

Mass

Ann Lynn

A friend says, *Let's not use the word mastectomy.*
Another says, *One in eight of us will get it.*

Mass no longer suggests the holy
but instead my grandmother

opening her shirt to show me her scar
like Jesus to Thomas,

Put your hands in these holes.

Love Poem
Ann Lynn

for David

When I think of you in your snowsuit
watching your mother
hold your dead brother's body

I understand why there are times
you need to be inside me,

then turn away in silence.

I read about a Turkish writer
who started to stammer
when he saw his father slain.

Only by singing could he make it stop.

You ask how I know I love you.

I have no proof,
like the boy who tamed his fear of water
by swimming in the deep

where there was more to hold him up.

Grace

Richard Deming

1.

A horse raises its head towards the west,
towards the sharp cry of raccoons savaging
each other in the grass at pasture's edge.

2.

Stepping into the sudden night
air of late spring, stunned
I disappear into my own
life, other people I have been,
all wearing a singular name,
as easily as walking through rows
and rows of tall corn.

3.

We stumble upon ourselves the way, sometimes,
boys will find the bodies of bums
and hobos thrown from the city-bound midnight
B & O, bleeding in the underbrush, not dead
but, Oh Lord, not living either.

And with the ignorant violence our eyes
commit upon the world,
we sear into that vellum of flesh
the shapeliness of *presence* that gives
itself wholly to loss.

4.

Ashes drift past
the scorched stones
of a campfire. Night

quickens, and this

5.

is the last light, the cold light the stars
cast down over open fields.

It is like this.

On Becoming a Poet in the 1950s
Stephen Beal

There was love and there were trees.
Either you could stay inside and probe your emotions
or you could go outside and keenly observe nature.
Describe the sheen on carapaces,
the effect of breeze on grass.

What's the fag doing now? Dad would say.
Picking the nose of his heart?
Wanking off on a daffodil?

He's not homosexual, Mom would retort, using her apron as a potholder to
    remove the Apple Brown Betty from the oven.
He's sensitive. He cares.
He wishes to impart values and standards to an indifferent world.

Wow! said Dad, stomping off to the pantry for another. *Two* poets in the family.
Ain't I a lucky duck?

As fate would have it, I became one of your tweedy English teachers, what Dad
    would call a daffodil-wanker,
and Mom took up needlepoint, doing seventy-two kneelers for St. Fred's before
    she expired of the heart broken on the afternoon that Dad roared off with the
    Hell's Angels.
We heard a little from Big Sur. A beard. Tattoos. A girlfriend named Strawberry.
    A boyfriend named Don.
Bars and pot and coffeehouses, stuff like that.

After years of quotation by younger poets, admiration but no real notice,
Dad is making the anthologies now.
Critics cite his primal rage, the way he nails Winnetka.

Marilyn Makes Her Comeback
Stephen Beal

I

Oh all right, she says,
and all of us who fell in love with her as kids fall in love again.
Not because she's gorgeous or sexy but, this time around, because she's real,
a plump old doll of seventy-three with laughing eyes and a great smile and a way
    of walking that makes us old guys turn and grin and raise our eyebrows at
    each other.
Our wives love her, too. Same reason. She's plump. She's happy. She's real.
We all go to see her do *Hello, Dolly* at the Pasadena Playhouse.
Hey, now there's a show.

II

Oh all right, she says,
looking older and skinnier than Isak Dinesen,
looking like the addict that we know she was—Marilyn has never lied—and
    now she's playing the mother in *Long Day's Journey into Night*, to such effect
    that Bosley Crowther returns from the dead to say he's sorry, he was wrong,
    she *is* an actress, she's a good actress, maybe even a great actress, for Lord's
    sake, the woman gets a Tony,
and then Hollywood does the film again, this time a punk-rock musical,
    Madonna in the mother role,
and Marilyn is pleased as punch to have lost a part to a babe, to be considered
    too artsy-fartsy for Hollywood, to be a Broadway star at last.

III

Oh all right, she says,
stuffing her body into a red spangled gown
and perching on a stool in a single spot against a black curtain,
voice amplified by extra mikes in her bosom as she belts out the blues that she
    has earned the right to, three more husbands after Miller, the booze, the
    drugs, the stays at Betty Ford, the learning as her first beauty wanes that
    what we loved in the first place was her soul,
and, boy, does she give us soul now, this woman holds nothing back, we know
    where she has been and we are proud that she has made it through.
Sing it, Marilyn! we call. We are here for you!

Driving Home from the Zendo

M. Smith Janson

On the side of the road a small herd of deer
stand with their ears raised listening to the truck pass
and in my mind are still there two days later
grazing in the dark, their necks outstretched
the way God's arm might when reaching for his pipe.
God reclined and having a smoke with his world of fault
lines and phosphorus; extreme
tips of peninsulas, wind-swept or not.
Small towns midprairie at dusk.

Meanwhile the deer continue
to exemplify the discipline of practice
and the mind wanders
so far afield in big sky country it's no longer in it.
On the radio the usual
programming is interrupted with news that
in July the moon is called thunder.
Another staticky interlude in which a museum guide speaks
of beauty and its possession. A painting in oil
of a horse with tangled mane leaning its heaviness
against a gate's split rail, flanks heaving
as if there were another caught inside.

The way a person might regard a tree
going a few miles over the speed limit, thinking
maple or aspen because those are the given words
but meaning something more akin to *tiger or silver*
and the terraced mines from which it is hauled.
Including the backs of men as they strain to lift it
and the deer who stand with their ears pressed forward
in the universal language of the burst-upon,
the suddenly awake
ears open like the flues of chimneys
or cactus flowers in a Sonoran desert
so thin and fine and papery
the headlights of oncoming cars shine through.

How We Enter the Kingdom of Grief

M. Smith Janson

Doors that have been opened close.
Great oak doors made of wood hewn
at the edge of the forest, hauled past
the lowing of beasts, studded
with a rood of hand-tooled metal.

And then another door opens, this one
lowered on chains, slow as the moon
on its axis, skewered above the town
where people sit at planked tables,
waiting.

For the concertina heart to play its reel.
For the fatted lamb, prodded
along a corduroy road, taken from
the thicket where it has lain its whole
short life, feeding on wild thyme.

Once Again

Audrey Haerlin

I will start over—
give my mind to another round
of something like optimism
or at least, a little less wry
bemusement.
Hope's an exercise
in being six years old again
and hoping that the resident giants
will turn benign
and that the bird
who so plaintively sang
of summer
did at last rise
from its shaded branch
and silently wing home.

Too Soon to Sleep

Audrey Haerlin

As great a lassitude
as on those fabled isles
where legend says
mariners ate the lotus,
then drowsed their lives
away—
this over-ease, these quiet days
and nights, devoid of
dissension and difference
that gave life impetus
meaning and unease—
this sleepy tempo infects
the soul, makes us think
of endings—
days that should be marked
by striving
a sharp regret
or bitter joy.

Sterility

Audrey Haerlin

When I have moved away
from these sterile rooms
I will remember the blank face
of the building across the street
a shelter I suppose for those
who haven't come up
to expectations.
It has the institutional air
of bricks that hold in place
a random population
housed as inconspicuously
as possible
considering
they're still alive.

Finding a Place

Audrey Haerlin

The little matter of a roof
against the rain and snow;

and walls to keep the wind out;
and stairs into a place

away from trees and earth
at least for the night;

how to find them and
how to keep them

and then
how to let them go—

that's all of it,
isn't it?

Residence

Audrey Haerlin

I live within
the last resort—
(the It's-Too-Good-For-You
Arms)—
(it's so clean
it's so quiet
it's so nice)

for the recently redundant
the casually subsumed
the unredoubtable old—
don't tell me again
what a lovely community
this is—
it's a marked-down collection
of human antiques
a sanitized attic
for the superfluous old
the easily lost
the quickly replaced—

that shelters most tenderly
faceless investors—

and those who live here—
who had the poor judgement
to grow old
to be poor—

are told every day
with cool silvery smiles

my aren't you lucky—
you could be out on the street,
you know—

and we just won't mention,
now will we, old dear,
how you're just about
to run out of time?

Largo

Veronica Patterson

"He wrote the Bible seven times by hand."
                                    —Obituary

Largo
is what I was trying
to tell you. I have
to write slowly now
though I can quicken
as the forward did that night
when even his fever urged the ball
through the only net. Remember how
the diver entered the water—the molecules
parting in welcome? How the long jumper's heels
required the far sand of the pit?
Erase the athletes' faces and sinews—
I mean the famous thing
they know.

    Like that,

        but slower.

           No thrash and flutter
           like the bird just now
        in the window well. But also nothing
          silky, pleasing, and right. I live
         in light's affinity for dark, become
       custodian of loss upon loss—how each
      inhabits the other—and of refuges, old alphabets,
              fruitions. I love the word
            portabella, which sings
         in my ear *beautiful door*. I move
          like honey. I can't say this
           well, but one word
             of it is
             largo.

The Eye and the Navel

Veronica Patterson

The eye, which had little choice
but all day to swallow the world,
the trash, tree bark, and vomit of it,
needed somewhere to rest
and found it in the slow convolutions
of the navel, a fleshy whirlpool,
alive, but still, and always in shadow.
The eye knew the navel was a refugee,
that its quiet was the aftermath
of something. But it saw into the navel
only so far and then there was dark.
The eye grew to love that small gloom.
For its part, the navel was flattered
to receive such blue and radiant attention,
as it sat in its hollow, pondering. Once
it had lived in a softer country, before
some severing drama. Once there had been
a seething, busy red rope. All day the navel
tried to recall the pulsing words of an old language.
All night it dreamed of ears. And when
the eye wept in terror at the cruel sorrows
of its unavoidable witness, the navel held
the tears in its sleepy recesses, tendering
the only solace it had to offer.

Points of View
Roger Ladd Memmott

What if we were cave people
& lived in caves & ate
woolly mammoth
& had no language
except signing & pictographs
on debatable walls?

What if we loved rocks?

What would we think
when lightening struck
& trees came undone,
their imploring limbs swaying
like civilized dreams &
fire smoothed away the dark?

What if you loved me,
        would I bring you flowers?

What if we crawled into our TV sets
as though they were caves &
language meant nothing
        (except in its humming,
        its shimmer, its electric
        skittering, shaking itself
        loose & getting into
        some young boy, a girl,
        the stuttering beat of a heart
        like roots or grafts going deep
        into the flesh of generations)
& our emotions were as dull
as bread & the only thing left
was the curiosity of dogs sniffing
among the rubble for survivors
of another white hot blast
deep inside the guts of CNN?

What of our desire for rain?

If we were cave people & lived
in TV sets & ate the transistors
& had no way of communicating
except by graffiti on subway walls,
would deep thoughts and the language
of computers keep our children intact?

What if there was no way back
& gravity undid itself & the world entire
fell away & left us floating in space:
TV sets, automobiles, computers, the
fancy china of a five-star restaurant,
noodles & that sort of thing, a cow
floating by good as the nursery rhyme
that started it all, a saber-toothed tiger
gooey with tar & the little white blink
of the world eons toward eternity?

What if there was no way back
& when we flipped channels
reception was bad, even the
Flintstones—everything
scrolling
                    ghostly
                    & a high-pitched buzz.

A Custodial Strike in Orly Airport
Joy Dworkin

Five hours after our final goodbyes in St. Petersburg,
five hours after I left him for good…chicken
bones, chewing gum, cigarette butts,
greasy wrappers from fast-food
burgers, the burgers themselves…garbage
cans, unlidded, are brimming and spilling their heads
to the floor. I've just landed—I'm between
flights—but I'm getting high, drunk
on all this junk. Amidst
the filth, Parisians make their
dainty ways, deposit chic heels,
negotiate used tissues. In the glassed-in
heart of the airport, criss-crossing along smooth
escalator-tubes, Armani-suited
businessmen rise and fall.

Where the hell do I think I'm going?
I hate litter, but this rising river
of trash, this flood of everything
we try to forget, I adore
this exuberant Orly
garbage, orgiastic
refusal to be swept aside
inviting and (I know it
well) despising me so. You are right,
you crumpled news, you rare and ripped
burger. There's nothing clean or consistent
in my getaway, this second half of a so-called
round trip. And I can see him still, asleep
in stained sheets a thousand miles away,
and know there's nothing clean about love.

Blue Ridge Mountains

Joy Dworkin

Drenched. Ears taut
from steady torrents and sudden

crushes: drums
in and out of my
head. Thunder

makes me—just
for a split

second (then I'm
here again)—an impassioned
trampoline.

I stretch out an arm to water
onslaught and watch

as it quakes along the length
from shoulder to finger-
tips. I wish

I could bring back that moment or (if I can't
go back up) that rain could break me

down into air
molecules or the sound of the storm
could wash me clear

down the mountain, out of this insular
self and into the rush

on the bed below. But I think
I know why
the woods blush when a bolt fades.

It's because we can be stunned,
yes, by power's electric ut-

most, but then (more!) by how much
regret settles

when light does no damage,

leaves no gutted tree-
stump raging prophesy,

no gash, no flare, no out of this
world radical counter-argument to
rain, which doesn't strike me

hard enough, illuminates
nothing,

brings me closer
only to myself and won't take me
out of this time, this body. It's always another

element we long for.

Vergonha

Art Sousa

It wasn't that I didn't want to go to kindergarten. I did. Both Beth Barnowski and Paul Shoren started school that fall and there were differences in them afterwards. For one thing, they could no longer play as easily with each other. Boys! Girls! Yet a world of new language united them. "Mrs. Joseph says we are to watch our manners and change our underwear every day. Mrs. Joseph says my eyelashes are lovely. Mrs. Joseph caught Steven Fennara picking his nose this morning." Who was Steven Fennara? I didn't know, but Mrs. Joseph was their kindergarten teacher and I loved her very much. The way she read to them each morning after recess. Her constant pleas for a world globe (A classroom without a globe is simply bare. Bare! One of you must have a parent willing to make such a small contribution went Beth's impersonation, unintentionally funny and damning, and probably accurate, I think now although I never met Mrs. Joseph—she died the following summer, decapitated by an unlicensed fishing boat on her morning swim in the Sowams River). Even her favoritism was dear to me. There was no part of her or kindergarten that did not own my devotion.

But it was a love kept quiet. I would not give Beth and Paul another thing to lord over me. They already had so much. Beth: three dolls, one of which, her untouchable prize, stood three feet tall, had red hair and an orange dress, and took Frankenstein steps when held by the hand. Paul: a miniature Noah's Ark, the ugly brown deck lifted aside to store the animals, no bins, just an empty shell, the animals jumbled together like a mass grave. Both: bikes, various pieces of broken games, incomplete puzzles. What did it matter that they were all hand-me-downs? With me, Paul and Beth puffed with riches. So I never asked after their mornings at school and of course they knew. "Where you been? You've missed so much," Beth would say. Paul always cut her off, "Never mind. He doesn't know."

And I could not go to my mother with my kindergarten longing. What would she have said? "And who's fault is that?" I'm sure she would have said so in English although she normally scolded me in Portuguese. Because it wouldn't have been a reprimand, not exactly. More my mother's way of saying it wasn't her fault. She couldn't bear the blame for one more thing. She had already married for love. She had already defied Vovó. The first, marriage for love, was not unheard of, the second—unthinkable. And he was *American*. An elopement to Atlantic

City (a justice of the peace, the implications, terrible) where in a motel register my mother signed not only her new surname, Monahan, but her Anglicized name as well: Grace. When they returned to Rhode Island, she had never been born.

I might have grown up in the same town a stranger to her family if not for the near-death. My own. In brief: I had some difficulty with my bowel movements. This seemed bad, a disappointment, so I kept my predicament a secret. I continued to close myself in the bathroom for which I was congratulated upon exiting. Good boy, my mother said. How long did this go on? A few days, perhaps. I'm not sure. Some of these memories are vague; I was three. I do remember this clearly: walking with my back hunched forward eased the expanding pressure in my tummy; I took many naps. Then one morning, I woke, light as air I smiled into the kitchen, my bare feet feeling not at all the winter-cold linoleum. My mother screamed for what seemed a long, long time before I hit the floor. My lips, she told acquaintances for years, had turned bright purple.

In a hospital room I came to surrounded by eagerly stricken faces, the women wrapped in heavy coats and severely tied scarves, the men in shirts buttoned to their throats, their fedoras cocked low and to the side. I knew immediately they were Portuguese. Just beyond the metal sleep-guard stood Vovó. Did she have the beads then? She must have, she carried them everywhere. Perhaps she had them tucked inside a pocket, or perhaps they hung from a hand. I don't remember, they meant nothing to me then. Her solidness took me up, her proximity; before she'd been nothing but a smudge briskly crossing away from us on the street. While she stared down at me, I stared up at her. Her dress, coat, and scarf were black. Her eyes, enormous behind thick square glasses, were coated white like the gluey surface of heated milk. Three gray hairs grew from her chin.

"Mommy!" The loud croak of my voice surprised the room into laughter. My mother peeked from behind, her expression fearful, and, strangely, I thought, apologetic. I looked down at the hospital sheets; so white, so medicinal. When I spoke again my voice was a whisper. "Daddy?" Vovó arched one eyebrow, reached for a plastic cup on the nightstand, and stuck the bent straw to my lips (ginger ale, flat). "Papai," she corrected me.

On the ride home from the hospital, I lay constricted and sweating under several heavy blankets. My mother, in the determined, lilting way she spoke when she hoped to sound more American, repeated, again, "Shouldn't we show Aaron our new house?" Driving, my father kept his face straight forward. A ripple ran across his cheek as if he were chewing a meager, spent piece of gum. They were beautiful then. Not Hollywood beautiful, but beautiful. That year a construction worker, my father burned with a dewy layer of sweat, the skin of his neck pink and moist as if he had just been bathed. All his life he boasted that women found him irresistible, and this was partially true. Some women, yes. With her delicate name, small bones, and round brown eyes, my mother might have been compared to a bird, and indeed was when people observed her appetite. Graça, my mother, was no sparrow. With her jitteriness, her hunger to please, she most resembled a sad, nervous dog.

That was how we came to move from the second floor of one duplex to the first floor of another, how, consequently, I came to forfeit kindergarten. From Vovó's perspective, it was a lack of property that had made me susceptible to tragedy. Using her own tenement as collateral, Vovó secured a mortgage for my mother, loaning her the two thousand dollar down payment as well—for what a real-estate advertisement might call a "handyman's special with a built-in second income." So handy and so special, in fact, that the second apartment would remain uninhabitable for the first four years of our tenancy.

Vovó's loan would be repaid in fifty dollar installments on the first of the month, the same day the bank's payments were also due. From the beginning it was clear which entity would require payment first.

She had one already when we first moved to Birch Street. My mother, I mean—a job. That was OK—expected—in that part of Sowams. A wife who did not work was reviled. Such pretension. Everyone waited for the fall. But the cost of approval was more complicated than if one did or did not work, however. When my mother began cleaning homes in addition to her job at the Premier Thread Factory, the talk began. "Your mother thinks her shit smells better than mine, don't she?" Mrs. Shoren asked. Mrs. Barnowski restrained her comments to everyone putting pants on one leg at a time. Their tones were the same. Outraged betrayal. Ambition was just another kind of injury.

Hearing them, my skin bloomed red from the chest up. Justifying my mother seemed impossible. First, I would have had to explain why my father wasn't looking for another job after loosing his latest, and secondly, where he now spent all his time. One, I didn't understand. The other I wouldn't reveal.

I was four and three-quarters.

Then I turned five. You know what that means.

New shirts, new shoes, what will it be like?, and oh, wait till you get yours (from the soon-to-be first and second graders) was all I heard as

August slipped fast into September. I said not a word, knowing, knowing. How did I know? I don't know. Just that I knew. My mother said of the first day of school: "Go to Paul's house when it's time. You can go with him." Then she seemed to forget about it.

Paul lived on the second floor of the duplex next to ours. The stairs to his apartment were around back. Mrs. Shoren's muffled voice came through the door at the head. "I swear to God, Jason, if you make us late I'll kill you." Jason was Paul's next oldest brother, that day a third grader. "And you, you better get that smirk off you face, Mr. Wiseguy. Act up and I'll be visiting your teacher, just like this one." Paul was the fourth child, first days were nothing special.

I sat halfway up the stairs. Everything about me was stupid: the clam-digger's pants, the single peanut butter sandwich in the grocery bag, the too-tight patent-leather shoes—nice shoes my mother said in her unknowing Portuguese way, but no boy I knew wore them. Stupid stupid stupid. But worse, worse, worse were all the things I was missing. With my face cupped between my palms, I saw it all, so clearly it was as if I'd already been to kindergarten and sent home: the lunch boxes, the sneakers, the pads, the pencils, the vinyl folders with pocket dividers. The necessary paperwork.

Mrs. Shoren and Mrs. Barnowski had gone to American schools. They knew the proper procedures. Paul and Beth were enrolled. I was not.

"Vergonha." My mother's voice rang inside my head with the same bewildered condemnation she used to describe the Harold Moses' bathrooms. The Harold Moses' kept no help during the week. Their privacy was dear to them, Mrs. Moses said. They asked that my mother reserve Saturdays solely for them. That way, however long it took, it took. Her first months there, my mother scrubbed the bathrooms immediately, but the Moses' woke late—even the sixteen year old who should have been out, if not working at least playing. By the time they showered, shaved, and the rest, the bathrooms looked as if they had never been cleaned. My mother learned to attend to the bathrooms last, then escape in a rush. That way there would be no way to call her back. When she described the Moses' toilets, the source of her disgust was clear: that she, an outsider, saw and knew the way they lived—and worse: might and did tell.

Vergonha was richer and more powerful than shame. Shame was momentary, a brief discomfort. Vergonha—bottomless, endless. Vergonha could kill you.

I slid down the stairs when I heard Mrs. Shoren say, "Now come on, let's go!" I could not bear that we would be exposed. On the step outside, I reached with both hands to slow the closing door, instead battering it away with the forgotten grocery bag. Aluminum and glass slammed, as abrupt and shocking as an unexpected slap. "What the—?" I heard Mrs. Shoren say and I was gone, gone, gone, holding my breath as I ran down the driveway, gasping as I fumbled with the latch, and shaking, first a little, then a great deal when I dropped the key. Inside, with my back slumped against the door, it was a minute more before I remembered to breathe.

"You didn't go?" my mother asked.

I shook my head a fraction. Sister Bertrille stood tiptoe in the convent courtyard with her hand on her habit, her chin turned to the wind. Ready to fly. Somewhere off screen, her boyfriend Carlos drove a cramped, charming car up winding semitropical hills. I lay on my stomach a foot from the TV. I had been there all day. I had seen everything. *Captain Kangaroo, Romper Room, Donahue, The Price Is Right, All My Children, Jeopardy.*

"It was today?" Her accent was thicker than usual, or perhaps it was her tongue that was thick. Swollen with weariness.

I nodded.

"Why didn't you go?" A commercial for Tide. In an otherwise dark, bare room, blinking blue light lit my mother: a rough wool coat although it was not yet fall, a plastic mesh bag with tarnished mettle handles gripped as if the remains of her lunch and dinner were very, very heavy, a confused expression.

"But it was today?"

Closing music, scrolling credits.

She bent to lower the bag, but didn't let go or straighten. Estimating, measuring, weighing the risks. She disapproved of the other neighborhood children; malcriados—*badly raised.* But with them I would have walked to school in the morning, and returned to play in the afternoon. I would have had company, and company could pass for safety. But a child left alone all day—

In the periphery of my vision I saw all this weigh on her already drooping shoulders and though I was unsure where her measurements would lead, I was certain where they would not: she would not clarify with Mrs. Shoren, nor would she herself take me by the hand to kindergarten the next morning. I would not go to kindergarten. Not this year. I had missed the first day of school, how could there possibly be a second? Her logic and my own were identical.

As she rose and turned to leave the room, one tarnished handle slipped from her grasp. The bag hung open like a slack mouth, like my mouth at times when she instructed me to breathe through my nose. Cerrar teu boca—*shut your mouth*. Do you want people to think you are stupid?

"Tu va teu casa de Vovó," she said exiting. *You will go to your grandmother's house*. The punishment would be for both of us.

I nodded my head a fraction.

Six-thirty the next morning I stood with my hand on the cold metal lever that secured Vovó's gate. Just inside the fence, a parameter of pruned rose bushes guarded the property from the remainder of Water Street. The corridor of pink, white, and red blossoms seemed to admonish a neighborhood that might not have otherwise noticed its own neglect. In the driveways to the right and across the street, shoots of grass grew from beneath discarded couches and tire rims. Directly to the left was The Good Times Pub. The one window interrupting its cinder-block exterior remained shut behind blinds, as if it too were silenced by Vovó's fastidiousness.

"Go, go," my mother's call came from a half a block away where she continued without slowing. The Premier Thread Factory was past Cannon Ball Park, a long way away. "Vâ, vâ," she called, her voice hotter and smaller and I knew that I must. Lowering the lever, I tested the gate with my shoulder before continuing. I had been warned; if a stray dog found its way into her yard, Vovó would know who to punish.

Artificial grass carpeted the fourteen steps leading to the high first floor porch. Slipping on a patch of ice and plummeting down those steps was Vovó's greatest fear. She was sure it would mean a broken hip and a broken mind. Even in summer she recounted the stories of women to whom this had befallen. It was always women, it seemed. With a perfunctory slap of her hands she dramatized and dismissed the physical fall. The fall from reason she described slowly, listing the brutal details in a controlled, enthusiastic manner. These humiliations consisted of the slow dissipation of memory: names, faces, events, years, and, finally, bodily functions. The fallen women were forced to wear diapers; worse yet, to be cleaned by their daughters. Their houses were eventually sold to pay for nursing homes. In precaution, Vovó had laid her front steps with plastic grass which gave traction to shoes.

The tough, wiry blades sank and sprang against me as I climbed. The green carpet reached over the top step and continued for nine or ten feet to the far end of the narrow porch. There, two doors stood side by side. The right opened to stairs leading to the second and third floor apartments where two ancient widows lived. Through the screen door on the left I heard Vovó's disapproving voice filter.

"Magro," she said. *Thin*. Because I could not yet differentiate between the male and female forms of Portuguese, I was unsure if she meant my mother or me, or both. We were thin, skeleton thin; people said so. Before crossing the length of the porch, I looked over my shoulder. My mother hurried into the distance, her feet and arms moving jaggedly. It was true. A misplaced step would have broken her to pieces. Vovó recalled my attention: "Aanon," she said. She could not pronounce my name; it was American.

I turned towards her voice. Vovó's eyes were hidden through the mesh. The door opened. I passed through. "Magro," Vovó said a second time and pinched the back of my neck. My life as a liar began.

"No, that's not true," I said quickly and too late. "I was joking. I meant I meant—." Paul had asked Jeez, what do you do all day with your smelly old grandmother? and the answer came out as if it had been waiting all day for an invitation. She takes me toy shopping. She's rich.

Paul's eyes locked with Beth's in a sweet, conspiratorial understanding. It struck me then: observations were made in my absence.

"Why?" I repeated, my voice reluctant.

"Yea. Why? Why don't you have to go?" The smile Jason directed to his brother was smug, predatory. Paul leaned forward with his hands on his knees, wiggling gleefully from side to side. His brother's complicity seemed to him a form of approval.

Crouching down, I used a twig to scrape up more dirt from the shallow hole the brothers had begun. The ground was hard. The twig snapped. I spoke into my knees.

"What? What didya say?" Jason said as he used the side of his sneaker to wipe away the traces I had left. Paul knocked me off my haunches.

"I'm smart," I said. "I don't have to go. I'm smart."

"Sometimes we take the bus to Providence," I said, powerless to stop myself. "We go to the museum." Which museum? I didn't know there was more than one museum in the world, only that it was educational and that Stanley made his children go. Stanley DeWolf of the former ship-building DeWolf's, whose cottage my mother cleaned on Monday, Wednesday, and Friday afternoons. She reported on the ways of the rich to Vovó when retrieving me at night. An offering, I think.

"And we go to lunch," I called loudly. "We go to lunch!" Beth and Paul continued kicking leaves into the air as they skipped down the street. The next morning they would be going to The Roger Williams Zoo, their first field trip.

"She has a color TV," I said casually as I piled up snow at the base of a tree. I was building a fort. I was alone. "Oh, she let's me watch anything." My hands and feet were numb.

The Werewolf. The Fly. Mutated survivors of World War III. I preferred these to Dracula and The Mummy, though I sat glued to them as well. It was the happiest surprise of any week, when the Moses' had weekend guests and my mother and I stayed home on a Saturday. I could watch anything so long as I kept the volume low. I waited patiently through the morning cartoons and the hour of re-runs at noon for the best four hours of my life: The Creature Double Feature on Channel 56. Invading space aliens were my favorite. There was always the chance they were real, there was always the chance they would kidnap me.

"Did you eat?" my mother asked when she stumbled from her room in the early evening with puffy eyelids and sour breath, drunk on the combination of too much and too little sleep.

Yes, I answered. Yes, I did.

"You OK?" Beth asked and Paul stopped too. They had never seen me so still, so removed. I paused. Never before had I experienced such calm. I could have jumped from the roof of Beth's house to her carport, an abyss of three feet, without a flutter. This feeling was new, mysterious, wonderful. What was it? I didn't know; no one had taught me the word cunning. I decided it didn't matter.

"I can't tell you."

"Can't—tell—us—what." Paul said, punctuating each word with a hop. It was unseasonably warm and he exercised his new and temporary lightness. His legs were zombie white.

"About my Vovó." It was the first time I used Portuguese on them.

"Huh?" Paul stopped leaping at a low bare tree branch. Beth blinked slowly. Something was going on. She could see that.

"Grandmother. I can't tell you what my grandmother does all day. My Vovó." I walked in the direction of our duplex and said without turning, "It's too awful."

Vovó prayed the rosary at twilight. Sitting at the edge of her couch with her knees tightly together, her voice remained hushed and impossible to follow. Not that it mattered. It wasn't the words I wanted. In light the beads she counted decades upon were nothing special, cheap plastic the color of her eye condition, pterygium. But the dark—the dark made them fantastic. When a trip to the bathroom interrupted her cycle, I stole the beads from where she had laid them, bringing them close to one then the other eye in my cupped hands. The beads glowed like a pile of radioactive ant eggs, like a battalion of space ships descending in the midnight sky.

I returned the beads to a neat pile when I heard the toilet flush. No telling what she would do if she caught me playing with God.

"What's the matter?" Beth said in her Mrs. Joseph voice, babyish and concerned. I sensed Paul to the rear. Being the youngest had taught him to hold back. Beth was an only girl. Her father bought her Cracker Jack's.

I sat on the granite curb and Beth followed. "I can't tell you," I said.

Leaping over our heads, Paul screamed, "Why?" He clopped down, righted himself, then ran his momentum off. His smile wavered when he turned. Only Beth had been startled.

"It's a secret."

"Really?" Beth's mustard breath enveloped me. Her eyes widened.

"Really-schmeally. Big deal," Paul said from upside down and between his legs. He had bent in two. Kiss my cu. Beth picked dirt from under her nails. Paul was her fiancé, no matter what he said.

It was quiet.

"She beat you?" Paul's voice was different, both deeper and higher. Beth looked up. With his weight resting on one hip and an imaginary cigarette between the index and middle finger of his right hand, he had metamorphosed into his mother.

"Does she!?" He ran at me. I was almost at my door before he caught me from behind and wrestled me into a headlock. "Does she!? Does she!? Does she!?" The back of my head burned from his noogies.

Beth pleaded, "Stop it! You're hurting him! Stupid-face!" She loved him so much.

"Does she?" he gasped. He had to know.

"No," I said harshly. Then softer, "No. Worse." Beth took a step back. "My Vovó is a bruxa."

They waited.

"My grandmother is a witch."

On the night before I kicked her down the stairs, Vovó rested in her La-Z-Boy throne watching Bonanza. She loved Little Joe, as pretty and tragic as a woman. You didn't need to understand the words to see it. My mother came with her thin wrists and the plastic-mesh bag with the tarnished mettle handles. Later she would offer me what remained inside the recycled margarine containers, each at least half full, but for now the bag leaned in a heap at her calf. My mother came and sat close by me, saying we had to hurry, we had to go, but staying. She had stories to tell and she told them.

The endless supply of Pepsi in the cellar, the candy that could not end. The wife took care of it personally. Because if Stanley reached into that pantry closet and his hand came out empty, then that empty hand would have to be filled, that empty hand would demand the key to the liquor cabinet, Goddamn it! And the world would end. The clothes! The clothes! You would not believe it, Mamãe, my mother said holding my hand tightly because we had to hurry. The wife wears a dress once and never again.

"Repiraga estúpida," Vovó said as she stood from her chair. Stupid girl. I looked at the TV: Little Joe contemplating a dainty hand. Marrying Little Joe meant certain death. "Saber qua dia amanhã?" Vovó asked as she left the room. *Do you know what day it is tomorrow?* Could it be? Already? The first of the month? We had better go, my mother said when Vovó did not return from the basement. Rising I heard a female voice bark inside my skull; it said: *do something, dummy.*

Whose? I wondered. Whose voice? Mrs. Shoren's? Mrs. Joseph's? My mother's? No, I realized—it hadn't been in English. It had been in Portuguese. It had been Vovó's.

"I don't believe you."
"She does."
"I don't believe you."
"She does."
Beth hung her head and twisted her hands.
"I don't—" Paul said.
"She does. She eats children," I said.
Who knew the truth could be so useful?

My mother was nearly dry-eyed as we stepped towards the duplex which had been chosen for us. "Why are you singing?" she asked me, her voice accusing and brittle.

"Nothing," I said in a sing-song. "I saw something good today." I shivered. It could still get very cold at night.

She wiped her nose with the back of her hand. Her handkerchief was no longer of any use. "You watch too much television," she said, the authoritative tone in her voice clearly Stanley's. I continued to hum as if happily, an attempt, an effort, an entreaty to muster as much courage as possible.

I had decided to do something. I had decided to kill Vovó the next morning.

The next morning:

My feet dug into the artificial turf, my shoulders pressed one into each of the hard wooden door jambs at the far end of the porch. "Eu va dizer," I said. *I will tell.* Vovó continued without slowing until reaching the stairs.

"Va aqui, repirago," she said. *Come here boy*—no bother to whistle. I tried again. "Eu va dizer."

She reached for the railing and took the first step. "Va aqui, repirago."

"Eu va dizer."

Vovó took another step. Then another.

"Eu va dizer," I whispered.

She took another step.

"No," I said finally, though I no longer believed in silver bullets.

She stopped. A blustering March wind lifted the shawl away from her back, but left Vovó unmoved. She remained facing the street when speaking a moment later. Curious, perhaps tickled, she asked softly, "What? What will you tell? Hmm? What?" Her accent was nothing like my mother's. No hesitation, no regret. I did not even know she could speak English. Using up the rest of her amusement, she turned and asked again, "What?"

I lowered my eyes to the artificial lawn.

"Aanon, such a good little boy," she said sweetly, mimicking my mother. I looked up. The three hairs on her chin quivered. "You are nothing! Nothing! You are a little girl!" Yes, I thought, yes. Urine streamed hotly down the side of my leg. I was dying the death I had intended for Vovó.

She spat in a heavy arc over the stairs, then turned her milky eyes upon me. "Tell your mamãe, 'Anna.' Tell your papai." She freed her hand from the railing and gestured towards The Good Times Pub. "Go tell your daddy."

Disgusted, she turned from me. "You stupid Portigee." There—the unspeakable witchiness Vovó had performed upon me—spoken: I was Portuguese I was Portuguese I was Portuguese. I slumped deeper between the two door jambs. I did not think I would ever move again.

Vovó reached for the railing and with the shawl flailing behind her, fell the nine remaining steps.

The school department sent a truant officer to the house in May. There was no one home, of course. "He said you were in serious trouble, honey." Mrs. Barnowski ran from her stoop to tell us. "Serious." My mother washed her hair and borrowed Mrs. Shoren's phone to call in sick the next morning.

We walked to the Hope Street Elementary School, which seemed appropriate. "You need to go to the Administration Building. Do you understand? The Administration Building," the principal informed us, his lips pinched. Our ignorance embarrassed him.

"Do you realize how serious this is? The boy has missed a year of school. He'll be a full year behind. It is a crime to keep your children at home in this country." The superintendent tapped a pencil on his monthly planner as his secretary translated. My mother apologized profusely, first in English, then in Portuguese.

"He'll have to be tested now," he said, the threat obvious.

A week later, we returned as we had been told. The superintendent cleared his throat, leaned forward, cleared his throat, and leaned back. He laid his pencil flat. He glanced at the test results on the desk, then doubtfully at my mother, then, more doubtfully, me. "Well," he said finally. The secretary did not translate.

On the opening day of school the following fall, I was the only first grader at a urinal to pee with his pants around his ankles. I thought the metal column that sprung water into a round basin was a drinking fountain. Every time someone laughed at the back of the class, I sunk lower into my seat. Mrs. Cidel scolded me for not raising my hand. At the end of the semester, I was moved to Miss Gablinski's class in the second grade.

I walked steadily, wincing a little when the drenched material pinched where my legs met, stopping only a moment at the top of the stairs to mark Vovó, her arms sprawled, her shawl askew, her head only inches from the gate. She moaned a little. I held the railing stepping down, using the other hand to brush away any wind-blown hair that fell to my eyes. At the foot, I carefully lifted first one shoe than the other over Vovó's left leg which had caught on the bottom step. I crouched down by her shoulder. "Come on, Vovó." She groaned and lowered her forehead so it touched the pavement. "No, Vovó. Come on." She hefted herself a little and screamed out. The skin of her palms and wrists were pitted and streaked from pebbles. "Come on, Vovó," I clasped my hands under her armpit and tugged. "Come on." When she rose, I saw her chin was raw, the meat showing through in the shape of an egg. Her eye-glass lens were miraculously unharmed. With her hand on my shoulder, she tested her weight first on one hip then the other. She took a half step towards the stairs, then another, then halted.

She lifted her head, shuddered, and began sobbing with unrestrained grief. After a time we continued forward and up the stairs. At the door she reached inside her coat pocket and surprised me by bringing forth not her key but the glow-in-the-dark beads. She extended them before me, a gift. She had known all along.

"No obrigado, Vovó," I said in a voice wholly my own. She nodded and put them away.

Inside, Vovó took a towel from the linen closet and laid it vertically on the couch. That she did not ask for my clothes to wash seemed the greatest kindness anyone would ever offer me. After cleaning and disinfecting her cuts, she retired to the dining room where she crocheted without interrupting herself. I turned on the television and sat as the screen warmed up. It didn't matter what was on. Laying my head back, I consciously inhaled and exhaled. Then again, again, again, each time testing how deeply. For the first time in many months, it seemed I might be capable of breathing freely under the weight of my remembered life.

elegy
Mộng-Lan

& what if hope crashes through the door what if
that lasts a somersault? hope for serendipity
even if a series of meals were all between us
even if the aeons lined up out
of order
what are years if not measured by trees

Ballad of Greg Withrow

Alison Luterman

Greg Withrow was a young neo-Nazi who organized the white supremacist student movement in Sacramento in the 1980s. When he converted from hate to love, his own troops turned on him.

1)

Love blindsided me.
Crept up in those dumb white
sneakers they make waitresses wear
like they was nurses. This girl said,
"All those things I heard about you
just can't be true. You seem like such a nice guy."
And she put eggs in front of me. I ate them,
though by then I was
so dirty inside I couldn't hardly speak human.
Dirt with a pile of eggs in front of it,
Except she smiled or something.
So I went back. Went back for her smile
and later her phone number. Love crept up
on dirt.

2)

She was new to town and didn't know.
Thought she knew men, but she never seen
what I was up to. My job: big man on the hate rodeo.
Ride into town, get the white kids fired up
telling them how the niggers and spics
and Jews had all the money, all the jobs.
Why they weren't getting any.
Under my direction a few black heads might get smashed
like pumpkins the day after Halloween,
or the body of some gook
show up in the tall weeds outside of town
with no one but his family to notice him missing.
And they not even able to tell the cops in proper English.
I wanted to be like Hitler, or better, Genghis Khan.

3)

She didn't have family
either. My mother
split once I was born, enough of *that*
bastard, I think she said,
and my dad was a for-real bastard.
Kicked me downstairs from the time I could walk
until one night he kicked me out entirely.
On the streets, the Nazis became my family, they took me in.
Because I was Aryan white, like them.
And we was going to someday rule again.

4)

What happened before doesn't matter.
What happened after I take as payment
on debts past due.
But I'll tell you something:
Love opens you up worse than a knife.
I've been stomped with steel-toed boots,
punched in the stomach, had my head swung into a wall,
into a toilet. Love is worse.
There's nothing to hold onto.

5)

See, we was family to each other.
She had no idea, she didn't know.
Little by little love was ruining me.
How could I eat her eggs and go out afterward
and preach kill the nigger? Kill?
I'd lift my head and it was another man,
a black man, eating his eggs
with maybe someone who loved him waiting at home
in their bed for him to make her warm.
And I couldn't do it. Love was ruining me.

6)

I tried to get away quiet.
Out by the back door. But hate gets mad
when love is shining. Hate does not want to let you go.
And I owed
something, now. Would have to pay.
Still, when they came for me I was not ready.
Came with their baseball bats and smashed my jaw

so I couldn't talk to no more reporters,
and say that Hate thing was a mistake.
After, I wouldn't tell police who done it.
Hell, it was me who done it. I trained me to come after me
in the middle of the night and leave me in a pool of my own blood.
That's who done it.

7)

When I blamed her for my troubles she left
and I don't blame her. I'd have drove her to the station
myself, had I known what was coming next.
After the news that night when I persisted in telling
the wrong I done and that I was sorry. They got me good—
and nailed me to a six-foot piece of wood
like the saviour of hell, and I come stumbling through the streets of Sacramento,
the nails in my hands, and blood
running down my side. And the white folks passed me by.
Like this I know God has a plan.
And nothing happens that He don't see.

8)

Cause my own Aryan Nation had warned me.
I was as good as dead already,
and the others they were afraid I think. My own people.
And then the black couple come.
And the man says "Is this who I think—?"
And the woman says, "We've got to take him down."
And the man says, "Hell, we've got to, do you know who *this is?*"
And she says, "Course I know, everyone in this town who's got a radio
or a television knows. Jesus, lord have mercy, help me
with these nails."

9)

And like this I come to speak before you.
Except I can not talk right
on account of the jaw still being wired
and because I don't know hardly
what to say anymore. When I hated I knew
whose fault everything was
and how to fix it. Fix them. Now I don't know
nothing, except the things I told you.
Love opens you up
worse than a knife.

Wings

Carrie C. Frasier

I.

Why disguise it?
This poem is about
you, your plane-filled
thoughts, the fear of
not going fast,
some G-filled dream with me placed
on the page of blue paper
that is your sky.
Above the clouds you pull your
plane in a tight loop, punching
through as if you were
moving through your mother's cervix,
the moment of exit,
all rushing sun and
your belly back somewhere on the wing,
God's finger in the small of your back.

II.

I look up from my patio.
Overhead jets are noise lines,
dividing my sky with chalk.
Silly hopscotch routine.
The freeway traffic grabs
a frantic watch from its pocket.
The children shout from 2 doors down,
the yard full of their ballooned voices
melodramatic injuries and yellow offenses.

III.

This is how I will love you:
quiet on the couch and there
to brush your shoulder as you turn, pull
a white cotton throw higher on your neck.
And I will love you on a bare mattress,

us naked and pale in the world,
like the world
in her hues of blue,
veins running rivers
across the back of my hands
and over your eyelids,
my fingers placed over your
eyelids like coins, feeling
the roll of your eye, the fluttering
of a suppressed blink.

IV.

You fly your plane
like it was your own hand
over my skin, teasing
the ground with a slow descent,
lifting the plane's nose on the landing
as if settling your weight
between my thighs,
tender, deliberate.
Your shoulders and back tense,
all business now, as you are
when you kiss me with intent.
I won't change the sheets because
I can still smell you on my pillow.

V.

Behind this overlay of quiet,
there is the lens
of airplane lift-offs,
interstate close-calls,
the grocery cart rush,
all the people—couples
smoking out their petty drifts
in indifferent gray
exhales, and children's objections,
raggedy corduroy voices.
The sky a wrinkle.
A lulling plane ride.
Your strong hands leaving
fire in my hair,
a sun-stained jet trail.

Bowing the Bass

Barbra Nightingale

First it is plucked
like we're used to hearing,
low and blunt, a growl
of contentment, belly of cave.
But when it's bowed
oh when it's bowed
it moans and howls
shivers its strings
touched gently
    giving back
        giving back
            giving back.

One-Night Stand

Barbra Nightingale

Everyone knows the world
consists of random acts,
who we are
as accidents of birth,
yet surrounded by order.
Think of the slow arc
of the sun, the even slower
arc of the moon, all lies
of course, perceptions we choose
to make real,
like this candle,
this bed,
this lonesome scrap of love.

The Invocation of the Laurel

M. Rukmini Callimachi

I do not want to be touched with pain,
do you understand? Wood,
make room for this girl in your branches.
I am not being chased, although I run.
It is he who has ran from me, dark sun.

So take me into your trunk,
hide me for a while, let my hair
grow into the knots of branches,
my fingers, long leaves.

He will never find me here,
because he will never look.

River, my father, I am not running
from the god of the sun.
I want him badly, but he has another. Please,
speak to the wood. Beg it. Hide me:
that my cries can fall
like the last leaves of the laurel. Hide me:
it is almost winter—that the snow
may come, that I may forget this,
that my body may stiffen a little.

When summer returns,
it will be another chase.
Orb, you should have taken me
when you could.

Laurel, open your body and take mine.
In your wood, I will forget everything.

To Have and to Hold

Walt McDonald

Didn't they enter that marriage forever,
didn't they, though? To have and to hold each other
forever, forsaking all men in tuxedos
and elegant maidens waiting to catch the bouquet,
so clever to know it would last. Some friends
seem to say that, sadly or grandly at parties
and ballrooms, always surprised that it lasted
this long. We greet them and offer our toasts
to their brides or new grooms at receptions
with strangers and blooms like bouquets.
Years are like dances with friends changing hands,
new partners for foxtrots or waltzes,
or sitting it out. We're oddly off-guard
when they ask us to dance, odd couple oddly regarded
like wallflowers or parents, quaint chaperons
at mixed-family reunions, monogamous dinosaurs
back from the tar pits, quaint and club-footed—
how charming like sophomores, possessive
or scared, how daring like monks to love only one
or to grow old together thinking it's so. They watch us
for chinks in our armor, flirtations and waves.
Oh, he's the sly one, they probably say—
forsaking all others, ha, that'll be the day.
They watch her for bruises, for a drugged,
glassy gaze. Our children have babies
that hurry us dizzy from birthday to birthday,
already almost our age when we married—*always*
now down to decades or days. We're aging
amazed and surprised by how swiftly it passes,
no turning back—how awful, how destined, I see,
to leave her alone with my name behind deadbolts—
or worse, and unbearably so, to lose her
someday, not ever to hold her, not touch
that remarkable face, splotched with age spots.
How could I stand it, to suffer her gone,
not hear her call me, with gray in her hair,
not ever to rise and build fires for her early
or listen to jays in the garden at dawn.

Great Myths of Our Time

J. David Stevens

In his notebook he wrote:

*Mikey, the Life Cereal Boy, drank a Pepsi
and ate Pop Rocks at the same time,
and his stomach exploded.*

Of course his friends tried to talk him out of it. "Take a look around you, Jack," Rico began, "the doctors gave Laurence a new prescription just last week, state-of-the-art stuff." "And AZT," Howard pointed out, "we know some people in Atlanta pushing it cheap." "Nevirapine, too," Rico agreed, "next to nothing."

But he had decided. Even though mural painting was great work, the benefits sucked. And maybe he'd been crazy to let his insurance slide, but it wasn't like he'd been on some kind of power trip, thought himself invincible. He'd known the risks well enough and if not HIV, maybe leukemia or emphysema or something. Did the name really matter? (Which of course it did, but he wasn't going to admit that.) Because in the end it was simply a choice he'd made, for better or worse, like the one he was making now. He'd live with it. At least for a while.

"Insurance, shminsurance," Rico continued, "Jack, you got to fight." But Howard, a red-haired Irish Catholic who understood all about inevitability, saw how things stood, took his hand, hugged him. And Rico cried a little (and maybe he did too, he couldn't remember later) and they each carried a bag down the stairs and loaded them into his yellow VW bug and Howard said, "Where'll you go?" So he smacked the car and joked, "As far as she'll take me." And Rico said, "Call if you need anything, triple-A, cash." Though they all knew he'd pulled seven thousand dollars, his lifesavings, out of the bank just an hour earlier, and Rico ran one hand over his stubbly black hair, his dark eyes hazing over as if seeing all those black-market drugs they would never buy. Pulling away from the curb, he waved and even blew them a kiss, but decided not to call out something glib because he knew he might never see them again.

He stopped only at his sister's Soho apartment to tell her what he was doing. "You're a crazy fucker, Jack," she said at one point, her blond-dyed eyebrows lifting, creasing her forehead. "Just like you to go looking for trouble. Remember when you took that header off the carport? I thought that was the end." She frowned. "You should have died before now." Which was a crazy thing to say, they both knew, but it was Joanne and was in its own way an expression of love. Late for an audition, she kissed him good-bye, told him to write, then on her way out handed him the cordless phone. "Call Mom," she said.

So he did. And he told his mother many things of which all he could later remember was the phrase "to die with dignity," as if that were possible. And he thought what a great line that was, "Die with dignity," a great myth of our time, and how much better it might be to mix up a glass of Pop Rocks and Pepsi and listen to his stomach explode like a geyser, flash of glory death, people telling stories about him for decades. But then he remembered how he'd seen Mikey on a talk show just last month and that whole scam dying thing. "What a riot," Mikey had said, "just another show-biz myth." So maybe he couldn't die with dignity, but he'd damn well try. And when his mother made him promise to fly back when the real pain started, he didn't have the heart to tell her that pain came in various forms—that it had already "started"—but instead made her another empty promise which in his love probably meant something after all. Then from his bag he withdrew the living-will form that he'd bought at the bookstore and left a signed copy on Joanne's table to match the one he'd given Howard earlier, shoving several blank copies back into his bag. And his mother said, "Let me know if you find your father out there." And he thought again how people say the craziest things at a time like this....

But then again, maybe death gave everyone the right.

In Cleveland he wrote:

*Ozzy Osbourne bit the head off a live bat during a concert
then hung a midget on stage.*

And him with nothing but show tunes. Jesus H. Christ, how cliché. Plus the saddest part: They weren't even his. Ever since Joanne had landed that bit part in *Show Boat*, she'd trashed his car with Broadway tapes *du jour*, driving from audition to audition. Looking around the interior, he felt a strange satisfaction that she would get the car when he was gone. She almost had squatter's rights to it now.

He dumped the tapes into a trash can outside an Ohio Denny's: *Annie Get Your Gun*, *Forum*, *Cats*, *Grease*, *Chicago*, *The Fantastiks*, *Sunset Boulevard*. He kept *Aspects of Love*, though for what reason he couldn't say, then stockpiled on anthologies from the Fifties and Sixties at the Rock 'N' Roll Hall of Fame. He was humming "Tutti Frutti" when he dropped an armload of cassettes onto the counter, laughed at himself, then made the clerk's eyes bug out when he paid from a wad of hundred-dollar bills. Two full shopping bags later, he finally took the tour and got a British woman to snap a picture of him in a pelvis-thrust before the Elvis exhibit, then took one of her in front of The Shirelles. He convinced her to do a duet of "Momma Said" and even got her to dance for several Chinese spectators with Camcorders. Someone in back asked when they were going on tour, and he yelled that he already was.

Driving through the Midwest, he watched family farms and strip malls run together in a blur of pavement. He grew tired easily—fatigue had been his first clear symptom—so he sang along with Ritchie Valens and Buddy Holly to stay alert, and thought how dying wasn't much of a way to live. Okay, maybe refusing treatment wasn't the best idea, but he would die fast, wouldn't he? Fast.... Fast.... Faster, maybe that was the word he was looking for, all things being relative. AIDS, he said to himself, said it again, an innocuous little word, almost made him laugh the pain away. He had gone to the rallies with Rico, the parades, and felt the same stir of righteous anger as everyone else when Howard reported how A.G. Shapiro, VP of Operations at the bank, had asked him to remove the red ribbon from his lapel because it wasn't in keeping with their corporate image. Still, he wondered, was AIDS so much worse? His grandfather, his mother's father, had lingered for months with throat cancer, lost his voice, gone on oxygen, fallen into bed one day never to get back up. In the end they fed him with a needle through a tube, and his mother learned how to tap his arms for unspent veins to put in the IV, and he watched his grandfather become more machine than man, bag of tubes, liquid food that trickled straight into his throat, a larger tube running into the colostomy bag at the other end. He imagined one big tube running right through the old man that connected the tubes between.

It couldn't be that bad. Right? Not if you didn't fight it, if you let nature take its course. Not if you died with dignity.

Near Fort Wayne he scribbled:
Baseball, hot dogs, apple pie, and Chevrolet.

The living will weighed down his portfolio. He took it out and read it from time to time while driving faster than he had ever driven, surprised at his audacity, at the car's urgency. "Damned if I knew she had it in her," he told the Indiana cop, who pulled him over just before the Illinois border. He took the citation with a polite nod then withdrew one of the copies of the will that he had not yet signed, signed it, then asked the officer to sign in the space marked Witness. "You need two people to sign this, son," the officer told him, as if even diseases should be made official. "God's watching," he replied, "that's enough." To which the cop, scribbling his name, said, "I suppose, but I'm still not taking back that ticket."

In Chicago, he sat through a daytime double-header at Wrigley Field and remembered how Rico had mourned the day they installed lights in the park. Rico was from Chicago and said that Wrigley was the only place where he had felt welcome when young, not because he liked baseball so much, but just because the Cubs were so damn bad and it felt so damn good sometimes to be in a place where lost causes were so freely embraced. Sitting in the stands just behind left field, he thought he knew how Rico felt. He waved at the camera when it swung in his direction and imagined Rico and Howard spotting him in the stands (they had paid extra to get WGN in New York). When a fly ball curved in his direction, he leaped up with the rest of the crowd but was brought back to his seat by a clenching pain in his ribs and could only nod when the guy in the Harley t-shirt next to him asked if he was okay. He looked up to see the ball stay fair for a home run and heard the crowd roar when another fan tossed it back onto the field, since it had come off a Pittsburgh bat. Death with dignity, he couldn't help thinking.

The Cubs split the two-fer, 3-10, 2-1. As the fans cleared out, he opened his notebook and wrote "Tinkers to Evers to Chance," lingering over the last word. The guy in the Harley shirt, who'd been playing beer-an-inning through the second game, leaned over and asked, "What's that?" "Great myths of my time," he said, "something to let me know what I'm about." The man's eyes scrunched tight, "You aren't a Pittsburgh fan?" To which he smiled and replied, "I'll get back to you."

Later that night he called his mother and told her he was feeling better. She said, "You'd remember your father, Jack, wouldn't you, if you saw him?"

In St. Louis he decided on:
Trickle-down economics.

And what was this business with his father? He hadn't seen the man since he was three, couldn't even be sure if the pictures in his head were real memories or fabrications that he'd refined over the years until he believed they were true. Joanne didn't remember squat and liked it that way. "Let the bastard rot, for all I care," she'd say, "walking out on a woman and two kids, what kind of fucker does that?" But Joanne hadn't even been born when their father left. She didn't have memories to contend with, real or imagined.

He convinced a street musician to take several pictures of him with the Gateway Arch in the background, took the film to a one-hour fotomat, then drove to just outside the city where he sat on the bank of the Mississippi, eating a cheeseburger and watching small tugboats maneuver barges back and forth between docks. The brown water near his feet made him think of tainted blood, but blood still churning. He threw bits of cheeseburger bun into the air and watched as shrieking seagulls tore the food off the breeze.

His mother had blamed his father for everything, not viciously or even openly, but always. When he was young and did something wrong, she would say, "If only your father had been here." And even though over the years the phrase had fallen away, she kept a look that said more than the words ever could, and he could not bear that look when she turned it upon him, when he declined a graduate art fellowship at Columbia to paint murals, when he came home one Thanksgiving with Rodney, his first steady lover. Now AIDS. He couldn't go to see her after that, couldn't stand up to that gray tint which worked its way into her eyes even as she told him how much she loved him, that they would get through this together. The implicit line: "If only your father had been here." But he hadn't been, and who's to say his father's presence would have made a damn bit of difference? Who would have wanted it to?

In Kansas City he ate dinner near the stockyards and, for once, was glad to enjoy a steak in peace. "Red meat kills," Joanne would say, or as Rico mockingly put it, "Carnivore!" Still, eight ounces through the best twenty-ounce T-bone he'd ever tasted, he had to admit to himself that death was liberating in its own way. When he got around to the baked potato, he asked the waitress for extra sour cream.

Back in his hotel room, he flipped through the photos, arranging them in chronological order and writing the date and place on the back of each: the shore of Lake Erie, the golden dome at Notre Dame, the Sears Tower. If he got back to New York, he figured, he would buy a scrapbook and install the photos along with the pages from the journal he was keeping. Not that he believed the words and pictures would automatically come together to tell him something about himself. He had spent hours poring over the scrapbooks at his mother's house, filled with images of him and Joanne at the beach, letters from camp, programs from every one of Joanne's plays, certificates of achievement for each of the County Arts Festivals in which his paintings had appeared during high school. There were locks of hair and baby footprints and pictures of relatives whom he could not recall. But none of these ever explained the things he felt like he needed to know.

There was only one picture of his father, and it was not in the books. His mother kept it on top of her dresser—a scene from his own front yard—black-and-white image of a sharp-nosed man, thinning hair slicked down against his scalp, staring at the infant cradled in his pale bony arms. Holding the baby, the man looks uncomfortable, pained, as if the small body he supports is in fact some inexplicable tumor which has bubbled up from his own abdomen. The sun is shining somewhere to the camera's left. The slant of light gives the illusion of movement to the several cars parked in the background.

"If only your father had been here." In the hotel room, he could almost hear the words emanating from the photos that he clutched, testament to this foolish journey he had undertaken, which could have only one end. At first, he had seriously considered his mother's suggestion that he find his father. Since he did not know exactly what he was searching for, one quest seemed as good as another. But in the end he realized how his mother's idea testified only to her fears come true, how all the men in her life—father, husband, son—had left her in one way or another. And he realized how her admonition was not borne even slightly out of a concern for his welfare, but wholly out of a concern for her own: a last-ditch plea with the universe to return those things taken from her. To return the two men who never seemed complete when they were with her, but whom she could never stop caring about.

Bring them home, God. He reflected on the words with contempt yet understanding. Bring them home: safe, satisfied, whole.

Somewhere between Denver and Grand Junction, he scribbled:

Green M&M's make you horny.

And only God knew how he had tried. At fourteen, there'd been Theresa Mack, who slipped her hand into his pocket at a Connecticut Pitch-and-Putt, supposedly to find his keys. At fifteen, there'd been Sandi Holman, showing him her breasts behind the dumpster at Mike's Bowl America. At sixteen, Angela Stinson, the cheerleader, his chemistry lab partner, blond, leggy—in the bathroom at her birthday party, her parents at some political function, his hand up her skirt, hers down his pants. She went from low moan to high squeal like a Ferrari engine, until he felt ready to die (of fear? of guilt?) about the pain forming in his gut. Not that Angela could tell. He was harder than the steering column on his mother's Buick. But he was sixteen, for Christ's sake—a change in the breeze made him stiff. Was he excited? Sure, but with a feeling that couldn't be described as pain or even nausea. Just absence, a space like bruised fruit carving itself out of his abdomen, his own body betraying him, his own muscles pulling him apart.

(For a fleeting moment he even thought how the disease had brought things full circle—not a disease which attacked his body directly, like cancer, but turned that body on itself—unsexed him, his penis a mere piss spout—his gut turning into a void that would engulf him from the inside out.)

But mostly he just remembered. His mother telling him not to worry, that he just needed to find the right girl. And his trying to fill the emptiness with food: raw oysters, kumquats, green M&M's—plain and peanut, bags and bags worth. Looking back, he decided that maybe his teenage years hadn't been so bad after all. Not that he ever stopped feeling lonely, but most days his diet kept him too busy puking to worry about it.

He checked into a hotel at Grand Junction then went on foot with his camera to take pictures of the Grand Mesa and the rivers, the Gunnison and the Colorado. Where the rivers met he made his way to the bank, scooped up a handful of water, sniffed it, splashed his face. There was something meaningful he couldn't quite pin down to the smoothness with which the rivers came together. None of the colliding power suggested by the fact that over centuries the two had carved out the entire valley. Nothing, it seemed, of the terrible forces of nature that came in big and small packages. Just the flow, one line into another, as if neither could exist individually.

He thought of the men he had loved, relatively few but with passion. Lionel, the first, a British investment banker whose general uptightness made his sexual openness that much more surprising and powerful, who made great eggs benedict and quoted nineteenth-century poets when someone asked how he was feeling—Shelley for happiness, Byron horny, Wordsworth pensive, Tennyson angry. With Lionel, he was sure it would last forever; it ended in two months. Then came Sebastian, the marathon runner, who lacked stamina in bed. George, from Hoboken, who commissioned him to paint a mural of Alexander Graham Bell on the side of his electronics store. And Karl, an acquisitions agent at MOMA, who flattered him by comparing his work to early Van Gogh. All of them sudden, all before he told his family, all gone in a matter of weeks.

Rodney, the marine biologist, lasted almost a year, introduced him to Howard and Rico, insisted on meeting his family, wrestled with Joanne on their living room rug, then promptly cut out for Oregon when a position came open at an Oceanography Institute near Portland. At first he agreed to follow Rodney to the west coast in a year, then they decided to do the permanent commute, then settled for phone calls, then wrote, then lost touch altogether. "Bad love, Jack," was Rico's thought on the subject,

"I never really liked him anyway." "You told me," Howard interjected, "that you would have danced naked for him in a pool of Karo syrup." "What has that got to do with liking him?" Rico retorted, then thoughtfully, "Love was never an option with him, even if you could bounce a quarter to China off his ass."

With Bruce, the chef, things were different, both of them on the rebound, both of them knowing that things were destined to end but willing to ride out events as long as they could. They parted on good terms after two years. Nevertheless, it was Bruce who had called four months earlier and told him without apparent emotion to get tested. Before he received his results, they met for lunch in a downtown café, where he could barely recognize the man he had once loved: trembling hands, gray fedora failing to cover several forehead lesions, green eyes that seemed already dead. They drank espresso, tried to identify the languages spoken by passing tourists, eventually talked about love and fear, held hands, cried a little. When they parted, Bruce said, "Make sure you call me when you find out." But deep down they both knew what the results would be. He had already noticed the first symptoms: weakness, nausea, dizziness. Further conversation would have only put old lovers through unnecessary misery.

After he snapped off another roll of film, he let his hand drag in the river, felt the current hidden there. A chain of men, he thought, whose sins and scents and secrets he could never shake, who had entered him, become him for a time. In a way he pitied the heterosexual men he knew, who would never understand what it was like to be penetrated— sometimes painfully, sometimes pleasurably—but always to feel someone else made part of him if only for a moment. To understand another in a way that required the most intimate and fragile of connections, to receive.

And so he was part of a chain, part of many chains, linking and unlinking to form the story of his life. He thought about his father, then, and wondered what that man beyond others had passed on to him, what heredity could account for and what it could not. He remembered how, while Rodney had wrestled with Joanne in their living room, he had confronted his mother in the kitchen, stopped her from slicing chunks of Velveeta onto Triscuits for hors d'oeuvres. How at one point, among the other words that passed between them, he had drawn up short and said, "That's it, isn't it? That's why Dad left. Because he was gay." To which even his mother, even then, had to laugh. "Him?" She shook her head. "He couldn't handle things, is all." She picked up the knife again, held it delicately like a pencil. "Nothing unusual about him. He was a goodenough man in theory, I guess. Just never could handle one blessed thing."

In the middle of the Painted Desert he stopped to write:

The second gunman on the grassy knoll.

He erased and re-wrote the line three times before letting it stay.

Rico, who was into conspiracies, believed in the second gunman. Rico had known about the CIA bringing crack into the cities before anyone. The government tests on monkeys and illegal aliens, the missile sites outside Albany, the secret agreements of the pharmaceutical company heads—Rico had all the dirt. Though he had protested with Howard to get gays and lesbians into the local St. Patrick's Day parade, Rico admitted on the side that their plan would never fly. "It's the Pope, man. He's fixed the city elections through 2012. Got that bad Jesus mojo magic. Gets a rise out of anybody."

Nevertheless he had his doubts about conspiracies.

The second gunman: nothing more than a gray photographic blob in a collage of distorted blobs, like clouds that resembled other things but could never be the things themselves. Once he'd attended a rally in Central Park, and his picture had landed on page three of the *Daily News*. Only the reporter had gotten his name wrong in the caption, called him Joe or Jerry. And even though he had told his mother a thousand times who and what he was, she still called to ask, "It's not you, right, Jack? It can't be. The name...the name...." Until even he wondered who the person in the photo was, then wondered how deceitful his eyes must be to make him disbelieve himself.

And who was he to worry about the second gunman, anyway? It would be three more years after Kennedy's death until he plummeted into the world. Still, remembering Rico, he figured that maybe the event itself mattered little. What mattered was the way the event lingered in memory, the way it became larger than itself with each re-telling. The old myths were the strongest, he supposed, the oldest conspiracies the hardest to shake. The conspiracy of the body against itself, the disease he felt within him, like history, the weight of the past set down on his less-than-Atlas shoulders.

That's how it was at the Grand Canyon. On the south rim, he shut his eyes and tried to imagine himself as the first Spanish soldier to stumble onto the place. Literally, as one story went, a Spanish soldier, half-drunk, crawled through the bushes looking for El Dorado, reached one hand out to find only air, then cleared the brush from his face to stare out over what could have been the end of the world. Brutal, beautiful reality presenting itself in a way that no words could touch. A limit of earth and imagination. Despite the literal grandeur, he kept his eyes closed, breathed in slowly, pushing that myth (of discovery?) to the extremities of his body—feet, hands, hair. Eyes still closed, he drew the camera from its bag and pressed the shutter a dozen times, letting his mind guide the lens. When he looked again, the red walls, red rock had become more than themselves, the air more than absence, the sun more than light. Old myth, first earth. A beginning even as it was an end.

That was the thing about a myth, he decided. Once created, it stayed in the blood, refused to go away. The myths of his time would now be the myths of all time, just as the myths preceding him were part of him in a way he could never fully understand. At the precipice, he stared out and thought maybe this sense—of immersion, of connection—was what he had been seeking. Not just since the disease, but all along.

The sun, noon high, seared its image into the world below, and for some reason he thought of the mural he'd been hired to paint on a hang-gliding store in Queens—Daedalus and Icarus—a strange image, he thought, for people in the business of keeping others aloft. The store's owner, nineteen, a CUNY dropout, was emphatic about what he wanted: "Big flames, man. Crash and burn." And so he had painted the picture he remembered from his elementary school reader—Daedalus looking up, surprised—the boy, Icarus, wings ablaze, falling.

But looking over the emptiness of Arizona red, he told himself that he had gotten it all wrong. He imagined Icarus suspended in air, that moment between ascent and fall—feathers, wood, clothes burned away. And Daedalus, his father, beneath him, thinking only of escape. What had possessed the boy to fling himself toward oblivion in this one futile heroic act—suspended before the sun, if only for a moment, its champion? And what had possessed the father to think only of some distant shore, some life of ease, such that he hardly noticed the naked wordless form hurtling past him?

He spread his arms, let the sun beat against him, and almost believed he could fly.

In his motel room in Flagstaff, he rubbed his eyes then wrote:

Masturbation makes you go blind.

Chains of myth, of blood, of love and desire. They linked the moments of his life together, and linked that life indelibly to the great work of time around it. In the bathroom, he felt his penis move smoothly through his hand, the warm surge of liquid against his palm. Ejaculation did not occur without some pain now—not in his groin, but around his scalp, a pressure behind his eyes wanting to be let out. Opening his fist, he stared at the white gummy mass as if it held some key to his quest. So small, so deadly—except to him. He lifted his hand to his mouth and rested his tongue lightly against his palm, tasted salt. He had consumed the semen of other men before, but never his own, and thought how odd it was that he chose to do so now, when he was the only one his sperm would not kill. He closed his fist again and considered that strange power, birth and decline perhaps, but more than these the links between him, his parents, his lovers, and all the world that had gone before, combined in his body at invisible levels, embedded in that taste of salt which he only now wanted to understand. Even the disease slowly killing him, that was part of the story, a part of all their stories, the countless billion specks of humanity which commiserated in his blood. Him, here, now—a single strand in the great myths of all time, whether other people wanted to believe it or not.

He turned on the faucet and washed the rest of the semen away with difficulty, having to scrub hard with soap and the fingers of his other hand. Moving into the bedroom, he picked up the phone and thought of Joanne, Rico, Howard, others. But finally he called his mother, never saying exactly where he was.

"Did you find what you were looking for?" she asked at last.

"I'm not sure. Maybe. In a way, I guess."

"Then you'll be coming home?"

A pause. "No, not yet."

She cleared her throat. "Jack, we love you, you know. Your sister and I."

"Yes," he admitted. "I ... I just wanted you to understand, whatever else you might think, that I'm handling things."

"Of course you are..."

"No. Mother, no. I want you to understand. I'm handling things."

A sound almost like choking came from the receiver. Later he would convince himself that it had been a glitch in the line. "Well, I guess I'll wait for your next phone call, then."

"Yes," he replied, though he might have said more, then hung up.

From the portfolio he took the notebook and turned to the last page, ignoring the numerous blank pages before it. "And they all lived happily ever after," he wrote, then shoved the remaining copies of the living will and as many photos as he could fit in between the pages. He secured the whole thing with several rubber bands, opened the drawer of the bureau, and laid it next to the Gideon's Bible, thinking how the two works fit together somehow—martyrdom, eternity making and unmaking itself, blood and bodies merged to become both more and less than they could be on their own. Outside several children's voices punctuated the grind of a car engine, then disappeared. The sun descended another fraction, sweeping away the rivulets of light sliding past the heavy curtains. His towel dropped off as he laid back in the bed. Running his hands the length of his naked body, he took in the silence like a lover, felt himself pressed down then lifted by the settling air.

Some Days I Wake up Walking over the Desert

James Tipton

Some days I wake up walking over the desert
and see pieces of me everywhere:
in these knuckles of ancient trees,
in that tumbleweed of soul in this spring wind,
in the tiny flowers rooted on heart rock;
even a piece of sleep that I thought was mine flew
in the blue wing of day out of a dead limb.

Ah, this gathering and gathering of self,
this brown joy in the eyes of a beloved dog,
this dust that dances into blossom,
this little notebook that is the earth,
this endless love that when we least expect it
knocks on our door and says
let the day begin.

Insisting with the only life I know
on some peace at the end of solitude
and desperation, I have arrived
here, at this desert place,
where a magic that few would want
rings light around me, where grace
comes toward me, one step at a time.

Algunos Dias Me Despierto Caminando en el Desierto
by James Tipton (translated by Isabel Allende)

Algunos días me despierto
caminando en el desierto
y veo pedazos de mí por todas partes:
en los nudos de árboles antiguos,
en ese revoloteo del alma en el viento primaveral,
en las flores diminutas
enraizadas en el corazón de la roca;
incluso un trozo de sueño que creía mío
salió de un miembro muerto
volando en el ala azul del día.

Ah, este juntar y juntar partes de mí,
esta dicha color avellana
en los ojos de un perro amado,
este polvo que florece danzando,
este pequeño cuaderno que es la tierra,
este amor inacabable que cuando menos se espera
golpea a nuestra puerta diciendo:
que comience el día.

Insistiendo
con la única vida que conozco,
en algo de paz después de la soledad
y la desesperanza,
he llegado aquí,
a este lugar desértico,
donde una magia que pocos desearían
me envuelve en su luz
y donde la gracia me llega,
un paso a la vez.

I Wanted You in the Kitchen of My Heart
James Tipton

I wanted you in the kitchen of my heart;
and there, after many cold lunches,
I found you; and there, like herbs
undressing in soup, I came to love you;
and there, like a delicate tea
of mangoes and marigolds your mouth
opened, and your words, flecked with gold
and the eroticism of your Latin blood,
flowed, like the blood I longed for, into me.

And how could I lose you among these cups
and spoons, among these golden candles,
these jars of honey lined along the window?
And what forget-me-nots in winter
tie me to you still? I could die in this bread
I have made without you. For you I would burn
this dry brain for incense; I would
serve you the wine inside the night; I would
drink the sea to give you salt.

Te Quería en la Cocina de Mi Corazón
by James Tipton (translated by Isabel Allende)

Te quería en la cocina de mi corazón;
y allí, despés de muchos almuerzos fríos,
te encontré; y allí, como hierbas
desnud·ndose en la sopa, lleguè a amarte;
y allí, como un delicado té
de mangos y caléndulas, tu boca
se abrió y tus palabras, salpicadas de oro
y del erotismo de tu sangre latina,
se derramaron, como la sangre que añoraba, en mí.

¿Y cómo podría perderte entre estas tazas
y cucharas, entre estas velas doradas,
estos frascos de miel alineados en la ventana?
¿Y qué nomeolvides en invierno
me atan aún a ti? Podría morir en este pan
que he hecho sin ti. Por ti quemaría
como incienso este cerebro seco; te serviría
el vino de la noche; bebería
el mar para darte sal.

Eating the World
James Tipton

I was born with my mouth open...
entering this juicy world
of peaches and lemons and ripe sun
and the pink and secret flesh of women,
this world where dinner is in the breath
of the subtle desert,
in the spices of the distant sea
which late at night drift over sleep.

I was born somewhere between
the brain and the pomegranate,
with a tongue tasting the delicious textures
of hair and hands and eyes;
I was born out of the heart stew,
out of the infinite bed, to walk upon
this infinite earth.

I want to feed you the flowers of ice
on this winter window,
the aromas of many soups,
the scent of sacred candles
that follows me around this cedar house,
I want to feed you the lavender
that lifts up out of certain poems,
and the cinnamon of apples baking,
and the simple joy we see
in the sky when we fall in love.

I want to feed you the pungent soil
where I harvested garlic,
I want to feed you the memories
rising out of the aspen logs
when I split them, and the pinyon smoke
that gathers around the house on a still night,
and the mums left by the kitchen door.

(continued on page 312)

Devorando el Mundo
by James Tipton (translated by Isabel Allende)

Nací con la boca abierta...
entrando a este mundo jugoso
de duraznos y limones y sol maduro
y esta rosada y secreta carne de mujer,
este mundo donde la cena está
en el aliento del desierto sutil
en las especias del mar distante
ue flotan en el sueño tarde en la noche.

Nací en alguna parte entre
el cerebro y la granada,
saboreando las texturas deliciosas
de cabello y manos y ojos,
nací del guisado del corazón,
del lecho infinito, para caminar
sobre esta tierra infinita.

Quiero alimentarte con las flores de hielo
de esta ventana de invierno,
los aromas de muchas sopas,
el perfume de velas sagradas
que por esta casa de cedro me persigue.
Quiero alimentarte con la lavanda
que se desprende de ciertos poemas,
y la canela de manzanas asándose,
y el placer simple que vemos
en el cielo cuando nos enamoramos.

Quiero alimentarte con la tierra acre
donde coseché ajos,
quiero alimentarte de memorias
surgiendo de los troncos de álamo
cuando los parto
y del humo de piñones
que se junta en torno a la casa en una noche quieta,
y los crisantemos en la puerta de la concina.

(continued on page 313)

I want to feed you the colors of rain
on deserted parking lots,
and the folds of delirious patchouli
in the Indian skirt of the woman
on Market Street in San Francisco,
and the human incense of so much devotion
in tiny villages in Colorado and Peru.

I want to serve you breakfast at dawn,
I want to serve you the bread
that rises in the desert dust, serve you
the wind that wanders through the canyons,
serve you the stars that fall over the bed,
serve you the Hopi corn one thousand years old,
serve you the saffron in the western sunset,
serve you the delicate pollen that blows its lullaby
through each lonely wing of flesh;
I want to serve you the low hum of bees
clustered together all winter
eating their honey.

Quiero alimentarte con los colores de la lluvia
en estacionamientos desiertos,
y los pliegues de patchouli delirante
de la falda india de la mujer
en la calle Market de San Francisco,
y el incienso humano de tanta devoción
en pequeñas aldeas de Colorado y Perú.

Quiero servirte desayuno al amanecer.
Quiero servirte el pan
que sube en el polvo del desierto,
servirte el viento que vaga por los cañones,
servirte las estrellas que caen sobre la cama,
servirte el maíz Hopi antiguo de mil años,
servirte el azafrán en el atardecer del oeste,
servirte el polen delicado que silba su cancíon de cuna
a través de cada solitaria ala viviente;
quiero servirte el zumbido de las abejas
agrupadas juntas todo el invierno
comiendo su miel.

Untitled
Linette Lao

1.

I woke up this morning
with oysters for eyes and
saw you there, a crown of
guppies around your head
their translucent hearts beating
in small finless bodies.
Your live ankles pumping
warm tea through
the sleeves of your best dress
into the tips of your plain hands.

Once we called you earth eater,
chicken diver,
mushroom heart,
envelope tongue,
forest fire.
Now we call you grandmother, and
your names still curl around us
like cigarette smoke.

Your electrical heart stops watches.
It swings through these dull plaster
walls. Your stubborn ear is at the door,
and your breath calls at the window.

Listen.

2.

When you were young
you discovered mars.
It's simply another
cracked surface.

3.

You married a bird watcher,
electrical taper, water tapper,

book binder, pipe maker,
bone digger.
The duck egg, photograph corner,
meat and scissor,
mint and zipper, pie and ice cream,
broken watch man.
Words are orange and green
flying from your mouth to hang
upside down from the ceiling.

4.

Children crawl across the floor and
shake the folds of your clothes.
Language is a red wire,
in an empty mouth.
Language will not describe this
black candy heart,
this space between ribcage
and throat.

5.

Dishes are singing,
kitchen chairs unfold.
The onions have your name
on their soft lips.
You stand at the counter,
a blurred contraption of knitting needles,
knives, hot oil and elbows,
a seamless intervention
from an unopened embassy.

A clay pot cracks and I am
born to the sounds of
squid ink draining,
gentle scratches of claws
against the inside of pots and
live fish hammered in dishtowels.

6.

You are lead
pouring into heavy shoes,
a rounded belly,

a collection of stones
arranged in a safe deposit box.

Targets, flags,
numbers and maps—
there is a plan written lightly
on the back of your hands.

It will not involve
the red Cadillac
the icebox
the aquarium
or the scooter.

It will not include
children, the milkbox,
the mailbox, rock salt,
sawdust, vinegar,
nylon or chocolate.

7.

The cure for magnets
will appear in hearts of palm
or in carnation bouquets
on an untuned television
across the faces of neighbors
in a yard of fresh snow.

8.

Like a sleepless animal or
a long lost alphabet, you walk
the long halls of the house,
the blue-gold eye of a carp rolling
in your mouth like a single word
on the tongue, a secret that crawls
across history to find its home.

Two Boys

David Dodd Lee

1.

I never met the boy who drowned.
He lived in the next block, another, a distant tribe.
But kids I knew were there
and said he flew on his sled as if no weight at all caught
in the winter wind
blowing him high off the lip of the lathered cliff of ice,
telling how he hung in the air
like he and his sled were one for a few miraculous flying seconds....

I'd been on an ice flow
for years, drifting through my own circadian rhythms,
so I knew how the boy felt,
how he imagined, and even saw,
while flying or sinking,
the robin hop and turn its head over the thick lawn
while nearby leaves crinkled as a blue racer
poured itself down a small hill.

At the peak of his flight the snow that had been falling
clung to him like magnetized insects huddling for warmth.

2.

Snow is warm.
My mother finally believed so after years of pain
and she died smiling curled on her bed
while her room grew small and dark. "It was like thunder
or a deep voice. God
makes an enormous clattering when he lets slip
a little breath inside the retina.
And a light the color of honey swings through the glass
to transport you." She was talking
about a snowplow.

I've fallen through before, and came up dry
two miles downstream
where I arrived escorted by something like pilotfish.

I think they were walleyes,
rubbing my eyes with their soft dorsals,
snuggling up warm inside my jacket.
                                    I walked dripping
rainbows of freezing water
back to my car.
I took off my clothes
and wrapped myself inside a wool blanket,
the passenger seat filled to overflowing with broken icicles,

2.

The ice in Lake Michigan
flows together like manatees, bumping heads.
Overnight the wind takes out its welding torch after the deep floes
perform their own version
of plate tectonics,
giant sheets of ice thrusting into broken peaks over the sea-colored water,
with licks and licks
the edges smooth,
a collision of mammalian foreheads, whales hibernating,
spits of water whipping sideways out of their blowholes....

3.

I found the boy's sled. It was wedged into a hunk of ice
bobbing in the deep water
like a ship going down. I sailed through the nights
with a flag of red flannel. I talked
to my mother for company. She said I shouldn't be afraid.
When she died
a doctor couldn't figure out how she'd remained limber.
My father came back to see if what he'd heard was true
and picked up my mother
and she hung limp in his arms like a sleeping girl.

The boy sank and sank lit up a comet
before resting on the sandy floor of the lake.
His picture in the newspaper grew indistinct
in the shadows
of the drifting snow that wrapped its arms around the junipers.

4.

I opened my windows for a while after that, hitched up my sheets
to a cane pole
                  and flew through the lake—
effect wave after wave until I was actually moving
toward something
that might envelope me with such purposeful silence beyond mere
     accident,
or a long enduring, drawn out lack of will.

A Gang of Crows Takes Over the Neighborhood
Susan Becker

The solid bodies of crows
patrol the streets five abreast,
strutting like wrestlers full of blood and bluff.
Crow feathers, packed smooth as oiled pompadours,
grease the air as they march along,
and the smell of crow fills dank alleys
in the fetid aftermath of summer rain.
They swoop at children
from poplar perches
and keep dogs in line
with rocks pushed from rooftops.
Like black holes, they cast no shadows.
Grubs slide down their gullets
like rotgut whiskey.
When they fly past,
they leave behind the rasp of doors closing.

Dust
Susan Becker

Hot, high summer at dusk.
Languid neighbors slump
on porches in damp cotton
or swelter and wilt
where they meet along the parched road.

Too hot to shuffle home to airless parlors,
they talk of nothing
with the desultory aimlessness
of nursing home patients
waiting to grow young.

Only the thick roadside dust does not sweat.
By the curb, a small girl sifts cool dust
through tender brown fingers,
then rubs it along her thin arms,
coating herself with talc.

The hairs on her forearms spring out,
pale and powdered as geisha dancers.
Legs next,
toes to thighs,
until she is bathed in the glory of dirt.

Later, there will be heat lightning
and the gleam of windowscreen
in starlight to ease her way to sleep,
but first this stubbly ghosting of her limbs
soothes her like the blessing of cool sheets.

My Son Tells Me Not to Wear
My Poet's Clothes

Maria Mazziotti Gillan

My son tells me not to wear my poet's clothes. "They're weird," he says. He wants me to look like an old-fashioned grandmother, someone out of an L. L. Bean catalog in a preppy sweater and a corduroy skirt, the kind of clothes that would have been all wrong for me even when I was 20 years old and 104 pounds, I love thin flowery dresses that float around me when I walk, long colorful scarves with fringe on them. My son does not say it out loud, but I know he thinks I'm the wrong kind of mother and that I should act my age and give up my poetry because it is strange for me to be running off to all those poetry readings and giving workshops and working so many hours a week at my job. Sometimes I think we should trade places. He could be the staid, conservative mother and I the recalcitrant son. When we talk on the phone, I hear how he shoulders the responsibilities of his life: his wife, his children, his job, the house, the yard. "John," I say "You're only 31. Give yourself a break." I hear him sigh, that expelled breath fraught with meaning that is the sound I make when I am anxious or bored, and I am saddened when I hear it coming from him over the wires across all that distance, not only the landscape that separates us but the language that fails us so I cannot find a way to make him understand that I love him, this son who needs to be far away from me so that it's as though I am chasing him down a path but he's always faster than me. I see him sitting with his son Jackson in his arms, Jackson who looks just like John did at two, and I see the way they lean together, Jackson so relaxed and trusting, his ear pressed to his father's heart.

The Ghosts in Our Bed

Maria Mazziotti Gillan

to my husband who has early onset Parkinson's disease

The mahogany four-poster bed your mother left us
is high up off the floor. It folds us into
the smell of lavender in sheets sprinkled with violets
the thick blue and green comforter.
For years we are happy in it,
lusty and young and so alive together,
this safe place to which we return each night
to lie in each other's arms, warm
and exactly where we want to be.

Now, when we climb into our bed, those people
who for so many years were ourselves,
the ghosts that we live with, sleep between us.

You have become so fragile. You are always
cold and need extra blankets, and you sleep
so quietly, your arms folded across your chest,
that when I wake up in the night, I have to reach out
to find you because I'm not certain you're there.

You used to take up so much space, with your energy
and strength, the big bones of your body,
I pile blankets on you now,
your face rigid and frozen even in sleep.
The ghosts of the future hover over us, reminding us
every night of how much more we have to lose,
even as out old ghosts whisper, "Remember, remember."
I fall asleep with my hand on your shoulder,
to keep you with me as long as I can.

About the Artists

ANITA CHENG, the dancer featured in William Rutledge's photography, received her BA in English from Colorado College, and her MFA in dance from the University of Michigan. In 1991, she received a Fulbright in choreography to complete her post-graduate studies at the Hong Kong Academy for Performing Arts. In 1997, she was recognized with a New York Emmy award as graphic designer for the series, "The City," for Thirteen/WNET New York. In addition, Cheng's video and DVD installation piece "D'Invenzioni," in collaboration with artist Ronaldo Kiel, premiered in Sao Paulo and was then invited to be part of the opening exhibition of the Santandar Cultural Center in Porto Alegre, Brazil. The website for Anita Cheng is www.chengdance.org.

AMOS MILLER studied at the Art Institute of Chicago, the University of Arizona, the Cleveland Institute of Art, and the Cooper School of Art. His work has been exhibited all over the country, and has been collected by numerous art centers, corporations, and individual collectors.

WILLIAM RUTLEDGE lives in West Chester, Penn. He has done many types of commercial and art photography, including still-life, corporate, fashion, and reportage. His work appears frequently in display, in print, video, and on the Web.

About the Contributors

KATHY CANTLEY ACKERMAN was born in Beckley, W.V., and grew up in the industrial midwest near Toledo, Ohio. She studied creative writing as an undergraduate at Bowling Green State University, then went on to receive an M.A. in English from the University of North Carolina at Charlotte in 1985 and a Ph.D. in American Literature from the University of South Carolina in 1991.

"My return to poetry is a return also to my family's heritage: the Appalachian Mountain region, which has been tormented by misunderstanding and exploitation. These themes recur in my poems. I cannot remember a time when I was unaware of the exploitation of working-class peoples—a symbol of which was the "black lung" check my grandmother received, compensation for the disease which forced my grandfather, too late, out of the coal mines. My father and his brothers migrated north from the hills as soon as they were old enough to learn a skilled trade in Ohio. Many of my poems come from my need to reclaim a small piece of the heritage they left behind."

ISABEL ALLENDE is the author of numerous books, including *House of the Spirits*, *Paula*, *Aphrodite,* and *Portrait and Sepia*. She is one of the foremost writers in the world. This is her first published translation.

JOY ARBOR-KARNES's work has recently appeared in *Hayden's Ferry Review* and *Santa Barbara Review*. Having graduated from Mills College's M.F.A. program, she studies British Romantic poetry in the doctoral program at University of California, Davis. She and her husband live in Sacramento with their three cats.

JANE BAILEY works as a registered nurse in Salem, Ore. She holds an English degree from Portland State University (Oregon) where she received the Academy of American Poets Prize for three consecutive years (1994–96). Her poetry has been published in a number of journals, including *CALYX*, *Calapooya Collage*, and *SLANT*. She is working on her first novel.

EDWARD BARTÓK-BARATTA grew up in Jersey City, just outside Manhattan. A poet and fiction writer, he has published in *Beloit Fiction Journal*, *Harvard Review*, the London-based magazine *The Month*, and *Manoa*, among others.

ANN BARRETT is a mother of four—one Jamaican stepson and three children of her own. She considers herself a "career student" and is in the creative writing program at the University of North Carolina in Asheville. Ann has won contests in both poetry and nonfiction. A collection of her poetry was nominated for The Persephone Poetry Book Publication Award sponsored by the North Carolina Writers' Network. Her writing, in addition to several local journals, has appeared in *The Caribbean Writer* and *Troika*. "Two Bad Bulls" won the 1999 Wilma Dykeman Prize in Non-Fiction at UNCA.

STEPHEN BEAL, raised by Miss Havisham's younger sister in Evanston, Ill., went to Williams and Oxford, made cartons in a nail factory, taught college English, ghostwrote books—among them *I Was Al Capone's Caddy*—served as a cook and chauffeur, wrote advertising copy, managed a yarn store, sold textbooks in Texas, and published five nonfiction books. His poetry regularly appears in *Hanging Loose* and his collection *The Very Stuff* received the 1997 poetry award from the Colorado Center for the Book.

SUSAN BECKER has a B.A. in English and American literature from Brown University and currently is the archivist for the Maria Rogers Oral History Program in Boulder, Colo.

LISA SHAW BLACK was raised in the small town of Crestview, Fla. She graduated from the University of West Florida and now lives in Kingston, Tenn., with her husband, four children and "Skipper the Flying Dog." She is working on her first book of poetry.

"After a discussion with friends on the topic of reincarnation, I was entranced by the notion of imagining why prominent personalities of history would return, assuming the choice was theirs. Mary, Mother of Jesus was one of the first to come to my mind and the one who would not let me be without exploring her options. There were, of course, many others and the possibilities still tempt me. I wouldn't be surprised if this idea took a turn towards the serial."

GREGORY BROOKER's poems have appeared in or are forthcoming in the *Iowa Review, Berkeley Poetry Review, Proliferation,* and *Puerto Del Sol*. His chapbook, *Spirit's Measure*, was published by Second Story Books.

DEBORAH BYRNE lives on a deadend street in Cambridge, Mass., with her sweetie Marc and her cat Emily D. She has won a Grolier Poetry Prize, the Edgar Allan Poe Award, and the Michael Gerhardt Memorial Poetry Prize. Her poems have been published in many journals including *Cimarron Review, Crab Creek Review, Heartlands Today,* and *Whiskey Island*. In cyberspace, her poetry can be seen at Zuzu's Petals. She dances the mango tango.

M. RUKMINI CALLIMACHI is originally from Bucharest, Romania, but has been educated in Switzerland, England, and the United States. She is a graduate student at Oxford University where she is studying theoretical linguistics and philosophy of language. Formerly, she was a Stadler Poetry Fellow at Bucknell University, an Ezra Pound scholar at Castle Brunnenberg, Italy, and Poet-in-Residence at the Kalani Honua Institute. She has been awarded the Galway Kinnell Poetry Award and most recently the Keats & Shelley Prize from the Royal Society of Literature, Great Britain. When she is not writing, she enjoys learning languages especially Sanskrit and Tibetan, and high-altitude trekking, and was sponsored to undertake a solo expedition to the Kyimolung valley of southern Tibet. Her work has appeared in *Black Warrior Review, American Scholar*, and *Midwest Poetry Review*.

NEIL CARPATHIOS teaches high-school English in Massillon, Ohio, and is an adjunct professor of English and creative writing at local universities. He is the recent recipient of an Ohio Arts Council Individual Artist Fellowship in poetry, and is a Pushcart Prize nominee whose work has appeared in a variety of nationally distributed anthologies. Recent work appears in *Poetry, Southern Poetry Review, Poet Lore, College English*, and *Cape Rock*.

MICHAEL CUMMINGS's short stories and essays have appeared in more than fifty well-respected literary reviews including *Alaska Quarterly Review, Berkeley Fiction Review, Kansas Quarterly, Maryland Review*, and *Southeast Review*. He has also reported business news for five northern Virginia weeklies and freelanced magazine articles for *Utne Reader, Buffalo Spree*, and *Portland Monthly*.

MARJORIE CARLSON DAVIS lives and writes in a Victorian house rumored to have a ghost. She teaches writing at Western Illinois University. Her work has appeared in *Baltimore Review, Thema, Sassy*, and other publications. She has completed a novel and is editing a short-story collection.

RICHARD DEMING divides his time between Ohio and Western New York and has work appearing in *Confrontation*, *Sulfur*, and *The Journal*.

CATHERINE DENUNZIO-GABORDI has been published in *American Poet and Poetry* and in the *Mystic River Press*. She has degrees in English (B.A.) and English education (M.A.) from the University of Connecticut.

QWO-LI/PAUL DRISKILL grew up in Glenwood Springs, Colo., and completed his undergraduate work at the University of Northern Colorado. He hopes to continue his education in Seattle, Wash. He is of Cherokee, Osage, African and Irish ancestry and a Queer/Two-Spirit activist. He is also a member of the Wordcraft Circle of Naive Writers and Storytellers, and has been printed in their newsletter, *The Moccasin Telegraph*. Qwo-Li's work will also be included in an upcoming *Queer Youth* anthology edited by Amy Sonnie.

"I began to write when I was fourteen in order to save my life. I believe writing is often the only thing that keeps me sane, alive and joyful." "Song of Removal' comes from my rage as a Native person at the invisibility of our lives and issues as people who are still dealing with the military occupation of Turtle Island. 'Another AIDS Poem or *Why do I have to write this*' came out of the frustration of seeing too many Queer Kids practicing risky behavior in the age of HIV and AIDS. 'Wild Indians' is simply a warning."

JOY DWORKIN teaches creative writing and world literature at Missouri Southern State College. Her poems have appeared in *Beloit Poetry Journal*, *Paris Review*, and *South Dakota Review*, among other journals; her translations from Polish and Russian have been published in *Conjunctions* and *Cross Currents: A Yearbook of Central European Culture*.

ERIC P. ELSHTAIN teaches at both Metropolitan State College and Arapahoe Community College in Denver. His work has been published in the *Denver Quarterly*, *Interpoetics*, *Fence*, *ONTHEBUS*, *Fine Madness*, and other journals.

DORIS FERLEGER, Ph.D. is a licensed psychologist specializing in helping female trauma survivors to heal, a published poet, a spouse, mother, and a daughter of Holocaust survivors. Her work has been published in anthologies entitled *MotherPoet, Journey into Motherhood, An American Anthology of Magazine and Journal Verse*, and *Edge of Twilight*. Her work has appeared in, *13th Moon, Jewish Currents, Changes, College English, Kerf, Mangrove, Northeast Corridor, Seattle Review, Visions*, and *Jewish Exponent*. She has studied writing with Carolyn Forche, author of *Against Forgetting*, who teaches "poetry of witness," and with Natalie Goldberg, author of *Writing Down the Bones*, and *Wild Mind*, who teaches creative writing and memoir. Ferleger has led workshops in "Using Writing as a Therapeutic Tool," and in "Expressive Writing for Sons and Daughters of Holocaust Survivors."

JEFFREY FRANKLIN's poems have appeared recently in *Asheville Poetry Review, Cumberland Poetry Review, Hudson Review, Southern Poetry Review*, and *Third Coast*. His book, *Serious Play: The Cultural Form of the Nineteenth-Century Realist Novel* is available from the University of Pennsylvania Press. He lives in Greenville, N.C. with his wife, Judith Lucas, and their children, Tyler and Emma.

CARRIE C. FRASIER spent her childhood in the foothills outside Fort Collins, Colo., and received her M.F.A. in 1994 from Colorado State University. Since then, she has wrangled horses, waited tables, stained histology slides, and now makes her living as a telecommuting multimedia specialist in Phoenix, Ariz. Her work has appeared in *Literary Review, Mid-West Quarterly, Plainsong, Seattle Review, Colorado Anthology of the Fantastic, New Voices,* and *Negative Capability.*

DAISY FRIED was awarded a $50,000 grant for her poetry by the Pew Fellowships in the Arts in 1998. Her poems have been published/are forthcoming in *American Poetry Review, Antioch Review, Beloit Poetry Journal, Colorado Review, Cream City Review, Mudfish, Pemmican, Threepenny Review,* and elsewhere.

CAMERON K. GEAREN's work has appeared in *Crazyhorse, Third Coast, Hawai'i Review,* and elsewhere. She was awarded third place in the *Painted Bride Quarterly* 1997 Poetry Contest. The two poems published here were written about her two-year stay in Thailand. She is on leave from the M.F.A. program at Indiana University (Bloomington); she and her husband are spending a year in Beijing.

MARIA MAZZIOTTI GILLAN is the founder and director of the Poetry Center at Passaic County Community College, editor of *The Paterson Literary Review* and is co-editor of *Unsettling America: An Anthology of Contemporary Multicultural Poetry.* She has won numerous awards, including the New Jersey State Council on the Arts fellowships, and a Chester H. Jones Foundation Award. The author of six books of poetry, her most recent is *Where I Come From: Selected Poems.* She has had poems in *The New York Times* and *Christian Science Monitor* and has appeared on National Public Radio's "All Things Considered," Leonard Lopate's "Books and Co.," and Garrison's Keeler's "Writer's Almanac."

"These poems come from a new manuscript of poems called *Learning Grace* that deals with the grief experienced by the long married when one of the partners contracts a disease that gradually robs him of his ability to move and remember. It also deals with the failure of language to bridge the chasm between parents and their grown children, and with the search for a way to accept our losses."

LISA GLATT has had work published in many literary journals and anthologies, among them *Columbia, Indiana Review, Crab Orchard Review,* and *Bust Guide to the New Girl Order* (Viking/Penguin). She teaches in the Writers' Program at UCLA. Her second book of poems, *Shelter,* was recently published by Pearl Editions.

J. EUGENE GLORIA was born in Manila, Phillipines and was raised in San Francisco. His collection of poems, *Drivers at the Short-Time Motel,* was selected by Yusef Komunyakaa for the 1999 National Poetry Series and was published by Viking Penguin. He also received the 1999 George Bogin Memorial Award from the Poetry Society of America. He lives with his wife, Karen, and teaches at DePauw University in Greencastle, Ind.

LEONARD GONTAREK is the author of two books of poems, most recently *Van Morrison Can't Find His Feet.* His poems have appeared in *Poetry Northwest, Exquisite Corpse, Quarterly, American Poetry Review, Hanging Loose,* and *New England Review.* He is the recipient of a poetry fellowship from the Pennsylvania Council on the Arts.

RAY GONZALEZ received a 1997 PEN/Oakland Josephine Miles Book Award in Poetry for *The Heat of Arrivals* (BOA Editions) and a 1998 Fellowship in Poetry from the Illinois Arts Council. His fifth book of poetry, *Cabato Sentora,* is available from BOA. He is the editor of twelve anthologies, most recently *Touching the Fire: Fifteen Poets of the Latino Renaissance* (Anchor/Doubleday Books). After teaching at the University of Illinois in Chicago, he is now on the M.F.A. faculty at the University of Minnesota in Minneapolis.

ALLISON GRABOSKI is a writer of poetry and fiction from Denver, Colo. She has had two stories published in *Walkabout*, the creative writing magazine at University of Colorado at Boulder. She has also been published in the Poetry Guild's 1998 *Celebration of Poets*.

CAROLYN KIEBER GRADY manages a seventy-acre wood lot in western New York and is finishing her Master's thesis at SUNY Fredonia. During 1993-4 she was the Writer-In-Residence at the American School of Bombay, India. Work has appeared recently in the *Comstock Review* and *Buffalo Spree Magazine,* as well as the *Best of Ore Anthology*.

ROBERT GREGORY is the author of two poetry collections, *Interferences* (Poltroon Press, 1987) and *Boy Picked Up By The Wind* (Bluestem, 1992).

JILL GREENE received her M.F.A. at Colorado State University. Her poems have appeared in *Poetry Northwest*.

STEPHANIE ELIZONDO GRIEST is a Latina whose acute wanderlust took her to Moscow in 1996 to study Russian, freelance and volunteer at an orphanage, and then to Beijing in 1997-1998 to teach journalism and edit the Chinese Communist Party's mouthpiece, *China Daily*. She has written about male belly dancers for *The New York Times*, religious cults for *The Washington Post* and Dead Heads for *The Seattle Post-Intelligencer*. She is currently chasing 181 Texan congressmen across the capital and writing about their upcoming legislative session for the Associated Press. When she's not writing, she is belly dancing with her troupe at restaurants and showcases in Austin.

AUDREY HAERLIN lives in Denver, Colo. Her work has appeared in various publications.

JEAN HANSON's essays and short stories have appeared in numerous magazines including *North America Review, Zoetrope, Indiana Review*, and *Creative Nonfiction*. A graduate of the Iowa Writers' Workshop, she has received an artist fellowship from the Colorado Council on the Arts, the Hackney Prize in the short story, and a Poets & Writers award for emerging writers.

EILEEN HENNESSY is a native of Long Island and has spent his life there and in New York City, apart from residence for several years in France and Austria. He holds an M.A. in creative writing from New York University, and is a Ph.D. student in the Arts and Humanities Education program at NYU. Hennessy began her professional writing career as a translator of books, chiefly in art history, and now specializes in translating legal and commercial documentation into English from several West European languages. She is an adjunct associate professor in the Translation Studies program at NYU. In terms of creative writing, apart from a few incursions into writing non-fiction articles and fiction, she is a poet first and foremost. Her work has appeared in various literary magazines, including *Paris Review, Western Humanities Review, Prairie Schooner*, and *New York Quarterly*, and in several anthologies.

TRENTON HICKMAN's poems have previously appeared, or are forthcoming, in *Southwest Review, Negative Capability, River Styx*, and *Tar River Poetry*, as well as other publications. Recently, he also translated Venezuelan poet Rafael Cadenas' work with Brian Evenson. *The Spaces of Silence*, the result of their work, was published by Pyx Press.

ANDREW HOFFMANN's works have appeared in numerous publications. He was a winner of the Utah Original Writing Competition and other awards.

RANDY HUNTSBERRY's work has appeared in numerous publications. He works as an executive coach and lives in Boulder, Colo.

ROY JACOBSTEIN, a public health physician and consultant in international development, has had poetry appear in a number of venues, including *Witness, Threepenny Review, Quarterly West, Puerto del Sol, Prairie Schooner, Poetry Northwest, Marlboro Review*, and *Beloit Poetry Journal*. He received Mid-American Review's 1999 James Wright Poetry Prize and his chapbook, *Blue Numbers, Red Life*, won the 2000 Harperprints Poetry Chapbook Competition.

M. SMITH JANSON's poetry has been published recently in *Harvard Review, Prairie Schooner*, and *Cream City Review*. She lives on the north shore of Massachusetts with her husband and daughter.

MARY CHI-WHI KIM received her M.F.A. at Bowling Green State University. She was an assistant editor at *Mid-American Review* and served as featured reader at Columbus-area cafés, Oberlin College, and University of Missouri. Her work has appeared in *Heartlands Today* and *Asian Pacific American Journal*.

MELISSA KIRSCH has studied creative writing at the University of Virginia and New York University, where she recently completed her Masters. She lives and teaches in New York City.

ROBERT KRUT completed his M.F.A. from Arizona State University in 1999. His work has received two Swarthout Awards from ASU and an Allen Ginsberg Poetry Award from the Poetry Center in N.J. He lives in Atlanta, Georgia.

LINETTE LAO work has appeared in numerous publications, including *Caliban*.

PATRICK LAWLER's collection of poetry *A Drowning Man is Never Tall Enough* was published by the University of Georgia Press in 1990, and a second collection, *reading a burning book*, was published by Basfal Books in 1994. His work has appeared in *American Poetry Review, Apalachee Quarterly, Epoch, Iowa Review, Ironwood, Literary Review, Many Mountains Moving, New York Times Book Review, Nimrod, Shenandoah, Southern Humanities Review*, and many others. Lawler was awarded a grant from the New York State Foundation for the Arts and received a fellowship from NEA. He is an associate professor teaching literature of nature and communications courses at SUNY College of Environmental Science and Forestry.

NEIL LEADBEATER was born in Wolverhampton, UK in 1951. He is an English graduate from the University of London. He is married and lives in Edinburgh where he works as a Health Care Policy Manager for the National Health Service. A relative new-comer to the poetry scene, he won first prize in the Scottish-based Understanding Poetry Competition in 1994. His work has been published in a number of leading literary magazines throughout the UK.

DAVID DODD LEE is the author of *Downsides of Fish Culture* (New Issues Press, 1997), and a chapbook, *Counting Backwards* (Bee & Flower Press, 1999). He currently lives in Kalamazoo, Mich., and teaches English at Western Michigan University.

JOSEPH O. LEGASPI was born in Manilla, Philippines and was raised there and in Los Angeles. He holds degrees from Loyola Marymount University and New York University's Graduate Creative Writing Program. His poems have appeared in the *Seneca Review*, and *Poet Lore*, among others. Legaspi lives in New York City, working for a nonprofit organization.

LYN LIFSHIN, whose most recent prizewinning book, (Paterson poetry award) *Before It's Light*, published fall 1999 by Black Sparrow Press, following their publication of *Cold Comfort* in 1997, has published more than 100 books of poetry, including *Marilyn Monroe, Blue Tattoo*, won awards for her nonfiction and edited four anthologies of women's writing including *Tangled Vines, Ariadne's Thread*, and *Lips Unsealed*. Her poems have appeared in most literary and poetry magazines and she is the subject of an award-winning documentary film, *Lyn Lifshin: Not Made of Glass*, available from Women Make Movies. For interviews, photographs, more bio material, reviews, interviews, prose, samples of work and more, check the Web at http://www.lynlifshin.com.

KIRSTEN LILLEGARD's work has appeared in various publications. She lives in Tennesse.

JEFFREY ETHAN LEE (formerly Jeffrey Loo) is a Philadelphia-born poet who won the Tupelo Press Literary Fiction Prize for *The Autobiography of Somebody Else* (forthcoming Spring 2002). He has a poetry CD, identity papers, available from Drimala Records [www.drimala.com], and he received a Greater Philadelphia Cultural Alliance grant (2001) to perform this work. He published *strangers in a homeland*, a poetry chapbook with Ashland Poetry Press (www.ashlandbookstore.com), and more than 150 poems, essays, etc. in publications such as *Crazy Horse, Inkwell Magazine, Many Mountains Moving, Crab Orchard Review* and others. He is a visiting assistant professor at Franklin & Marshall, teaching creative writing, Asian-American literature and romanticism. He volunteers for the board of Asian Arts Initiative of Philadelphia, a 501(c)(3) nonprofit arts organization, and co-produces the NotCoffeehouse Poetry and Performace Series (www.notcoffeehouse.org).

ALISON LUTERMAN is a poet in the schools in Oakland (available for workshops wherever—have poetry, will travel). She is a freelance journalist, has worked with recovering drug addicts and done H.I.V. test counseling.

"I came across Greg Withrow's story in *PEOPLE* magazine about ten years ago and was haunted by it, but it took a long time before I was ready to write the poem. I don't know what happened to him, if he's even still alive."

ANN LYNN's poems have appeared in *River Oak Review* and *Graffiti Rag*, and are forthcoming in *Defined Providence* and *Christian Science Monitor*. She has worked as a social worker, editor, and freelance writer, and is now teaching poetry to children.

"'Love Poem' is about the risks we take in being human. 'Mass' is for all women everywhere who have had or will have breast cancer."

JACQUELINE LYONS is a native of Wisconsin who lived in Boston, Portland, and Missoula, before settling in Fort Collins, Colo., where she received her M.F.A. in poetry at Colorado State University. For nearly three years she lived in Lesotho, Southern Africa, where she taught English language and literature to high school students as a Peace Corps volunteer.

"I traveled all around Southern Africa, have since been back to visit, and hope to return there for a lengthier stay in the near future. I fell in love with the place, and much of my recent poetry and nonfiction is based on my experiences there."

JACK MARTIN lives in Ft. Collins, Colo. His poems have appeared in *Agni, Black Warrior Review, Dry Creek Review, Fine Madness, The Journal, River Styx*, and other magazines. His chapbook is *Weekend Sentences* (Pudding House, 1997).

"'Fluid Mechanics' springs from the time I spent self-medicated during the Reagan years."

KHALED MATTAWA is a native of Benghazi, Libya, and is the author of a book of poems, *Ismailia Eclipse* (Sheep Meadow Press), and the translator of two books of Arabic poetry, Hatif Janabi's selected poems, *Questions and Their Retinue* (University of Arkansas Press), and Fadhil Al-Azzawi's *In Every Well a Joseph Is Weeping* (*Quarterly Review of Literature* poetry series). Mattawa's work has appeared in many literary reviews and anthologies including *Paris Review, Poetry, The Kenyon Review, Ploughshares, Pushcart Prize*, and *Best American Poetry* (1997) and was awarded an Academy of American Poets prize, the Vachel Lindsey Award, the Alfred Hodder fellowship at Princeton University for 95-96, and a Guggenheim fellowship for 1997-98.

GLEN MAZIS lives in Marietta, Penn., and is a professor at Penn State Harrisburg. He has published two books of philosophy on similar themes to those expressed in this poem. His poetry has recently appeared in *Spoon River Poetry Review, Sou'wester, Mangrove, Xanadu*, and many others.

WALT MCDONALD is the author of numerous books, including *Counting Survivors* (University of Pittsburgh Press, *After the Noise of Saigon* (University of Massachusetts Press) and *Night Landings* (HarperCollins). His work has been published in countless publications.

ROGER LADD MEMMOTT, from Willows, Calif., taught creative writing and contemporary literature at the University of Cincinnati. He is Vice President of Marketing for MegaMax Systems, Inc., a large-format theatre development and motion picture production company. His fiction, poetry, and articles have appeared in *Sou'wester, Confrontation, Cumberland Poetry Review, BYU Studies, New Millennium Writings, Black Warrior Review, Byline*, and *Paintbrush*, among dozens of others. He is the recipient of a William H. Taft Creative Writing Fellowship.

"'Points of View' is a skewed look at the world we live in from a long way off, satirizing our new millennium penchant for wondering ("What if...") and how language continues to fail us in this marvelous age of communication—or something like that."

MỘNG-LAN's poems have appeared in the *Kenyon Review, Manoa, Iowa Review, Pushcart Prize Anthology XXIV*, and other publications.

GEORGE MOORE teaches at the University of Colorado, Boulder. His most recent collection of poetry, *The Petroglyphs at Wedding Rocks*, was published by Edwin Mellen Press in 1997. He has also written a critical book on Gertrude Stein and his poems have appeared widely in many journals, including *The Atlantic, Poetry*, and the *North American Review*.

NIKKI MOUSTAKI has an M.A. in creative writing from New York University and an M.F.A. in the same from Indiana University. Nikki's poetry has appeared in *Alaska Quarterly Review, Cream City Review, Spoon River Poetry Review*, and *Quarterly West*, among others. She lives in New York City where she works as a freelance writer.

ELISABETH A MURAWSKI's chapbook *Troubled by an Angel* was published by Cleveland State University Poetry Center. Moon and Mercury was published in 1990 by Washington Writer's Publishing House. She's had poems featured on Poetry Daily's website. Her poem "Mother and Daughter" appears in the Best of Web del Sol. Her work has appeared in *Grand Street, Doubletake, Virginia Quarterly Review*,

American Poetry Review, and other publications. Her poem "Thoughts on St. Agatha" won third prize in this year's Anne Stanford Poetry Prize competition.

BARBRA NIGHTINGALE holds a doctoral degree in higher education and is an associate professor of English at Broward Community College, South campus, Florida, where she was recently (April 17, 1997) awarded the James Knight Endowed Teaching Chair. She has had over 100 poems published in numerous poetry journals and anthologies, such as *Birmingham Review*, *Chatahoochee Review*, *Crosscurrents*, and *The Poet*. She has had three chapbooks published, *Lovers Never Die* (1981), and *Prelude to a Woman* (1986), and *Lunar Equations* (1993), and is competing for publication of two major collections, *Sweet Insomnia*, and *Singing in the Key of L*.

"'One Night Stand' was conceived after becoming familiar with e-mail and writing to a lot of people. It is pure fiction yet universally true. 'Bowing the Bass' was conceived watching a jazz concert where the bass fiddle was bowed instead of plucked, as I've usually seen it done. I was very impressed with the fiddler's style."

JENNIE PAK is enrolled in the M.F.A. program at Cornell University. Her poetry has been published or is forthcoming in the *Oakland Review* and *Alligator Juniper*. Her poems received the first place poetry prize from the *Oakland Review*.

VERONICA PATTERSON has published one collection of poetry, *How to Make a Terrarium* (Cleveland State University Poetry Center) and one collection of poetry and photography *The Bones Remember: A Dialogue* (with photographer Ronda Stone, Stone Graphics Press). Her work has appeared in many publications including *Southern Poetry Review*, *Louisville Review*, *Sun*, *Madison Review*, *Malahat Review*, *Indiana Review*, *Another Chicago Magazine*, *Mid-America Review*, *Willow Review*, *Bloomsbury Review*, *Colorado Review,* and *Georgia Review*. She has been awarded a residency at the Ucross Foundation and a 1997 Individual Artist's Fellowship from the Colorado Council on the Arts. She received first place in the Peregrine Poetry Contest (Amherst Writers and Artists) and first prize in the 1997 Salt Hill Journal poetry competition (Syracuse University).

PRUDENCE PEIFFER was the 1996 Junior Scholarship Winner from Hampton Shorts magazine. In 1997 she won second place in the Amy Award, a poetry contest open to women aged 30 or younger residing in New York City or the east end of Long Island. In 1998 she won first place in the same contest. Prudence was also the winner of EarthMatters 1997 environmental poetry contest. She co-created the magazine *andy's wings*, devoted to all the arts, and has taught a poetry workshop for young children at her local library.

LINDA TOMOL PENNISI is a graduate of Le Moyne College in Syracuse and of the M.F.A. in writing of Vermont College. Her work has appeared in journals such as *Paintbrush, Nightsun, Midwest Quarterly, Spoon River Quarterly* and *Louisville Review*.

JON PINEDA received an AWP Intro for poetry. His poems are appearing or forthcoming in *Asian Pacific American Journal*, *Crab Orchard Review*, *Haydens Ferry Review*, *Poetry Northwest*, *Puerto del Sol,* and elsewhere.

KAREN PROPP's poems and essays have appeared in *Antioch Review*, *Lilith*, *Ploughshares,* and many others. "On Losing One's Virginity Again" is a chapter from *The Pregnancy Project*, a book about infertility and reproductive technology— how both effect women's sense of their bodies, self, and sexuality. Karen Propp lives in Cambridge, Mass. In September, 1997, she gave birth to a baby boy.

Many Mountains Moving

"I walked around for several weeks with the title for this essay in my head. in an early version, I described an imaginary art piece: a glass box that displays syringe, condom, speculum, ultrasound photographs of a woman's uterus, vials of blood and semen. I wanted it all arranged in a classical still life composition, with a bedsheet falling in voluptous folds in the background. But as I worked further with language and my memory of the experience, I remembered the plumber coming to fix the pipes in my house. That's when the piece began to take off. Then I worked to synthesize the narrative with the more theoretical points I wanted to make. Reproductive technology offers women so many more choices now; I think we as a society have barely begun to articulate how medicalized conceptions effect our life decisions and definitions of life."

CAROL QUINN's poetry has appeared in *Midlands*, *Poetry Motel*, and *Philomela*.

PHILIP RAMP is an American living in Greece, translating from Greek into English and writing, poetry mainly. His poems and translations have appeared in a number of magazines and anthologies. A selection of his poems called *JONZ* was published in England by John Lucas's Shoestring Press in 1994. The full collection of *JONZ* was published in a bilingual edition (English/Greek) in Athens in 1997.

ANGELA REGAS is an English major at Boucher College. She still reads herself bedtime stories.

PETER REYNOLDS work has appeared in numerous publications. He lives in Seattle.

RICHARD ROBBINS was born and raised in Calif. and Mont. As an undergraduate at San Diego State University, he studied writing with Glover Davis, Rick DeMarinis, and Carolyn Forche, and as a graduate student at the University of Montana, he studied with Madeline DeFrees and Richard Hugo. Robbin's work has been awarded the Robert H. Winner Prize from the Poetry Society of America, as well as fellowships from The Loft, the McKnight Foundation, the Minnesota State Arts Board, and the National Endowment for the Arts. Individual poems have been published in *Poetry Northwest, Nation, North American Review*, and other journals. His first book of poems, *The Invisible Wedding*, was published in 1984; *Famous Persons We Have Known* was published in 2000. He directs the creative writing program and Good Thunder Reading Series at Mankato State University.

BERTHA ROGERS' poems appear in journals and in her collections *Sleeper, You Wake* (Mellen, 1991) and *A House of Corners* (Three Conditions Press, Maryland Poetry Review Chapbook Contest Winner; Fall, 2000). Her translation of "Beowulf," the Anglo-Saxon epic poem, was published by Birch Brook Press. She has received residency fellowships to the MacDowell and Millay Colonies, Hedgebrook Foundation for Women Writers, and Hawthornden Castle International (Scotland) Writers Retreat.

"I wrote the poem while in residence at Hedgebrook Foundation for Women Writers on Whidbey Island in Washington; the cottage/studio where I worked, the firs and cedars were the inspiration."

JAY ROGOFF is the author of *The Cutoff* (Word Works, 1995), winner of the Washington Prize for Poetry. His next collection, *How We Came to Stand on That Shore*, will appear from River City in 2002.

RICHARD RYAL, a producer of poetry events at South Florida bookstores and Nova Southeastern University's Writers' Bloc, is an activist for poetry in daily traffic. Experience has taught him that the temptations of capitalism are most easily resisted through taking up a poet's career.

"'The Arc of Our Reach' was inspired by a session with my osteopath, Dr. Elisa Ginter, a true holistic healer. I appreciate anyone who can raise skills and relationship to levels that overflow mundane experience. The artist Anna Homler once described such moments as 'getting big.' That's a wonderful way to see it."

MARGOT SCHILPP has had work published in *Denver Quarterly, American Letters & Commentary, Gettysburg Review, Crab Orchard Review, High Plains Literary Review*, and others. She was a fellow at The MacDowell Colony and at the Virginia Center for the Creative Arts. She is working on a Ph.D. in creative writing at the University of Utah, where she edits *Quarterly West*.

JOANNA C. SCOTT is an Australian-American writer living in Maryland. She is the author of two novels, *Pursuing Pauline* and *Charlie and the Children*, and a nonfiction collection, *Indochina's Refugees: Oral Histories from Laos, Cambodia and Vietnam*. She was awarded *The Lyric*'s 1996 New England Prize for Poetry and won awards with the Chester H. Jones Foundation, the National Writer's Association, Treasure House, New Millennium Writings, and in ARTSCAPE, Baltimore's Literary Arts Competition. Steve Parish Publishing, Australia, featured a selection of her poetry in its photographic calendar, *Rainforests of Australia*.

ALISON SEEVAK's poetry and essays have appeared in various journals and anthologies including *The Sun, Lilith, Rosebud*, and the collection, *What Have You Lost?* (Greenwillow Books) edited by Naomi Shihab Nye. She teaches creative writing to young people through San Francisco WritersCorps. Her poetry received a nomination for the Pushcart Prize.

KATHLEEN SEROCKI's work has appeared in numerous publications. She lives in New Hampshire.

MARY SHARRATT, originally from Minneapolis, has been living in Europe for the past ten years. Her work has appeared or is forthcoming in *International Quarterly, Long Story, Emrys Journal, Evergreen Chronicles, American Writing*, and *Writing for Our Lives*. She received a 1998 Pushcart Prize Nomination for her short fiction. Her novel, *The Gold Rain Tree*, was published by Coffee House Press in Spring 2000. She also publishes *Another Country*, a Munich-based literary journal.

MIRA SHIMABUKURO earned her M.F.A. in creative writing from the University of Washington in 1997. She teaches creative writing on and off for Seattle Central Community College and for an alternative public high school, The Middle College, in Seattle, Wash. In 1996, she served as part of the Young Women's Editorial Collective for CALYX Journal's 20th Anniversary Issue, *Present Tense: Writing and Art By Young Women*. Her writing has been published in *International Examiner, Raven Chronicles, Writing For Our Lives, CALYX, The Seattle Review*.

"'Before you were called" was written as a response to the whole anti-P.C. rhetoric that was going on while I was in school."

VIVIAN SHIPLEY is the editor of *Connecticut Review* and a professor at Southern Connecticut State University. She won the 1997 Lucille Medwick Prize awarded by The Poetry Society of America and the 1997 Right Kind of Trouble Poetry Contest from Ain Air. In 1996 she was awarded the Sonora Review Poetry Prize from the University of Arizona, the Defined Providence Poetry Prize and the Gretchen Warren Award from the New England Poetry Club. In 1995, she won the Ann Stanford Poetry Prize from the Master of Professional Writing Program at the University of Southern California and the Marjorie Lees Linn Poetry Prize from Elk River Review. Her poems appear in *Anthology of Magazine Verse* and *Yearbook of American Poetry, Southern Review, Pleiades, American Scholar, Quarterly West, Christian*

Science Monitor, Southern California Anthology, New Letters, Indiana Review, Flyway, and others. Her first book, *Poems Out of Harlan County* was published in the Ithaca House Poetry Series by The Greenfield Review Press. *Devil's Lane* was published by Negative Capability Press and was nominated for the 1996 Pulitzer Prize of Letters. Raised in Kentucky, she has a Ph.D. from Vanderbilt University.

MARY MCLAUGHLIN SLECHTA is a poet and fiction writer whose work has appeared in many journals and anthologies, including *New to North America* (1997) and *Identity Lessons: Learning American Style.*

KATHERINE SMITH received an M.F.A. from the University of Virginia, and lives with her daughter in Knoxville, Tenn., where she teaches at Pellissipi State Community College. She has been published in *Wind, Berkeley Poetry Review, Little Magazine,* and a previous issue of *Many Mountains Moving.*

ART SOUSA was born on the island of San Miguel in the Azores, but grew up outside of Providence, R.I. He graduated from Rhode Island College and received his master's degree from the University of California, Irvine. He now lives in San Diego, Calif.

ALEX STEIN is the author of *Dark Optimism,* published this year by Emerson's Eye Press. He lives in the fictional town of Boulder, Colo. His work has appeared in a previous issue of *Many Mountains Moving.*

JEFF P. STEIN was born at the Indy Speedway in Indianapolis, Ind., in 1968. He was educated at Beloit College, earned a masters in English from the University of Northern Colorado, and is currently working on an M.F.A. in Creative Writing at Colorado State. He has lived and traveled in Kenya, Tanzania, Zanzibar, Korea, Costa Rica, Canada, and Israel and worked as a college administrator, community college professor, ESL instructor, youth director, hotel desk clerk, and preschool teacher. He has written a book, *Finding Our Skins.*

"My wife and I knew so many friends who seemed to just look at each other and get pregnant. After a year of trying to get pregnant, this miscarriage rang, like a bell, out of the quiet world for which we had not prepared. For many months I struggled at pieces of poems trying to talk about the loss. Pulling the pieces together into one poem mirrored all my awkward attempts to think it through, all the fracturing and questioning of that time; and the process seemed to help me through my own grief period as well."

ART SOUSA was born on the island of San Miguel in the Azores, but grew up outside of Providence, R.I. He graduated from Rhode Island College and received his master's from the University of California, Irvine. He now lives in San Diego, Calif.

"How any of my stories manage to be born is mystery to me. Mostly what I do is write on a daily basis—apparently with diligence, apparently with discipline— loads and loads of nothing. Empty, conscious and self-conscious plots which could not and should not be called stories, but then, suddenly, one line will appear. One startling line. Always uninvited and unexplained. Always enigmatic, daunting. And then the real work begins. "Vergonha" came into life in just this way.

MELISSA S. STEIN received an M.A. in creative writing from the University of California, Davis, and is currently a book editor in San Francisco. Her work has appeared in *American Poetry Review, Faultline, Terra Nova, Blue Mesa Review,* and others, as well as several poetry anthologies. Stein received fellowships from both The MacDowell Colony and the Villa Montalvo Center for the Arts for artist residencies throughout Spring/Summer 1998, and was awarded Second Prize in the Villa Montalvo Biennial Poetry Competition.

J. DAVID STEVENS is Assistant Professor of Creative Writing at Seton Hall University. His most recent stories appear or are forthcoming in *Paris Review*, *North American Review*, *Iowa Review*, and *Witness*. Stevens was born and raised in Richmond, Virg., the grandson of two Southern Baptist ministers. He attended Duke University as an undergraduate then went on to receive a Ph.D. in American literature from Emory University and an M.F.A. in fiction writing from Penn State University. Presently an Assistant Professor at Seton Hall University, he lives in Sleepy Hollow, N.Y., and splits his time between writing, gardening, and watching unhealthy amounts of TV.

ALISON STONE's poems have appeared in *Poetry*, *Paris Review*, *Ploughshares*, *Catholic Girls,* and a variety of other magazines and anthologies. She is the winner of *New York Quarterly*'s Madeline Sadin Award. She is also a painter.

MARILYN TALAL received her Ph.D. in creative writing from the University of Houston where she was a Stella Erhart fellow. She won an NEA creative writing fellowship in 1991. Her poems have appeared in *New Republic*, *Poetry*, *Southern Poetry Review,* and many other publications. She teaches at the Gemini Writers Workshops in San Antonio, Tex., and in New York.

CYNTHIA THATCHER received her M.A. in English from the University of Colorado—Boulder. She received the Barker Award for Poetry from the university. She is an acupuncturist and traditional Chinese medicine practitioner. Her poems have been published in various journal but this is first published translation.

JAMES TIPTON lives on a high mesa in western Colorado where he keeps bees and writes poems. His work is widely published, including credits in *The Nation*, *South Dakota Review*, *Southern Humanities Review*, *Greensboro Review*, *Esquire*, *Field*, and *American Literary Review*. He is also included in various anthologies and other works, most recently *Aphrodite*, by Isabel Allende (1998), *Bleeding Hearts*, edited by Michelle Lovric (1998), and *The Geography of Hope*, edited by David J. Rothman (1998). His most recent collection of poems, *Letters from a Stranger*, with a foreword by Isabel Allende (Conundrum Press, 1998), won the 1999 Colorado Book Award in Poetry. He is working on a new collection, *The Alphabet of Longing*. Tipton is a popular speaker and reader at conferences and workshops, and he may be reached at 970-858-5014 or jtpoet@aol.com.

CHRISTINA VELADOTA studied creative writing at Emerson College and earned her M.F.A. from the University of North Carolina at Greensboro. Her poetry has appeared *Alaska Quarterly Review*, *Greensboro Review*, *Free Lunch*, and *Poem*.

JOHN WILLSON is a recipient of the Pushcart Prize and awards from the Academy of American Poets, the Pacific Northwest Writers Conference, the Artist Trust of Washington, and the King County Arts Commission. His chapbook, *The Son We Had*, was published by Blue Begonia Press in 1999. A 1995 finalist in the National Poetry Series, John lives with his wife on Bainbirdge Island, Wash., where he works as a poetry instructor and as a bookseller at an independent bookstore.

EDWARD W. WOOD, JR. has received two Wurlitzer Foundations Grants and an award from the National Council of Senior Citizens. He is the author of the memoir *On Being Wounded* (Fulcrum) and lives in Denver, Colo.

Good News about the Contributors

ROBERT BLY's poetry collection, Holes the Crickets Have Eaten in the Blankets, is available from BOA Editions. $7.50. ISBN 1-880238-58-6.

DEBRA KANG DEAN's collection of poems, *News of Home*, is available from BOA Editions, Ltd. (www.boaeditions.org). $12.50 paperback. (ISBN 1-880238-66-7).

HARVEY HIX's collection of poems, *Rational Numbers*, is available from Truman State University Press (www2.truman.edu/tsup). $22 cloth (ISBN 0-943549-80-9)/$15 paperback (ISBN 0-943549-79-5).

TONY HOAGLAND's poetry collection, *Donkey Gospel*, is available from Graywolf Press. $12.95. (ISBN 1-55597-268-3). It won the James Laughlin Award of The Academy of American Poets.

B.D. LOVE's chapbook, Meat Wisdom: Sonnets & Variations is available from Pudding House (www.puddinghouse.com). $8.95. (ISBN 0-944754-97-X).

BERTHA ROGERS did an interdisciplinary exhibit as artist/translator at the New York Public Library this year for her translation of *Beowulf*.

ELLEN DORÉ WATSON's poetry collection is available from Alice James Books (207-778-7071). $9.95. ISBN 1-882295-12-9.

Prairie Schooner

may be 70 years

old, but we're still

running strong.

What's the secret? Well, it has to do with horsepower.

Prairie Schooner is still one of the leading literary magazines today because we haven't changed the essential fuel that makes us run.

Excellence.

Prairie Schooner publishes the best contemporary poetry, fiction, essays, and reviews four times a year. While hundreds of other magazines have sputtered and died, *Prairie Schooner* continues to collect kudos from the likes of Best American Short Stories, Essays, and Pushcart Prize anthologies.

Contribute to a natural resource. Subscribe to *Prairie Schooner*.

Send $22.00 for a one-year subscription (4 issues) to:
Prairie Schooner, 201 Andrews Hall, University of Nebraska, Lincoln, NE 68588-0334 (make checks payable to *Prairie Schooner*)

DETAIL FROM A PHOTOGRAPH BY PILIĀMO'O

MĀNOA

Seeking the unexpected? You'll find it in this beautiful, ground-breaking journal—writers from Japan, the Philippines, New Zealand, Australia, Viet Nam, Korea, and the rest of the international Pacific and Asia...including the United States. *"Vitality and surprise"*—W. S. Merwin. *"Access to some of the best voices in world literature"*—Small Press. **Visit our website at www2.hawaii.edu/mjournal and see why** MĀNOA is unlike any other American journal.

Published every summer and winter by the University of Hawai'i Press, 2840 Kolowalu St., Honolulu, HI 96822. TOLL-FREE TEL 1-888-UHPRESS / TOLL-FREE FAX 1-800-650-7811 / E-MAIL mjournal-l@hawaii.edu.

MMM ORDER / SPONSORSHIP FORM

Two-issue subscriptions are $16 ($29 for four-issue subscription)*,**. Gift subscriptions make a perfect gift. The first issue of gift subscriptions will be sent with a card in your name. If you are not completely satisfied, we will promptly send you a refund.

*Canada add $3.00 to each single issue or $6.00 per 2-issue subscription. *Other countries add $5.00 to each single issue or $10.00 per 2-issue subscription.*

** *Colorado residents add ONE of the following tax amounts for journal purchases: Boulder—7.36%; Denver Metro—3.7%; CO outside of Denver area—2.9%.*

Please begin my subscription with ❏ the current issue (#12) / ❏ next issue (check one)

Subscriber's name _____

Street/Apt. No. _____

City/State/Zip _____

Phone _____

Subscriptions (circle one)

$16 for 2 issues

$29 for 4 issues

$44 for 6 issues $_____

Gift subscriptions:

Recipient's name _____

Street/Apt. No. _____

City/State/Zip _____

Sender's name _____

Sender's addr/phone _____

Gift subscriptions (circle one)

$16 for 2 issues

$29 for 4 issues

$44 for 6 issues $_____

❏ **Yes, I would also like to order individual issues of Many Mountains Moving**

Inaugural issue, #2, #3, #4, #7, #8, #9, #10
(circle requested issue #s)   ___ @ $6.00 each $_____

Tribute to W.S. Merwin (#11)   ___ @ $9.00 each $_____

Current issue #12 (Vol. IV, No. 3)   ___ @ $9.00 each $_____

Additional charge for foreign purchases* $_____

Subtotal $_____

Colorado tax** $_____

Become a sponsor. We invite you to become a sponsor of Many Mountains Moving by making a tax-deductible contribution (contributions are tax-deductible minus the $16 value of the 2 issues). Sponsors receive a two-issue subscription to the journal and will be recognized in those issues for their contributions.

❏ **Supporting subscriber ($30)** ❏ **Donor ($50)** ❏ **Patron ($100)** ❏ **Benefactor ($250)**

Tax-deductible sponsorship donation $_____

Total amount enclosed $_____

Send check or money order to:
Many Mountains Moving, 420 22nd St., Boulder, CO 80302 U.S.A.

Phone (303)545-9942; Fax (303)444-6510
mmm@mmminc.org
www.mmminc.org

[#12]

In upcoming issues...

Nature issue, Luis Alberto Urrea and Brian Andrew Laird, eds.
Literature of Spirituality issue, edited by Cathy Capozzoli
William Aiken
Aliki Barnstone
Natasha Bruckner
Michael Calvello
David S. Cho
David Chura
Maria Gillan
Felicia C. Garcia
Ray Gonzalez
William Greenway
Sharon Hashimoto
Michael Henry
Cynthia Hogue
Mark Irwin
Christopher Luna
Joyanna Laughlin
Mari L'Esperance
Joshua McKinney
Beth A. Partin
Marge Piercy
Adam Sorkin
Virgil Suarez
Jay Veazey
David Williams